Reflection in the Writing Classroom

KATHLEEN BLAKE YANCEY
University of North Carolina, Charlotte

D0931812

UTAH STATE UNIVERSITY PRESS
Logan, Utah
1998

Utah State University Press
Logan, Utah 84322-7800

Typography by WolfPack

98   99   00   01   02   5   4   3   2   1

Library of Congress Cataloging-in-Publication Data

Yancey, Kathleen Blake
   Reflection in the writing classroom / Kathleen Blake Yancey.
     p. cm.
   Includes bibliographical references and index.
   ISBN 0-87421-238-3 (pbk.)
   1. English language—Rhetoric—Study and teaching. 2. Report
writing—Study and teaching. 3. Reflection (Philosophy) I. Title.
PE1404.Y36   1998
808'.042'07—dc21   97-45395
                                                 CIP

Reflection in the Writing Classroom

CONTENTS

PREFACE

THIS VOLUME GREW OUT OF A FOCUSED INQUIRY: *WHAT CONVERSATIONS,* I wanted to ask, *could we have around texts in order to foster reflective habits of mind?* What you'll read in the following pages constitutes my attempt at an extended answer. Because it is a book-length volume, I've taken the luxury of thinking about this question in multiple ways: theoretically, pragmatically, and—I hope—reflectively. I've located my responses to this focused inquiry within my own practice, to be sure, but I've tried both to theorize that practice and to make it visible so that others can read themselves into this story as well. Ultimately, as I hope is apparent, I'm as interested in the questions raised in the process of inquiry as I am in the answers we construct. They are foundation and means of reflection, both.

More specifically, what I've done here is to re-theorize Donald Schon's theory of reflection for use in the writing classroom, and in that process to think about how we might use reflection as a mode of helping students develop as writers. I've written this volume, then, because I think through reflection we can change both the teaching and learning of writing. What I also do here is show how we might begin making some of those changes, and suggest some of what we— teachers and students—could learn if we understood the writing classroom as a reflective practicum, as a new kind of writing classroom, one where students are writers, reflection is woven into the curriculum, and practice becomes art.

I was fortunate in having the support of many at my institution, the University of North Carolina at Charlotte. In particular, I want to thank the University, the Faculty Grants Committee, and Dean Schley Lyons for an academic leave to support this work.

There are several people whose contributions to this project I'd like to acknowledge. Michael Spooner, my editor and friend: (again) thanks. Also: Irwin Weiser and Afhild Ingberg, for reading sympathetically and resisting helpfully; Charles Schuster, for encouraging me in this intellectual work; Diana George, for helping me see that reflection provides one means of faculty development; Doug Hesse, Jeff Sommers, and Robert Calfee for their responses to some of my earlier work on reflection; the members of Portnet (especially Michael Allen, Pat Belanoff, Bill Condon, Mary Kay Crouch, Cheryl Forbes, Marcia Dickson, George Meese, and Robert Marrs) for listening to me talk about relfection endlessly (it must have seemed); Sandy Murphy, who encouraged me to link reflection to assessment more theoretically; Sam Watson for pointing me toward Donald Schon; Brian Huot and Meg Morgan, for keeping me straight; Connie Rothwell, Fowler Bush, and Al Maisto, for encouraging my work in reflection in the honors program; my colleagues Mike Pearson, Christie Amato, and Mike Corwin, for inviting me into their classes and allowing me to work with their students.

No project like this—no writer like this—could exist without her students: thanks, most especially to them. No project like this is worth more than those who saw its development, day by day: thanks to my husband David, for his abiding belief in me; to my daughter Genevieve, for her welcome companionship; to my son Matthew, for his always-irreverent appreciation.

If you are lucky, you get to write a book that brings together what you believe and what you know, and that connects to what you do: it's a project in reflection.

Kathleen Blake Yancey
Charlotte, NC

CHAPTER ONE

On Reflection

We come to terms as well as we can with our lifelong exposure to the world, and we use whatever devices we may need to survive. But eventually, of course, our knowledge depends upon the living relationship between what we see going on and ourselves. If exposure is essential, still more so is the reflection. Insight doesn't happen often on the click of the moment like a lucky snapshot, but comes in its own time and more slowly and from nowhere but within. The sharpest recognition is surely that which is charged with sympathy as well as shock—it is a form of human vision.

Eudora Welty

In sum, no matter how objectively one thinks or writes, one does so in a storied context as a character acting in relation to other characters in some moment in time and space.

Walter Fisher

WE'RE THREE WEEKS INTO THE FALL TERM. IT'S STILL HOT AND SUNNY here in Charlotte, and today is Friday: the day when the first formal assignment, a narrative, is due in this course in first-year college composition. We've been writing (continuously, it seems) since the day the class started, but those texts were all preparatory. Somehow, they didn't count. Although the narrative due today won't be graded, it *will* count. The students understand that. The beneficiaries of twelve years' worth of schooling, they *know* what's going on, graded paper or not: *I'm going to see how they write.*

Before the bell rings, they're all in their seats, the 20 of them— men, women, black, white, Creole, Southern, Yankees, eager, distant. They flip through their texts, read them aloud to hear how they sound, laugh too obviously at nothing in particular. Kelly, the liveliest student, wears a vibrantly colored, bell-ringing jester's cap for the occasion. Although anxious about the impending evaluative moment, the students are also relieved, like runners at the end of a ten-miler. They've made it. School's about to be out for the weekend, and it's time to do something a lot more fun than writing.

Until I tell them: "Click on the word processor. We have one more text to write."

A *reflection*.

***

During the 1970s and into the 1980s, students in writing classes across the country were asked to take part in research focused on writing processes. The problem we wanted them to help us address was simple if a little disconcerting: while we in composition studies were supposed to be teaching students how to write, we didn't really know how they *learned* to write. We'd read how published authors learned to write, of course—or what they'd claimed as how they'd learned to write, usually in retrospective accounts that seemed to offer little if any generalizability. We'd done some interesting experiments in sentence-combining, hoping that we could change how they learned to write. We'd done a little investigation into creativity theory and thought about how that might be applicable to the teaching of writing. But ultimately, we didn't know much about the very thing we were supposed to be teaching: writing and the processes that create it. We certainly didn't know much about it from the point of view of those we were daily practicing upon: the students. As Janet Emig put it in outlining one of the first texts to redress this situation, *The Composing Processes of Twelfth Graders*, "The subjects for case studies have always been at hand, but, as teachers of writing, we have too often relied on tradition, ignoring the writers we are working with" (49).

If we had *too often relied on tradition* prior to the 1970s, we more than compensated afterward. In a period described by Sondra Perl as a shining moment, compositionists spent most of the 1970s and much of the 1980s investigating the composing processes of students. Perl's brief description of her case studies exemplifies the first and most popular approach:

> To gather my data, I observed five writers at work, and following Emig, I, too, asked them to compose aloud, tape-recording whatever they said. Since my interest was in documenting the sequence and flow of my students' composing, I devised a coding scheme to order and systematize what I was observing, which then enabled me to detect patterns of

composing within and among the students. Through careful coding, I discovered that students who produced flawed written products did, nonetheless, have consistent composing processes. (xiii)

Case study as methodology, then, and a focus on the individual student *composing aloud*, trying to get the writing right with the self: prime components of early research on composing processes. A second wave of research, more cognitivist in orientation, followed, led by Linda Flower and John Hayes. This research involved both novice and experienced writers as it focused less on how writers expressed themselves for themselves, and more on how the experienced writers approached the audience, so that what we learned from these latter writers could be applied to good effect in the classroom. Still, an irony: although these theories of composing derive from different understandings and value differently—the first, valuing the writer expressing him/herself (thus, called *expressivist*), the second, valuing the ability of the writer to create text for a reader—they resemble each other in their point of departure, a presumed ideal text, which determines the view of both process and product. As Joseph Harris explains,

> while they offer quite different views of the composing process, both Emig and Flower arrive at their sense of that process in much the same way: through positing an ideal text and working backward from that. The process you teach turns out to depend on the sort of product you want. The effect of process teaching thus becomes not an opening up of multiple ways of writing but an inculcating of a particular method of composing. (67)

More particularly, Harris claims, what was deleted from both models of composing was a powerful conception of *revision*:

> Both the expressivist and technocratic views of process lacked a dialogical sense of revision. For theorists like Emig and Flower, that is, the process of writing *ends* with the creation of a particular sort of text; they fail to explore in any real detail how writers might change not only their phrasings but their minds when given a chance to talk about their work with other people. To really change the teaching of writing, then, it seems to me that a view of process must go *beyond* the text to include a sense of the ongoing conversations that texts enter into—a sense, that is, of how writers draw on, respond to, and rework both their own previous writings and those of others. (68)

Current theories of composing—a third wave of work in this area, often based on cultural studies and sometimes called post-process—

do just that: study the effects of larger discourses on students and posit "end points" of earlier models (such as submission of text) as sites for revision. As put by Perl, then, composing process theory now has shifted to include a pluralized context (Harris's *ongoing conversations*) as a defining feature of writing and writer. "Studies of composing have led us then not to fuller and more detailed models or to larger and longer taxonomies as we once suspected they might. Rather, we are arriving at an understanding of the complex relationship between writers and the contexts that shape their lives" (xvii).

∗∗∗

Reflection has played but a small role in this history of composing. A single published article links reflection and composing process: Sharon Pianko's "Reflection: A Critical Component of the Composing Process," published in 1979. A quick review of the text, itself a synopsis of an unpublished dissertation, speaks of the behavorist orientation of the times and of the kinds of classroom practices new models of composing would eventually displace. Pianko first describes how the data were obtained, under what were *fairly usual classroom conditions* of the time. "All the writing episodes took place under fairly usual classroom conditions: the stimulus was provided by teachers; the writing had to be completed in one afternoon; the minimum length of the paper was specified; and the writing was done in a single enclosed room" (275). Reflection, according to Pianko, is indicated by a writer's *pauses and rescannings*, and distinguishes the *able* writers from the *not so able*.

> The act of reflection during composing—behaviorally manifested as pauses and rescannings and heretofore ignored as a component of the composing process—is the single most significant aspect of the composing process revealed by this study. It is reflection which stimulates the growth of consciousness in students about the numerous mental and linguistic strategies they command and about the many lexical, syntactical, and organizational choices they make—many of which occur simultaneously—during the act of composing.
>
> The ability to reflect on what is being written seems to be the essence of the difference between able and not so able writers from their initial writing experience onward. (277-278)

Reflection here is used, of course, in a way consonant with the times: as a mode of *behavior* indicative of *growth of consciousness*. When I asked my students to write a reflection, nearly 20 years later, I too wanted to see *growth of consciousness,* but not defined behaviorally as *pauses and rescannings.* Rather, I was interested in reflection as a means of go[ing] *beyond the text to include a sense of the ongoing conversations that texts enter into.* To get at that reflection, I had indeed bootlegged into my class a key tenet of the methodology of early process research: the idea of students as authoritative informants.

In retrospect, what the early researchers did seems pretty obvious. You want to know how students learn to write? *Try asking 'em.* (And a postmodern question: You want to know how they arrive at certain conclusions, what discourses they are drawing on? *Try asking 'em.*) These researchers did ask—in person, on tape, as they wrote, after they wrote. As students talked and as their talk was taped, *it became text.* As text, it was visible, it took on the status of text, invited the mechanisms of text—reading, interpretation, understanding, evaluation. From the very beginnings of research into composing processes, then, student writers were regarded as a crucial, informed, authoritative source, and some might say as the primary source.

In the years intervening, we've seen diminished interest in composing process research. Partly, this is a function of politics: the sense that process itself, without considerations of how knowledge is made and of the role that ideology plays, isn't enough ballast for an intellectually respectable investigation; and/or that process is too positivist/individualist/expressivist in nature, that it needs to become post-process. I don't really disagree with these observations. But we shouldn't lose sight of a key rhetorical move here on the part of the early researchers. In crediting *students* with knowledge of what was going on inside their own heads and in awarding it authority, they did something very valuable and very smart. These students are the ones who have allowed the rest of us, the teachers, to investigate, to understand, *to theorize our classroom practice.*

One purpose of this volume, then, is to recover this strand of student talk, but to do so in a new setting and to use it quite differently: to ask students to participate with us, not as objects of our study, but as *agents of their own learning,* in a process that is product that is becoming known, quite simply, as *reflection.*

***

One often undervalued and little understood method of identifying what we know and of understanding how we come to know involves what, in the last ten years or so, has been called "reflection." The word itself reflects and refracts what the Russian psychologist Vygotsky would call many senses of the word. It can mean revision, of one's goals, or more often, of one's work (Camp 1992; Weiser); it can mean self-assessment, sometimes oriented to the gap between intention and accomplishment (Conway); it can mean an analysis of learning that takes place in and beyond the writing class (Paulson, Paulson, and Meyer); it can entail projection (eg, goal-setting) that provides a "baseline" against which development can be evaluated (Sunstein); and it can mean all of the above (Black, et al. 1994a).

What I'll mean in this text when I say reflection will be 1) the processes by which we know what we have accomplished and by which we articulate accomplishment and 2) the products of those processes (eg, as in, "a reflection"). In method, reflection is dialectical, putting multiple perspectives into play with each other in order to produce insight. Procedurally, reflection entails a *looking forward* to goals we might attain, as well as a *casting backward* to see where we have been. When we reflect, we thus *project* and *review*, often putting the projections and the reviews in *dialogue* with each other, working dialectically as we seek to *discover* what we know, what we have learned, and what we might understand. When we reflect, we call upon the cognitive, the affective, the intuitive, putting these into play with each other: to help us understand how something completed looks later, how it compares with what has come before, how it meets stated or implicit criteria, our own, those of others. Moreover, we can use those processes to theorize from and about our own practices, making knowledge and coming to understandings that will themselves be revised through reflection. As Donald Schon suggests and as we shall see, "from our reflection upon the particular, we learn about the prototypic" (1995, 85).

Reflection, then, is the dialectical process by which we develop and achieve, first, specific goals for learning; second, strategies for reaching those goals; and third, means of determining whether or not we have met those goals or other goals. Speaking generally, reflection includes the three processes of projection, retrospection (or review), and revision. For writing, it likewise includes three processes:

1. goal-setting, revisiting, and refining
2. text-revising in the light of retrospection
3. the articulating of what learning has taken place, as embodied in various texts as well as in the processes used by the writer

Accordingly, reflection is a critical component of learning and of writing specifically; articulating what we have learned *for ourselves* is a key process in that learning—in both school learning and out-of-school learning (although I'm not sure the two can be—or should be—separated).

***

In the last decade, various constituencies within education have come to reflection as a means of doing something old better, or of doing something new.

> Students and their teachers have come to reflection in large part because of portfolios: collections of work that are narrated or interpreted by the composer in a *reflection* (see, for instance, Yancey; Black et al.; Yancey and Weiser).
>
> Teachers have come to *reflection* as a means of enhancing their teaching and/or changing curriculum (Applebee; Brookfield; Hillocks).
>
> Assessment researchers have come to *reflection* as a necessary component of evaluation, arguing that evaluation is only valid to the extent that it links back to curriculum, and that reflection provides one means to do that (Lucas; Camp 1993; Moss).
>
> Leaders within both higher education and K-12 have come to *reflection* as a vehicle for changing education on a large scale and in a systematic way, involving both students and teachers (see Hutchings; Myers and Pearson).

In sum, there are multiple reasons that the members of the educational establishment have come to the same place: *reflection*. Reflection brings with it an underlying promise: that it can provide a means of bringing practice and theory together (Phelps). In so doing, it makes possible a theorizing of practice based on practice, a means of extending and differentiating earlier practice, and then of theorizing anew. As Robert Brookfield, an advocate of reflection as a defining characteristic of good teaching, puts it:

> Theorists of reflective practice are interested in helping teachers understand, question, investigate, and take seriously their own learning and

practice. They argue that professional education has taken a wrong turn in seeing the role of practitioner as interpreter, translator, and implementer of theory produced by academic thinkers and researchers. They believe instead that practitioners, including teachers, must research their own work sites. This involves their recognizing and generating their own contextually sensitive theories of practice, rather than importing them from outside. Through continuous investigation and monitoring of their own efforts, practitioners produce a corpus of valuable, though unprivileged, practical knowledge. (215)

Much like the writing across the curriculum movement, work in reflection has been motivated, then, as much by interest in changing teacher practice as by interest in assessing student work, with faculty *recognizing and generating their own contextually sensitive theories of practice*. As Brookfield suggests, such reflection posits an intelligent agent engaging in frequent and deliberate self-awareness—what Patricia Carini calls agency and the witnessing of agency—in order to understand and learn from our own informed experience.

What Brookfield claims for teachers is also true for students. They too are *intelligent agent*[s] *who can engag*[e] *in frequent and deliberate self-awareness*, theorizing and learning from their own practice. In this text, several students *engag*[e] in various kinds and diverse forms of reflection. These students are not extraordinary. If they were, this would be a different kind of book, and more to the point, I couldn't suggest that what these students do, other students also can do. While these students, then, are quite ordinary, *what they are doing, through reflection, is extraordinary*.

As they learn, they witness their own learning: they show us how they learn. Reflection makes possible a new kind of learning as well as a new kind of teaching. The portraits of learning that emerge here point to a new kind of classroom: one that is coherently theorized, interactive, oriented to agency.

***

Brookfield also reminds us of what others–e.g., Dewey and Vygotsky and Polanyi–have said about how reflection works to help us understand and theorize our own learning. Those thinkers also provide a(nother) convenient stopping place for thinking about reflection.

John Dewey has written extensively about reflection, most explicitly in *How We Think: A Restatement of the Relation of Reflective Thinking to the Educative Process.* Here he defines reflective thinking as "the kind of thinking that consists in turning a subject over in the mind and giving it serious and consecutive consideration" (3). Reflection, he says, is goal-driven; since there "is a goal to be reached, . . . this end sets a task that controls the sequence of ideas" (6). Put definitively, reflection is the *"Active, persistent, and careful consideration of any belief or supposed form of knowledge in the light of the grounds that support it and the further conclusions to which it tends"* (9). Reflection is defined here as goal-directed and sequential, controlled by the learner because he or she wants to learn something, to solve a real problem, to resolve an ambiguous situation, or to address a dilemma (14). It relies on a dialogue among multiple perspectives, as the learner contrasts the believed and the known with presuppositions and necessary conclusions.

Reflection, Dewey also says, is habitual and learned. "While we cannot learn or be taught to think, we do have to learn *how* to think well," he says, "especially *how* to acquire the general *habit* of reflecting" (34). Since language "connects and organizes meanings as well as selects and fixes them" (245), it follows that reflection is language-specific. Dewey claims that there are three uses of language, chronologically developed and applied: first, the attempt to influence others; second, the entering into of intimate relations; and only later, the third: the use of language "as a conscious vehicle of thought and language" (239). The task for the educator is, therefore, to "direct students' oral and written speech, used primarily for practical and social ends, so that gradually it shall become a conscious tool of conveying knowledge and assisting thought" (239).

***

Lev Vygotsky too sees the exchange characteristic of interplay and dialogue as the foundation of reflection. According to Vygotsky (1962), "Reflective consciousness comes to the child through the portals of scientific concepts" (171), i. e., through the formal concepts typically learned from adults and/or in school, which are juxtaposed with "spontaneous" concepts, those that are unmediated by external language or systematic representation. To illustrate, Vygotsky uses the task of tying a knot:

> The activity of consciousness can take different directions; it may illuminate only a few aspects of a thought or an act. I have just tied a knot—I have done so consciously, yet I cannot explain how I did it,

because my awareness was centered on the knot rather than on my own motions, the *how* of my action. When the latter becomes the object of my awareness, I shall have become fully conscious. We use *consciousness* to denote awareness of the activity of the mind—the consciousness of being conscious. (170)

Reflection, however, requires both kinds of thinking, the scientific and the spontaneous, the strength of scientific concepts deriving from their "conscious and deliberate character," the spontaneous from "the situational, empirical, and practical" (194). Speaking generally, Vygotsky says, "the two processes . . .are related and constantly influence each other. They are part of a single process: the development of concept formation, which is affected by varying external and internal conditions but is essentially a unitary process, not a conflict of antagonistic, mutually exclusive forms of thinking" (157). We especially see these processes in dialogue at certain times of development, he explains, as during the period when children are between seven and twelve. Then,

> the child's thought bumps into the wall of its own inadequacy, and the resultant bruises—as was wisely observed by J. J. Rousseau—become its best teachers. Such collisions are a powerful stimulus, evoking awareness, which in its turn, magically reveals to a child a chamber of conscious and voluntary concepts. (165)

Learning thus requires scientific concepts, spontaneous concepts, and interplay *between them*. As in the case of tying a knot, we use this dialogue to focus on the end—the knot—as well as on the processes enabling us to achieve the end.

For Vygotsky, as for Dewey, language is critical for reflection: "The relation of thought to word is not a thing but a process, a continual movement back and forth from thought to word and from word to thought." (218). This interplay, then, is both foundational, in terms of our being human, and continuous. It begins at the moment of birth, as the child engages with–interplays with–the others of his or her environment, and according to Vygotsky (1978), it is through this communal play and interaction that the child develops individuality:

> Piaget and others have shown that reasoning occurs in a children's group as an argument intended to prove one's own point of view before it occurs as an internal activity whose distinctive feature is that the child begins to perceive and check the basis of his thoughts. Such observations

prompted Piaget to conclude that communication produces the need for checking and confirming thoughts, a process that is characteristic of adult thought. In the same way that internal speech and reflective thought arise from the interactions between the child and persons in her environment, these interactions provide the source of development of a child's voluntary behavior. (89-90)

In other words, we learn to understand ourselves through explaining ourselves to others. To do this, we rely on a reflection that involves a *checking* against, a *confirming*, and a *balancing* of self with others.

***

Knowing and learning—and therefore reflection—occur within the context of a problem. Michael Polanyi, like Dewey before him, identifies the *finding of the problem* as another key feature in reflection. Polanyi suggests that the problem definition itself is the first critical step in any creative act such as reflection.

To hit upon a problem is the first step to any discovery and indeed to any creative act. To see a problem is to see something hidden that may yet be accessible. The knowledge of a problem is, therefore, like the knowing of unspecifiables, a knowing of more than you can tell. But our awareness of unspecifiable things, whether of particulars or of the coherence of particulars, is intensified here to an exciting intimation of their hidden presence. It is an engrossing possession of incipient knowledge which passionately strives to validate itself. Such is the heuristic power of a problem. (131-32)

A scientist, the knower here of whom Polanyi speaks, controls his or her own problem, motivates him or herself by the questions the self poses, weaving back and forth between the felt and the known, the unarticulated and the explicit, what Vygotsky might call the spontaneous and the scientific, what Carl Sagan has called dual modes "cohabiting" in the mind.

***

Collectively, Dewey, Vygotsky, and Polanyi understand reflection as a social process by which we think: *reviewing*, as we think about the products we create and the ends we produce, but also about the means we use to get to those ends; and *projecting*, as we plan for the learning we want to control and accordingly, manage, contextualize, understand. We learn to reflect as we learn to talk–in the company of others. To reflect, as to learn, we set a problem for ourselves, we try to conceptualize that problem from diverse perspectives—the scientific and the spontaneous—for it is in seeing something from divergent perspectives that we see it more fully. Along the way, we check and confirm, as we seek to reach goals that we have set for ourselves.

Reflection becomes a habit of mind, one that transforms.

***

Writing has always been understood as unpredictable–as what Aristotle called the art of the probable. To write well, as Lloyd Bitzer argues, is both to understand and to respond appropriately to a rhetorical situation: to an exigence, or occasion, calling forth the writing, and to an audience engaging in that exigence with a writer. Guided by heuristics rather than rules, writing is not an exact science. But to learn—about how we learn to write, about how we know when a text suffices, about how to help others learn—*is* exacting. Hence, the problem: *how to know which methods of teaching and learning are best, how to know when a method works well.* Reflection offers one way to know that.

The philosopher Donald Schon offers another, more recent theoretical perspective within which to view both the teaching of writing and the learning of writing, the perspective that frames much of my work in this project. Known principally for his definition of the reflective practitioner, Schon argues that it is by reflecting on our own work—by knowing it, by reviewing it, by discerning patterns in it, by projecting appropriately from those patterns, and by using such projections to hypothesize a new way of thinking about a situation—that we theorize our own practices; that we come to know and understand our work and perhaps thus to improve it. In other words, reflection is *rhetorical.*

In explaining his epistemology, Schon begins by distinguishing between two kinds of knowing: that of the technical realm and that of the non-technical. The world of technical rationality, Schon says, allows for a knowing by way of causal inference that is controlled: the lab experiment, for instance, that confirms the presence of an antibody in the blood. This world is neat, is clean, is controlled and therefore managed quite nicely.

The second world is the world in which we *live*—and it is certainly the world of the classroom—the world where causal inference is a judgment call, no matter how well informed. Such knowledge relies upon the expertise of its participants, who, through reflection-in-action–a rethinking "lead[ing] to on-the-spot experiment and further thinking that affects what we do" (1995, 29)–become skillful improvisers. Given that they work in this second world–the world of teaching and learning–they must find effective ways to ground and to exercise both inquiry and judgments. As important, Schon says, it is only through reflection that they–and we–are better able to accommodate ourselves to the next iteration of a similar instance:

> In normal social science, the choice of questions, the selection of variables, and the design of experiments are all designed to produce externally valid causal generalizations of the covering law type. In contrast, causal inquiry in organizations typically centers on a particular situation in a single organization, and when it is successful, it yields not covering laws but prototypical models of causal pattern that may guide inquiry in other organizational situations—prototypes that depend, for their validity, on modification and testing "in the next situation." "Reflective transfer" seems to me a good label for this kind of generalization." (97)

Key to Schon's perspective are the two concepts of reflection-in-action and reflective transfer; these form the philosophical backdrop to this book.

More specifically, in this book I take those two central concepts, re-theorize them as three discrete but inter-related concepts and apply them to the teaching and learning of writing: *reflection-in-action* becomes a means of writing with text-in-process; *constructive reflection*, like Schon's reflective transfer, applies to the generalizing and identity-formation processes that accumulate over time, with specific reference to writing and learning; and *reflection-in- presentation* appears as the formal reflective text written for an "other," often in a rhetorical situation invoking assessment. Our definition of reflection in the writing classroom, then, involves these three kinds of reflection:

> *reflection-in-action*, the process of reviewing and projecting and revising, which takes place within a composing event, and the associated texts

constructive reflection, the process of developing a cumulative, multi-selved, multi-voiced identity, which takes place between and among composing events, and the associated texts

reflection-in-presentation, the process of articulating the relationships between and among the multiple variable of writing and the writer in a specific context for a specific audience, and the associated texts

Reflection-in-action and constructive reflection are separate constructs, though they often work together. In the composing of any text, the writer attempts to create novel responses based on new ways of seeing the situation, the purpose, the audience, the genre, and hence the material. Reflection-in-action includes those processes of review and revision and hypothesizing within a composing event— including all activities that go into a final text. It is always tacit. It can be made explicit; made explicit, it assists the writer in composing.

As reflection-in-action is focused on the single composing event, constructive reflection grows out of successive composing events. This second kind of reflection takes place tacitly as a composer writes to different rhetorical situations over time, so it is always implicit. Constructive reflection can take place quite explicitly as well, however, as when a writer is directed to consider the effect on him or her of multiple composing experiences, for example when a writer is asked to choose a set of texts to share with a public audience. Oriented to the writer-qua-writer, constructive reflection focuses on such questions as "who writes here?", "is this the same writer as before?", and "how does this writer know?" Constructive reflection is thus cumulative, taking place over several composing events. As it takes place, of course, and as response to composings are provided, such reflection has a shaping effect; it thus contributes to the development of a writer's identity, based in the *multiple texts* composed by the writer, in the *multiple kinds of texts* composed by the writer, and the *multiple contexts* those texts have participated in.

Reflection-in-action, then, can be private or public: its purpose is to understand the single composing event in progress and to make sense of it. Constructive reflection, as often as not, is private, often is unarticulated, the result of multiple composing events that themselves shape a writer.

Reflection-in-presentation is public: the image of the writer that is projected by the composer to an other. Commonly, we see reflection-in-presentation in portfolios–writing portfolios and teacher portfolios and capstone portfolios. Reflection-in-presentation takes place in the reflective letter that opens the portfolio and the reflective essay that closes it. The genre contouring reflection-in-presentation—the letter or the essay—is significant, for any genre will at once privilege and efface certain observations and modes of knowing. We also see reflection-in-presentation in two other situations. More and more frequently, especially in testing situations, students are asked to write a reflection to *accompany* a more canonical kind of text, for instance, an impromptu essay (Harrington). And not infrequently, students are asked to write a final, cumulative reflective essay at the term's end (Perl 1997, Marshall). In all three cases, because reflection-in-presentation is linked to public ways of knowing, it is typically associated with evaluation, with the judgment about the writing and the writer made by a reader. Thus, reflection-in-presentation brings with it discursive and epistemological issues associated with the ways it may be framed as well as evaluative issues associated with the ways it is read.

Teachers also are reflective practitioners; for them reflection is key to understanding performance. Another purpose of this book, then, is to explore how reflection can be employed to enhance the teaching of writing from the teacher's perspective. Individual teachers, like writers, use reflection-in-action to adjust their teaching, engage in constructive reflection over a set of teaching experiences, and project reflection-in-presentation when they present themselves publicly as teachers: in interviews for jobs, for instance, and in teaching portfolios for employment and promotion. In other words, teachers' practice, like writers' practice, is known, reviewed, understood and enhanced through reflection.

***

This project developed inadertently, at least initially. I didn't plan to do research on reflection (if that's what this is), and I certainly didn't plan to write a book on it. Like many teachers, I came to the topic interested in seeing if and how reflection could help students learn. I liked reflection for what it promised (but often failed) to add to portfolios, and I understood that for students to write a reflection-in-presentation that satisfied, they would have to write more than that single reflective text, on the quick, at the end of the term. In other words, reflection would need to be integrated within the curriculum.

It's also true that as I reflect upon how I came to reflection, I understand that I also came to reflection quite differently, in another context altogether.

In the late 1980s, I directed the Office of Writing Review, a center for writing assessment at Purdue University, whose mission was to "certify" the writing proficiency of all graduate students and some undergraduates. One of the difficulties in the job involved the high-stakes nature of the assessment. If the students' proficiency couldn't be sanctioned—and the scoring system we used placed an inordinately high value on surface error—students either wouldn't graduate or couldn't continue in their chosen field of study. Ethically as well as professionally, this put me in a bind. I do think that students—and more to the point, graduates—ought to write well. From that perspective, I was in accord with the purpose of the requirement. Writing well in this situation, however, meant writing an impromptu essay; this was an institutional constraint that I began to try to change, but in the meantime was a given. In sum, I didn't (and don't) particularly want to be part of a system—worse, in charge of a system—that denies students the right to continue based on a single impromptu essay. I'd prefer to focus my attention on devising ways of helping them meet whatever the requirements are, in a reasonable manner. Given the parameters of the situation and my own disposition, then, I had to find a way to help these students meet the requirement.

In practice, what this meant was that I met with most (if not all) of the very challenging cases: the student whose writing outside of the testing environment meets all conceivable standards but whose writing fails inside a testing center; the learning disabled student; the student who suffers from test anxiety; the student who just can't seem to find something to say on the proverbial assigned topic. In talking to these students, I learned. For instance, in the case of one student, what appeared from the text to be primarily a syntactic and usage problem turned out, after some discussion, to be rooted in rhetoric, more specifically in an absence of invention strategies. For another student, what the text suggested was a problem in coherence, but what we found together was a problem with the information base, a problem that the text did not properly signal. In other words, as I met and talked with these students, I began to see that *there was too little correspondence between my reading of their text and their accounts of what went into the making of that text.* Not that my reading was totally wrong, you understand, but that it was perilously incomplete. With their talk—with what I am calling reflection—the reading became fuller, at least.[1] We had a common, more stable place to start our work together, one informed by multiple perspectives, one informed by reflection.

Now, it's true that the students I was working with were what we might tag as the weaker students, at least in this rhetorical situation. It also occurred to me, however, that I was reading the texts my "classroom" students submitted the same way: in the same kind of isolation—as a reader in the garret. Assuming, then, that I would read these texts "better"—i. e., in a more informed way—if I asked the students to talk to me about them, I did. I asked them in many ways, at many times. *Reflection.*

In sum, I began to see reflection as a component not only threaded through, but *woven into* the curriculum.

***

Perhaps what was most interesting about these diverse reflective texts, when I began to reflect on them in a process analogous to what I'd been asking my students to do—to see them as a body of work, to think about what the stories that body of work claimed—was the story that they told about the writers of those texts. It was a story about how they learned and what they learned, about how that both dovetailed with what I'd planned, and departed from that agenda. From reading these texts, I began to understand from *the students' words* what was obvious: there was a lot more and other going on in my classes than I'd understood previously. So I began to ask about that—what's going on here?—sometimes abruptly, without warning, without really knowing what I was asking, much less what I expected to learn. Then I asked more carefully, became better able to read student cues as signals teaching me what was important, what needed to be asked. In time, which questions to ask of students, how to ask them, when to ask them became not a way of research apart from the classroom, but a means of learning for students and teacher *in* the classroom, and a different way of teaching for me.

Partly, this text is also that story: about learning to ask questions, about the power that asking good questions confers, about the value of doing this collaboratively so that we learn with and from each other. Reflection is, as I've learned, both individual and social.

Partly, this text is about what happens when we ask students what they think they are learning or have experienced or when we put that answer in dialectic with theory, when we put those in dialectic with what we observe and interpret, and when we begin to explain this to others so that we can explain it to ourselves. In other words: *reflective research*.

Finally, then, this project is also the story of what I have learned, which I can here preview:

> We tend to assume that we offer a single curriculum. But as Jennie Nelson has suggested, we have more than the one we offer. By my count, we have at least three curricula that operate simultaneously. The students bring with them their *lived curriculum*, that is, the product of all their learning to date. In the classroom, they engage in the *delivered curriculum*, which is the planned curriculum, outlined by syllabi, supported by materials and activities, and so on. The delivered curriculum, however, is experienced quite differently by different students: it is the *experienced curriculum*. The intersection among these three curricula provides the optimal place for learning; reflection is one means of establishing the location of that place.

> Historically, students have not been held accountable for their own learning, or for their own texts. The school model, rather, has gone something like this: students are responsible for learning; teachers are responsible for judging. Pragmatically and ironically, what this means is that students are not responsible at all for *knowing* their own texts: teachers will do that—come to know the texts—in the process of judging them. Rather than know their own texts, then, students are distanced, even alienated from their own work (which if you think of school as factory and about what Marx said about the alienation of workers from the product of their labor makes a certain amount of sense). Through reflection, students are asked to know their own texts, to find in them what is likeable, then to critique those texts, then to revise, not in the linear fashion I've just outlined, but like writing itself, recursively, and within a social setting.[2]

> Through reflection students articulate their own native language, a combination of discourses infused with idiolect, the multiplicity of which is what they bring into class with them. We can

see this at rare moments: a student with an interest in science talking about *variables* in writing, talking, in other words, about writing through the lenses and language of science. Like all languages, a student's native language is inhabited by metaphor and image: this too moves from tacit to explicit through reflection. How we should continue to invite such metaphor is a key question.

Reflection is both process and product. The *processes* of reflection can be fostered in several ways. Inviting students to reflect in multiple ways is inviting them to triangulate their own truths, to understand and articulate the pluralism of truth. Given what William Perry explains about maturation for the typical college student—that she/he moves from a dualistic stance to a relativistic stance to a reflective stance[3]—such invitations seem particularly appropriate. They allow students to articulate two opposing views; to bring in a third way; to consider the promises and effects and ethics of such an addition. In other words, reflection provides a place for such considerations to occur on a regular and systematic basis. The *products* of reflection are often informal, sometimes formal, not always explicitly marked as reflective. That reflective discourse can be found within the academy, in portfolios for instance, is by now a truism. What's as intriguing is that increasingly, it is found outside the academy as well, as we'll see.

Students can theorize about their own writing in powerful ways. Through reflection they can assign causality, they can see multiple perspectives, they can invoke multiple contexts. Such theorizing doesn't occur "naturally": as a reflective social process, it requires structure, situatedness, reply, engagement. When treated as a rhetorical act, when practiced, it becomes a discipline, a habit of mind. When treated as a rhetorical act, it has ethical implications.

One of these implications, one fundamental to this study, was pointed out to me by Affhild Ingberg. She suggests that this project is permeated by "a paradox which I see as central throughout: the tension between the different agencies that seem inevitable once one decides that it is essential to attribute agency not only to teachers (as designers of curriculum and as evaluators of student performance) but also to students." I agree: this tension defines the classroom. I think it always has, but it's simply more available through reflection. And Ingberg raises other, related questions that such a project needs to address: "Can one ASSIGN or REQUIRE of students that they be agents of their own learning?" And to "put this in another way," she asks, "is part of the value of reflection for YOU in this work that you didn't really know what you expected to learn? If so, what is the difference if someone else tries to 'design' your learning experience?"

No, I don't think we can require agency of anyone, theoretically or otherwise; like other teachers, I've had far too many students resist my idea of agency (which, however, doesn't mean they aren't exercising their own). Besides which, even if possible, the idea of requiring agency stikes me as oppressive (in a Foucaultian way). Still: *classroom as a place to make possible*, that's the idea. Reflection as means toward making possible, to help students learn about writing as they learn to write. So some insistance, yes: I am trying to insist that they do their own learning (as opposed to regurgitating mine), but I'm not designing it. I'm prompting it. I'm asking them to design it based on the prompt. The prompt is supposed to constrain what would be complete freedom otherwise, to effect a balance between freedom and constraint that leads to insight and surprise and creativity.

Reflective classrooms, where we teach writing "reflectively"—by which I mean using reflection as a means *and* an end—are places where we teach much differently than is typically the case. One way to think about it is to say that while many of us advocate student-centered pedagogy, we are still struggling to see how to get the student into that center. Instead of doing that coherently, in a theorized way, we rely on discrete, often scattershot techniques—say, an effort at self-assessment here, some small group work there—that taken together don't compose a whole—theoretically or pedagogically. Reflection—because it's theorized in a coherent way, and because it assumes an agency and authority—responds to that dilemma in a systematic, generative way.

***

This text includes eight other chapters. Here, I've set out the foundation for what follows, and in each of the next chapters I take up a particular dimension of reflection. In chapter two, "Reflection-in-Action," I look at reflection within a single composing event, focusing on several ways of asking students to reflect on that event, reading many student responses, and then talking about what we can learn from this kind of reflection. In chapter three, "Constructive Reflection," I work in a parallel way as I take up this more cumulative reflection, define it more completely, work with student texts, and think aloud about the identity formation that such reflection fosters.

Chapters four and five, in some sense, are also parallel chapters. Chapter four, "Reflection-in- Presentation," addresses the text reflection-in-presentation, with specific application to classroom situations, demonstrating its similarity both to scientific method and to autobiography. And again, I read student reflections here as a way to talk about what doesn't work in such texts and, as important, what does. In chapter five, "Reflective Reading, Reflective Responding," I distinguish between reading and response and explore what our aims in each might be. Then I again read some student texts, with an eye toward how students read their own work and how we might want to respond to those readings; how, in other words, our readings and respondings change to accommodate student readings—how our responses might become more reflective as well.

In chapter six, "Reflection and the Writing Classroom," I bring reflective processes and texts together as I read the work and the curricula of a college first-year writing class. My reading emphasizes the kinds of questions we might ask of students and theorizes from some answers about how it is that students think they become writers and not; it raises several questions as to the stances students take: learner, counterlearner, and overlearner. In "Reflection and Assessment," chapter seven, I move outside the classroom to discuss reflection in the high stakes assessment context, taking note especially of reading processes and the role they play in assessment that includes reflection, of the directions we provide in such assessments, and of the textual qualities we seem to value.

In "Literacy and the Curriculum," chapter eight, I conduct another kind of reflective reading: a reading of what it is that my students know about literacy when they enter the classroom. In doing this, I also talk about the nature of literacy and curriculum as I move back and forth from today to yesterday in a kind of reflective narrative. And chapter nine, titled "Reflective Texts, Reflective Students," concludes the book. In addition to summarizing the argument of the volume, it expresses cautions, it raises questions, it provides my final over/view. And it also provides one other reflective reading, of two texts, one from a recent *Harper's,* one from a student, to show that reflection is not only aside the drafts, but within them.

***

Here, then, is a story of reflection.

Notes

1. Of course, I might have known this from my work in the Purdue's Writing Lab, where I had enjoyed similar discussions with students. I should also indicate that I was assisted in this work by the finest staff possible, including Bob Child, Susan Carlton, Harriet Crews, Theresa Moore, and Mark Zamierowski.
2. Peter Elbow had it right about students needing to like their work before being able to work on it. See his essay "Ranking, Evaluating, Liking."
3. Of course, William Perry's study included only Harvard students, who as white males hardly constituted a representative case. Nonetheless, the movement toward multiple perspectives and reflective consideration of them is one the academy seems to value. I certainly value it; in some ways, it's the touchstone of my intellectual work with students.

CHAPTER TWO

Reflection-in-Action

Although most learning is thus subtle and unrecognized as such by either its recipients or its providers, a great deal of it does grow out of the more usual kind of conversation: direct verbal interchange between two people.

Sherwin Nuland

In the process of teaching the subject, composition, we are also composing the students.

Lynn Z. Bloom

IT'S FRIDAY; I'VE PICKED UP A SET OF ARGUMENTS FROM MY FIRST YEAR comp class. How do I read them? *Relative to an ideal text in my head:* how/do their texts compare with what I think is the model text for this assignment? *Relative to each other:* how does one student perform compared to the person he or she worked with? *Relative to what we did in class:* how well did those activities prepare them? *Relative to what a writer is capable of:* how would I know this? *Relative to what went into the making of the text?* What *is* the relationship between and among the making of text, the text, and the reading of it?

Suppose I began to ask some of these questions with my students, regularly. Suppose their answers were written, were visible. Suppose those answers contextualized my reading.

Reflection-in-action.

***

In *The Reflective Practitioner* and *Educating the Reflective Practitioner*, Donald Schon distinguishes between what he calls knowing-in-action and reflection-in-action. Many problems, Schon explains, are well defined, permitting (perhaps even encouraging) a "routinized" response. Such a response reveals knowing-in-action, a knowing that:

may be described in terms of strategies, understandings of phenomena, and ways of framing a task or problem appropriate to the situation. The knowing-in-action is tacit, spontaneously delivered without conscious deliberation; and it works, yielding intended outcomes so long as the situation falls within the boundaries of what we have learned to treat as normal. (28)

But much of writing, as we know, falls outside those boundaries, calls for novel responses based on new ways of seeing the situation, the purpose, the audience, the genre, and hence the material. Thus, the need for what Schon calls reflection-in-action:

Reflection-in-action has a critical function, questioning the assumptional structure of knowing-in-action. We think critically about the thinking that got us into this fix or this opportunity; and we may, in the process, restructure strategies of action, understandings of phenomena, or ways of framing problems. (28)

Through reflection, we can circle back, return to earlier notes, to earlier understandings and observations, to re-think them from time present (as opposed to time past), to think how things will look to time future. Reflection asks that we explain to others, as I try to do here, so that *in explaining to others, we explain to ourselves.* We begin to re-understand.

Reflection-in-action is thus recursive and generative. It's not either a process/or a product, but both processes *and* products.

***

To a certain extent, Schon's reflection-in-action seems to be composing process research, only dressed in new language. It seems to be what researchers of composing processes used to call the processes of "reviewing" and "monitoring" and revising as a single text is written. Although these processes weren't identified or defined as *reflective* in the Schonean sense in the models of composing that were created, what is currently called reflection-in-action—this thinking as we write, what Carl Sagan called a "co-habiting of dual modes of the mind"—was identified as a crucial part of the composing processes studied and described by Linda Flower and John Hayes, Sharon Pianko, Nancy Sommers, Sondra Perl, and Susan Miller. Regardless of the ways these researchers framed their observations, they all found the same thing: expert writers rely on this reviewing during composing and between drafts, finding in it 1) a means of invention and 2) a way to read as the other in order to communicate with him and her.

The observations made by Sondra Perl and Nancy Sommers are most germane to reflection-in-action. Perl constructed what we're calling reflection-in-action by dividing composing into two components, almost like two selves, calling the one *retrospection*, the other *projection*, calling them together the "alternating mental postures writers assume as they move through the act of composing" (Perl, 369). Retrospection, Perl and Egendorf say,

> refers to the way in which the writer turns back to lay hold of and take forward the sense, however, inchoate, of what is already there to say. Writing is the carrying forward of an inchoate sense into explicit form. This proceeds further when what has been written can be read, sensed anew and used to provide a further differentiation of the sense one has now of what one wants to say. (Perl and Egendorf, 126)

In contrast to retrospective structuring, they say, projective structuring

> depends on a writer's capacity to distinguish between a felt sense of what is intended and the formulations devised to say it. Only through this distinction can projective structuring succeed. One must be able (a) to lay hold of the sense of one's intention and (b) to compare it with one's sense of what readers will need to be told before they can grasp it, so as (c) to assess whether a given set of formulations provides an adequate vehicle for translating a private datum into publicly accessible form. (Perl and Egendorf, 125-26)

Accordingly, in the process of composing, the writer focuses on *both*: the relationship between the writer and the text; and the relationship between the reader and the text. Both focal points are generative.

During this same period (in the early 1980s), Nancy Sommers also posited two writers within the rhetor. Again relying (as was the custom then) on the expert writer for the model of felicitous practice, Sommers observed that

> experienced writers imagine a reader (reading their product) whose existence and whose expectations influence their revision process. They have abstracted the standards of a reader and this reader seems to be partly a reflection of themselves and functions as a critical and productive collaborator—a collaborator who has yet to love their work. The

anticipation of a reader's judgment causes a feeling of dissonance when the writer recognizes incongruities between intention and execution, and requires these writers to make revisions in all levels. (378)

Sommers thus also seems to be positing two actors working together within a single writer; the distinction between them is not only clear but necessary, forcing a detachment of the writer from the text, even as the text is being produced, a detachment that makes possible another perspective on the text.

Asking our students to reflect so as to adopt and adapt these perspectives invites them to behave as expert writers when they compose: to review their own texts, to read those emerging texts not only as writers but also as readers, to consider what strategies can be useful, to determine as they compose what truths they are to tell, what selves they are to construct and verbalize.

***

Reflection-in-action tends to be embedded in a single composing event, tends to be oriented to a single text, its focus squarely on the writer-reader-text relationship and on the development of that text. We can invite it in several ways.

***

One method of reflection-in-action is as familiar as composing process research, and not surprisingly, it takes the form of a description of writing process. One version of *the process description* is called a Writer's Memo. As outlined by Jeff Sommers, such memos are "'fresh' accounts of the composing process" that can bring the composing and responding closer together by showing how the primary text developed (181). More particularly, he says, it

> is this inquiring and reflecting—this looking back into the process leading to a completed draft, and reflecting on both it and the final product—that constitute the essential value of the writer's memo. All the other benefits grow out of increasing the student's awareness of the composing process— an awareness ultimately creating in the writer the capacity for internal response, for communication between the writer and the self. (185)

Descriptions of process, then, can be useful precisely because as first-person accounts, they provide a *record* of what happened; the record begins to make visible what heretofore was invisible. As important, in making this record, students begin to *know* their own processes, a first and necessary step for reflection of any kind. The principle here seems obvious, but it bears articulation: *We cannot reflect upon what we do not know.* And finally, as teachers, we can use that account, in the same way a mathematician uses a student's development of a proof, to inquire into how a learner moved from process to product, in this case from the processes of writing to final draft.

Not all accounts of writing processes are equal, of course. Some students seem to know their own processes, can mark them in a way that teaches. Others begin more tentatively. They don't seem to know how to talk about their own work, or perhaps they are only beginning to know it. When asked how he would prepare the current draft for submission after meeting with his peer group, for instance, one student remarked [1],

> My group did not find the things that I said would need to be changed but they did find some other things that would help out. First that I need to explain more on some of my details and second that I need to change one of my ideas and to use the world wide web instead of WWW. (Steve)

Does this student know his own work? How would we be able to answer this question, given, as Schon has said, that being able to reflect on a project in progress isn't at all the same as being able to verbalize that reflection (31). Perhaps the student here has a clear and detailed sense of how he is going to move from this draft to the next, but isn't yet able to externalize it on the page. But it's more likely— according to the research on expert and novice writers that Flower and Hayes have conducted—that the undeveloped scaffolding we see here—the general claims, the dearth of detail—indicates that Steve *hopes* he can move forward rather than *knows how.*

To the extent that specificity isn't *visible,* we—as readers, as responders, as teachers—aren't as useful as we might be. There's not much to comment upon—in terms of suggestion for continued writing, or response as to what might be working or not. Of course, one might also say that it's difficult to know which comes first—the process of writing, or the description of that process. For some writers, the process probably comes first; for others, exploring some detailed sense of what's possible *precedes and prepares for.* In both cases, asking for a process description is a good place to begin writing, to begin knowing one's work, to begin *reflection-in-action.*

Asking for a process description can also be useful after a submission draft is completed; it can provide another text for discussion among student and reader. A student in a tutoring class, for instance, told me more than she knew when she described the process she used to create a case study of a student she had tutored.

> The first thing I had to do was to decide on my student. After a question in class, I decided to do Carol and Alice. They work together in English 1101. The next thing I did was break up the categories into paragraphs. The categories were the student, issues, strategies, outcomes, and finally, what's new. Under each of the categories I put the main things that I wanted to say about the two different students. (Sarah)

This process description accompanied the formal text, what Chris Anson (1994) calls the secondary text, and it seemed to explain much of what I saw in the primary text: paragraphs that seemed like slots without integral or synthetic connections; paragraphs that identified categories and linked them to students, but that didn't seem to develop observations or activities; paragraphs through which the paper didn't progress. What, I still wondered, were *the main things that* [she] *wanted to say?*

When I looked at the process description, I saw the same material missing: *the main things.* What (little) process is articulated here seems highly mechanized as well as overly general (which given that my student was supposed to be tutoring others in how to write, was especially troubling). The good news: both texts—the process description and the primary text—told the same story, thus providing me with a starting place from which I could respond to the student.[2]

Even when process descriptions are detailed, insightful, and engaging—and thus *seemingly* unnecessary—they are still worth inviting. Of course, they are worth *reading* precisely because they are detailed, engaging, and insightful. They are, however, equally valuable to the writer, in at least three ways. First, in writing them, students frequently remember ways in which they generated material that they'd been unaware of. Consequently, in the process of recording the process, students learn: about the myriad of methods they use to recall, remember, re-create. And they have a *record* to which they can return. Second, describing processes can be generative: students often create scenes or themes or insights that they can use in a later draft. And third, in such describing, students continue to develop an authority, an *expertise,* about their own writing, about how it works when it works, as well as about how it doesn't. Deborah, also writing a case study of a student she is tutoring, provides us with a case study of process-based reflection-in-action:

> As I sat down to write about my student, Rachel, I tried really hard to focus on her as an individual—her facial expressions, her mannerisms, etc. I thought that if I could really recall the nuances of our sessions, I could give an overall impression of her. The reason is this: as she becomes more comfortable with her writing, her confidence level in our tutorials visibly increases.
>
> During our first session she was really uncomfortable. Dr. XXXX's comments on her draft just seemed to break her. She said, "I know what I'm trying to say, and I've never had problems writing before. What does this man want from me? After reading her paper, the first thing that came to mind was *a focus, perhaps.* Of course, I did not say it just that way, but after a brief conversation with her, I clearly recognized that she writes exactly the way that she talks—cyclically, constantly narrowing her circle until she finds her point. There is a point, but it takes her eons, it seems, to get there.
>
> So, as I said, I focused on her. I looked at her consecutive drafts. I noted the progress made in certain areas. Then, I just sat down at the computer and started to write. . . . I revised as I wrote, thinking some things not quite right, or a perception of her not quite on track. (Deborah)

Deborah's method of invention seems to involve many sources: 1) recall of the physical experiences and mannerisms of the student; 2) the student's description of what she sees as the problem; 3) Deborah's reaction to and analysis of the problem; 4) Deborah's interpretation of the changes the student went through; 5) a review of the student's texts. And in the course of describing the process, Deborah outlines the paper itself; the process description, in other words, acts as a means of invention, something against which she can check the final draft. As important, it may be only through such a reflection-in-action that Deborah herself will understand the multiplicity, richness, and textuality of the resources she is drawing upon. And then, too, I'm learning something. If the primary text is successful, I as responder have at least some idea as to how that might have come about, and I can link that process to the text in appropriate ways—by commenting on what I see as links between the two, by questioning Deborah as to what connections she sees, ask her to generalize from her own practice. And last but not least, I can move to generalize from this particular, use Deborah's reflection-in-action to help me plan: if this assignment works for Deborah, perhaps I can see through her words the kinds of task-specific strategies that I can recommend if I use this assignment again.

Yet another way to think about such process descriptions was developed over a decade ago by Lester Faigley, Roger Cherry, David Jolliffe, and Anna Skinner in *Assessing Writers' Knowledge and Processes of Composing.* To learn about composing processes, Faigley and his colleagues created a process log where students recorded descriptions of the processes they used in writing. When the researchers looked at these descriptions of processes, they saw that some were "better" than others in terms of students' control of composing, and they were able to identify gradations in the process descriptions. Adapting a scale used to show a developmental range of piano-practicing skills, Faigley and his colleagues developed a set of developmental categories for process descriptions:

> 1. *General-Intention Responses.* These responses are very general and give no indication of any knowledge of specific composing strategies. In addition, they often suggest only a student's abstract motivation to succeed in the writing task. General intention responses often take the form of such statements as "I really worked hard on this essay" and "I really tried to do my best."
>
> 2. *General-Strategy Responses.* These responses reflect a general approach that might apply to all writing situations. They are often mechanically employed and do not take into account the specific dimensions of the writing task or previous experience with tasks of the sort that are being commented on. Our research revealed such general-strategy responses as "I went back and corrected my errors," or "I made an outline for this essay."
>
> 3. *Task-Specific-Strategy Responses.* Responses in this category represent task-specific behavioral elaborations that have been adapted to meet the demands of the particular writing situation. We found task-specific strategies in such responses as "I wrote the rough draft of this essay very quickly since I wanted to have time to change my mind on this subject," and "I know exactly how someone feels in this situation since I have been in this situation many times before." (192)

Such a scale can foster reflection-in-action in two ways. In the first instance, when we as teachers ask for such process logs or process descriptions or writer's memos, we can begin to relativize student descriptions by plotting them against this guide so that we see what is included and what is absent, a guide through which we can identify and make sense of the gaps. Seen in this context, for instance, Steve has a starting place: he has moved beyond mere "abstract motivation" (pronouncements of time and effort spent) to include some general strategy responses—*explain some more of my detail,* as he says. Sarah, too: her description seems a hybrid of general strategy and task specific. In other words, I can call upon *the language and pattern of the scale* to talk to both students about the strategies they are using and about how we might make those less general and more specific to the task at hand.

Second, and as important, such a scale can help students themselves begin to relativize their own practice, to see how their own descriptions—like their own processes—can change from one task to another, from one text to another, from one occasion to the next. Given that writing doesn't develop in a linear fashion, and given that writers often take on new tasks that depart in intent, genre and audience from those of earlier tasks, it's not likely that we'll see a clear, straightforward progression from the Faigley group's category one to category three. But such a scale provides a language and a pattern against which a writer's composing can be mapped, understood, and reflected upon. It provides one frame for reflection-in-action.

***

A second means for reflection-in-action takes the form of a *companion piece,* a (secondary) text that is composed after a (primary) text is completed. Although a companion piece can be composed in diverse genres and have different local intents, its larger purpose is to comment in some way on the primary text *qua* text. Elsewhere, for instance, I've talked about Transmittal Forms, which are sets of sequenced questions—about writer intent, about the intended audience, about problems the composer had in creating the text—whose answers collectively set a context for the reader (Yancey, 1992). Sam Watson has talked about the *letter of reflection* he requests in which students can talk about whatever they think is important for the reader to know as she or he reads the primary text. Here I'd like to outline another kind of companion piece that is focused in two directions: toward self-assessment and toward multiple perspectives. It too facilitates reflection-in-action.

The original idea in this self-assessment companion piece, what I'm calling a Talk-To, was to invite students to reflect in two ways.

First, I wanted students to think about their text quite explicitly from diverse perspectives. Second, I wanted to begin to de-mystify how I go about reading and evaluating a text; I wanted to bring some awareness of my reading process into their thinking, again in some explicit way. I was convinced that *if asked,* students could in fact perform a teacher-like reading themselves; and that performing such a reading and putting it in dialogue with their own thinking about their text would be a good means of seeing *possibility* within that text. To work toward these two goals, I began by borrowing from Elbow's *Embracing Contraries* and asking students to write a Talk-To contextualizing a primary text in which they first, were to

believe that this is the best paper you've ever written

and then to

doubt that this text is any good at all.

This gave students two frames through which to see their own work, to see also that the same text—their text—didn't have to be either/or; it could be (and probably was) both/and. I also wanted students to think about their text from the perspective of another—in this case, from my perspective. So, I asked students to

predict Yancey's take on this paper.

As we know, texts aren't static commodities: even as teacher (some might say especially as teacher), I don't have a lock on how a text should be read. In other words, if writing and reading are the things we say that they are—by which I mean social and negotiated—then a space for such negotiation needs to be provided. So, I asked students to

agree or disagree with your sense of Yancey's take on this paper.

This set of stances—*believe, doubt, predict, agree/disagree*—acts as a heuristic; it provides a basic template to which other questions, as we'll see, can be added.[3]

One of the values of this heuristic is that while it taps into the wisdom of *Embracing Contraries,* it also moves farther, as it includes perspectives other than the writer's. The tension between believing and doubting can be generative: as a function of working within these two categories, writers can see their own texts differently; it is through such a crossing of frames that much invention and creativity are produced. As important, students are more likely to see their texts as complicated, as worth *both* believing in and doubting. The danger, however, in using such a set of contraries is that it will underscore a dichotomous view of writing that students already have, as

Elbow himself notes: as weak/strong, bad/good (Elbow, 1997), a point also discussed at some length by Chris Anson. As Anson suggests, students, particularly first-year college students (like their younger high school siblings), often operate in this either/or mode, as dualistic thinkers, unable to contextualize their work. Summarizing William Perry's schema of maturation, Anson says, "When students begin college, they often see the world of knowledge in polar terms: right vs. wrong, good vs. bad. Authorities (teachers) possess all the answers, because they strive to accumulate Absolutes in their role as givers of truth" (334). For writers, dualism means that "there is a 'correctness' both in the proper form and the proper content of a response to a task" (335). In other words, in composing a text, one succeeds, or one fails.

As students mature, though, they "begin to take on a more relativistic view of learning" (335), recognizing the ways that context influences what was previously regarded as right and wrong, beginning to appreciate the role that ambiguity plays in a world they start to understand as "pluralistic" (337), eventually moving to what Perry calls "committed relativism." Anson describes "the dominant epistemological view in this stage as *reflective*" (337). The purposes, then, in designing this sequence for reflection-in-action are multiple: to help students to *know*, but also to *like* and to *unlike*. In Perry's language, we help students move beyond dualism and toward a more complex, sophisticated view of their own texts. More specifically, the purposes for this Talk-To include:

- to encourage students to articulate their tacit understandings of their own texts
- to encourage students to assess their own texts, as practiced writers do
- to encourage students to predict how a specific reader will interpret and value that text, as experienced writers do
- to encourage students to articulate various ways of reading their own text, synthesize them in some way, and perhaps to use that to shape the additional development of a text
- to encourage students to make informed judgments, as experienced writers do

Ultimately, of course, what we are trying to foster here is reflective writing, produced by reflective writers.

Michelle's Talk-To illustrates how this form of reflection-in-action can work. A first-year African American college student, she is a strong student; and–rare for any student, I think–she has turned down an athletic scholarship to study. Like many first-year college students, she knows much more about literature than about writing. For this assignment, she has written a narrative about a trip to Spain she took as a high school track star; she focuses, as she says, on the plane trip itself. Her detailed analysis shows us also how she *under-stands* writing—as a process and as a phenomenon with certain characteristics she is beginning to understand as flexible. Michelle first *believes*:

> I believe that this is the best paper that I have written because I focused on one particular subject. During high school, I always wrote broad papers. They didn't have just one focus. They were mainly written over a long period of time. This paper focuses on one day; the day that I traveled out of the country.
>
> Another reason that I feel that this is the best paper . . . is because I put more time into it than any other. I sat down and planned this paper. I wrote out the things that I wanted to include in it. I remembered things about my trip that stood out for me and put them into my paper. Because of this, I found that my paper would be too long for the assignment. Therefore, after three Statements of Purpose [a planning document], I finally come up with the subject of what I thought could be a good paper. I jotted down a few details and began to elaborate on them. (Example: the food on the airplane episode and how the clouds and the land stood out to me.)
>
> Last I revised my paper more than I have ever revised other papers that I have written. Usually, I write a paper, then edit it for spelling, grammar and small things. This time, I changed sentences, added sentences, and did what I thought was good revision. I think that this helped my paper to be more focused on its topic, contain more detail and also made it more interesting.

Michelle begins by remembering the nature of her last writing experiences, in *high school,* and how they are different from the experience here: instead of taking a broad view, as she has in the past, she here *focuses on one day;* has spent *more time;* has written *three Statements of Purpose;* and has engaged in *revision* she thinks is *good*–one that entails not only editing, but *adding sentences* and *changing* them. In short, while Michelle wasn't asked to provide a process log, that's what we have here. It's fairly task-specific, and it's contexualized relative to her own practice. Without being asked, she's brought her past writing experiences with her and used them as a frame of reference. Interesting. But also interesting: Michelle believes the text is the *best paper* not because of any of its features (say, organization or detail) or because of its rhetorical effect (say, how it communicates to an audience, or what it communicates) but rather, because of the more elaborated processes she has developed. In fact, viewed from this perspective, *what Michelle seems to have learned in this assignment is how a writing task needs to be narrowed, just as how a writing process needs to be elaborated.* Had Michelle not explained this to herself, I'm not sure she would have "known" it. I certainly would not.

Michelle also *doubts*:

> I doubt that this is a good paper because I feel that I didn't cover enough details about what went on in the day. The only detail that I think that I fully elaborated on was the food episode. That was probably because it was the most memorable thing from my flight over to Spain and because it was my first "different" experience. Much more happened during my flight than I wrote about. I could have elaborated on the movies that I saw, the people, how I felt, and the athletes and made this a much better paper. My problem was in order to go into immense detail, you must have a lot of leeway to write. This was supposed to be a 3-5 page paper. If I would have elaborated more the things that happened on my flight, I could have produced a 6-8 page paper. Also, my use of words could have been improved. I feel that I ran out of words and phrases that would make my paper stand out from all others.

Again, here Michelle considers what's going on in the paper. She could have written *differently,* she says; she's not sure how to go into *immense detail* and still stay within what she understands as the parameters of the assignment. And she shows in this summary what else could go into the paper if it's to be revised: accounts of *the movies that I saw, the people, how I felt, and the athletes.* So not only has Michelle seen some gaps that might need to be filled, but she has also talked about 1) the nature of writing tasks and the flexibility of the parameters, especially for school tasks; 2) the desirability of including various kinds of material about her topic and in detailed form; and 3) her sense that her *words and phrases* aren't conveying the expression she is attempting.

What's also interesting is that we get to these more abstract issues—the nature of school assignments, the kinds of development needed—*through the specifics of a given text.* The particularized text and her reflection-in-action on it, in other words, help Michelle begin to develop her own theory of how her writing works and what it needs to do to work in this college rhetorical situation. As Schon remarks, we learn about the prototypic through the specific: Michelle shows us how.

Michelle also *predicts* my reading of her text:

> I think that you are going to read my paper and afterward have the feeling that I am a decent writer but have the potential to be much [better]. I could be better if I would make a better choice of words, make my statements more clear, and if I would go into more detail. You will think that this paper could have been better also if I would have made my audience see what was happening as I did instead of telling them that it happened. You will probably also think that I could have used better transitions throughout my paper. I feel that I sometimes jumped to different subjects without some foreshadowing.

At this point audience comes into play. When Michelle *believes,* she talks in terms of process; when she *doubts,* she talks in terms of textual features; when she *predicts,* she talks about *audience* and the need for her readers to *see what was happening as I did instead of telling them that it happened.* Even the need for transition is couched in terms of linking *different subjects* rather than as isolated textual feature. Also interesting here is the relationship between text and writer that Michelle pursues; she has a fairly sophisticated understanding of herself as a writer, apart from this text. Thus, although Michelle understands herself as a *decent writer,* she has the *potential* to be better. Michelle then explores how she-as-better-writer would do this— by writing the better words and sentences that she sees as missing from the text here. *In this reflection-in-action, Michelle begins to write her own curriculum for development.*

Finally, Michelle decides the extent to which she *agrees* with the assessment.

> I do agree with what I have written as your response to my paper. During the writing of my paper, I came to many points when I was at a loss for words. I also had to stop many times and just think about where I wanted to go next in the writing. So, I would agree if you thought that I should use better transitions within my text and choose better words. Also, in my paper, I know that some statements are unclear. I went over these during revising many times, but just couldn't find the phrases that would make the sentence sound better.

Here, Michelle continues to stipulate some of the terms for our discussion of her text: in this case, I concurred with the student's assessment in the Talk-To. As readers, we did need to *see* more than Michelle had shown, some of her words didn't seem quite right, and the text was surprisingly jumpy for such a focused piece. It's not always the case that as reader, I do agree, however; often I read text differently than the writer, especially at the beginning of our work together— which is one way of parsing a writing course, *as our work together*. Such a reflection- in-action gives us a place to begin that work.

***

A third means of fostering reflection-in-action is to continue the nominal dialogue that the text and a response create.[4] We like to talk about text and response as composing a conversation; however, what we often have is a predictable and *non*-conversational kind of sequence:

a student develops a text and turns it in;
I read it, I comment on it, I return it;
perhaps it returns to me in a portfolio, perhaps not;
case closed.

Or not? Suppose that when returning the text, I ask for a response to my reading. The wisdom of asking for such a *response piece* was brought home to me by Elizabeth Hodges's work on student response. Her project is to determine how students "unpack" teacher responses to their texts. The results so far disappoint and, from a teacher's perspective, dishearten. Put simply, whatever it is that students *unpack* in our responses, it certainly doesn't seem to be what it was that we thought we had *packed*. In the place of what we understood as specific responses and recommendations, students find uncertain readings, confusing advice, and another text altogether. Although Hodges's project is research, I saw it as another means of reflection-in-action. All it involves is asking students to "talk back" to the teacher when texts are returned. So the Monday after I heard Hodges's talk, I was returning a set of papers; as I did, I said, "Talk back to me. Tell me what you think I'm saying, tell me how you are reacting to what you think I'm saying, tell me where I'm clear, where you disagree, what you want me to know." They did.

As with other invocations of reflection-in-action, what writers will create in Talk-Backs varies; but all of it is text for conversation authorized by the student. Sometimes, for instance, the responses are surprisingly specific: "I thought that a comma can now be optional after a dependent clause?" and "The reason I chose to use the word 'peep' is that I thought it would appeal to my audience—they are feeling urges to peep into areas that adults have not wanted them to before." Other Talk-Backs take the form of summary, a kind of reality-check as to whether the writer understands what it is that is being communicated to her:

> You liked the specific details I included. Most of the recommendations you made were concerning clarity. You suggested describing the setting an then interpreting. You commented that one of my paragraphs is vague. You also suggested I begin one paragraph with a more effective word than "this." In two incidences you also recommended that I more clearly define my words where similarities had been drawn.

In such a summary, the student gains practice in reading and interpreting the comments of a reader. But such a summary can cause concern as well; sometimes students see such a record as a sort of "to-do" list, the completion of which, they assume, will assure an excellent paper—and grade. In such a case, judgment is somehow suspended between and among the items on the list. No dialogue is intended, and none ensues. The reflection does not work as intended. (It fails.)

Other times and more productively, the Talk-Back provides a chance to bring in multiple contexts that only the student would know; *the primary text's* intertexts *are articulated as the student makes sense of, interprets, and applies a teacher's reading.* Tasha, a particularly confident first-year student, knows the argument essay better than I. But the narrative, she is learning to write. She responds below to my reading of her narrative. I had asked three questions as a way to frame the Talk Back:

- What was valued in the text (by the reader)?
- Do you agree with this reading of it?
- What else would you like me to know?

Tasha replies:

> I think that Dr. Yancey did enjoy the overall story plot. She agreed with me when I wrote that I had some good imagery. She liked that I tried to

use slang and improper grammar to decrease the reader's distance [from the writer; to create a more intimate space between them]. She did like the paper for all the reasons that I thought she would. Also, the things I stated would turn her off to the paper were correct assessments, too. She definitely understood my difficulty in finding the exact words I was looking for to make my meaning complete. She suggested that I go to the WRC [Writing Resources Center]. I think that is a very good idea. I knew it was there for students, but I never considered going there because I thought it was for students who were doing poorly in their English skills. I guess it is for everyone regardless of their writing level and skills.

I do agree with Dr. Yancey because her comments were the same exact ones I thought she would give. However, I didn't realize how many errors I had in the paper. I will spend the holiday [fall break] looking over them and trying to detect, diagnose, and correct.

I am not overly grade conscious. I don't usually worry about my grades because I am confident enough to know that if I study I can do as well as I want to. Unfortunately, writing is different for me. It is not cut and dry at all. Studying more is not the key to it. The comments are very, very helpful because they give me a sense of direction. Also, it would be nice to have a "measuring stick" to compare each paper to. So I wouldn't want an actual grade but something to help me see where I stand and where to go. So maybe just a comment like passing, above passing, or something of the sort could be put on my papers.

Tasha's first observation focuses on the match between her reading and mine: she's pleased that I *enjoy* the *plot*, I like the *good imagery*, I like the *slang*. This language—*plot* and *imagery*, for instance—Tasha brought to class with her, and I'm assuming it's language she learned in a prior English, probably one devoted to literature. Here, she uses it as a starting language with which to talk about her narrative, and in some ways it's not a bad fit—a narrative tends to have a *plot*, and in class we had discussed *imagery* as it appeared in some of the narratives we read. Still, my sense is that these terms were bootlegged in from prior experience. (Perhaps the narrative assignment as a transitional essay makes sense, if Tasha's experience is at all typical: it provides for a kind of curricular overlap that could help bridge the transition from the high school to the college context.)

At the same time, Tasha is learning a new language that she can use to talk about texts, the language of composing—*detect, diagnose, and correct*. As Tom Hilgers points out, all students, even very young elementary students, *can talk about writing in the language of writing* if their classroom discourse is populated by such language, and we see such application in Tasha's remarks. She's also learning about composing itself—as she says, *writing is different . . . It is not cut and dry at all. Studying more is not the key to it.* In this reflection-in-action, we also see Tasha learning about both composing and the college environment when she observes that the WRC *is for everyone regardless of their writing level and skills.* The questions framing this Talk-Back, then, like the other *sequences of questions* fostering reflection, act merely as a scaffolding, a means to generate *student intertexts*: insight and dialogue about texts, composing, curriculum, and whatever else the student sees as germane.[5]

Although not all students are as specific or as elaborated as Tasha, most can still begin to negotiate their texts with teachers. They can "talk back": summarize and agree and disagree and set their own agendas. One college senior, for instance, was quite clear about how she would proceed after receiving my response:

> It does not surprise me to find "wordy" [the comment I had made on her text] in a couple of spots. In fact, I fully expect it every time I turn in a rough draft and sometimes a final draft. You mentioned being lost in the beginning—I was too. Guess I reflected that in my paper. I think I can fix it, though. I have read all of your comments, but I feel I need more time to decide if I agree with all of them. I can certainly see your point in all of them, but I want to play around with what I can do, say your way. I'll compare that with what I have and get back to you. Do not get me wrong: I love criticism, constructive or not. I take it all into consideration. (Judy)

The writer here seems pretty much in charge, ready to consider advice but interested in experimenting and seeing for herself *if I agree.* And she's not alone: a first-year writer makes the same kind of point:

> I also agree with Yancey that the last sentence of the paper isn't right. Yancey said it was too strong, but I don't think that is the problem. I think World War II did change the face of the world for the better, but I also think I could have stated this in a better way. (Sharon)

Both writers may choose not to revise; this too can be an appropriate decision. As Tom Hilgers puts it, "it is possible that evaluation can yield a decision not to revise. Expert writers frequently employ evaluative criteria as goals when they plan a piece of writing (Scardamalia, 1984). When such goals are effectively met in a draft, a decision not to revise may be perfectly appropriate" (54). The point here, then, is that when writers are treated as writers, they will need to be awarded the authority that comes with writing. They may make decisions that run counter to our recommendations, and if they do so for reasons that are rhetorically sound, then we will need to defer. Through reflection-in-action, we begin to negotiate; our practice changes in fundamental ways.

More generally, the student constructed in all these forms of reflection-in-action is not passive, may resist our authority, and in doing so—in terms of caring enough about a text to negotiate what happens to it in specific and informed ways—may be behaving exactly as we would wish. At the same time, there's no question: this isn't easy, especially not for us, even those of us who consider ourselves progressive. As Sarah Freedman reminds us, it's not easy to negotiate our own authority, and in these practices and texts, that's what's at issue. She relates forceful writing directly to audience expectations and permissions:

> one of the problems that many students exhibit when they write is a lack of force, a lack of commitment to their topics. I do not believe that most of us take into account how much the teacher-student role relationship militates against the student's ability to write with force and authority. The amount of force a student can show is most likely directly related to the student's power over the topic and the audience. The more the student thinks he or she knows as opposed to what the audience knows, the more forceful the student will be able to be. . . . Most important of all, once we ask for and get forceful writing, we must be careful not to show bias and penalize the writer inadvertently for what may appear to be a student's overstepping of his or her role. (309-310)

Here the issue of authority—which is a good deal of what assigning, responding to, and, ultimately, grading texts is about—will challenge many of us. But to fail to take up this challenge is, of course, to ignore our own rhetoric—not just about liberatory pedagogy, but about the rhetoric that we teach, about the negotiation from which meaning is constructed. As important, to fail to take up this challenge denies students the opportunity to engage in the very discourses that construct us all.

And Talk-Backs can accomplish one other purpose: they can generate the dialogue I had hoped for when I first used them. In other words, it's true that in responding to our students, we can ask them questions; they can, of course, return the favor, as Susan makes clear.

Well, I did feel better about this paper than my other ones until I got it back. I didn't predict how you would react to my paper very well at all. . . . You did agree that my sources were good, but I still didn't give enough illustration of my points. I agree with you, though, that examples and quotes from Julie Hill [a professorial source] would improve the paper. I knew that you don't agree with my position (What happened to truth?), but I do think that if I had put quotes and examples from my interview with Julie that it would have made my point stronger. I guess what I might ask you is "Whose truth?" That may be a point that I will want to bring up in the paper. To me, public relations is like law: they both DO have "party lines," take stands that they try to illustrate as truths.

    As far as my pronoun reference goes . . .

Whose truth indeed?

***

I need to be clear about the sequence I've typically employed in devising these texts for reflection. Usually, I've seen the need for such a reflective text for some reason that is rhetorically based if not theoretically driven; that is, I've seen that if I as teacher knew more and knew better, I could be more useful to students. And I've understood that *students do know more and know better*—about their thinking, their processes, their practices. We've assumed this in our research, but we haven't always assumed this in our classrooms. All I've done, in one sense, then, is to make the classroom a place where students can speak on their own behalf *so that they too can begin to see how they learn.* The rhetorical situation, then: please tell me as teacher what's going on.

    But it's also true that I see this reflective writing more theoretically than at first light, that framing these practices as reflection-in-action helps me see them differently, more deeply, more intertextually. I see that reflective practice, as I have defined and illustrated it here (and no doubt there are other ways of implementing such practices), asks student writers to do what experienced writers do: think and talk about their work. Furthermore, I think changing such student practice changes teaching practice as well, in at least four key ways.

    First, asking for such a context makes it less likely that we will read that primary text against some ideal text, against the one in our heads, against the one a student's colleague produced. We may still read with these contexts in mind, but we'll read a composer's primary text along with/as informed by at least one other, the written context that s/he has created. Not surprisingly, then, when it comes time to respond to the text, we can talk to both texts—the primary text and the secondary text, where we find some of the composer's perceptions about that text.

Second, when we invite writers to share their own context in these ways, we do more than issue an invitation; we likewise send a message, in this case about what it means to write. Good writers, for instance, do not produce good writing easily, even if they are good writers, but students often believe that they do. (As one student told me, "A good piece of writing is usually one that comes easily and quickly to the writer.") So the questions we ask—how did you write this text, what's working in it, what difficulties did you encounter in writing it, do you agree with the reading others gave it?—*suggest the kinds of experiences writers typically have.* In other words, we know that writers do consider audience, they do review their work, they do consider the effects of proposed changes, they do predict how readers will interpret their text and write with that prediction in mind. But students often don't understand that *these are the practices of writing.* Asking them about how they practiced as writers is asking them to become writers. As important, we should carefully consider which questions we want students to address, which messages we want to send.

Third, the observations students make contribute to a writer's identity formation. Often, students cannot characterize their own writing practices in any detailed way, probably because they haven't been asked to do so—nor have they volunteered. But much like the teacher who begins to learn his or her own teaching practice by keeping some kind of record of it, writers too can record their observations as one of several moves toward knowing their practice. Understanding themselves as writers means that they can discourse about how they engage in, create, revise text for multiple audiences and purposes, about which truths they hold. Such discoursing is an identity-building process, and it is a key part of any writing curriculum. (In fact, it's not an exaggeration, I think, to claim that all curricula are exercises in identity formation. If we approached our classrooms with that understanding, what other changes might we make?)

Fourth, the articulations that students make contribute to a kind of language about writing that informs us all. In one sense, it permits a writer to talk about his or her writing from a very personal perspective, thus linking the personal perception with the public activity, often in a unique way that allows the composer to narrate his or her own development. In another, Bahktinian sense, the language that a student uses brings traces of past learnings with it, and one goal, then, is to see how well this language adapts and can be made to work in the new rhetorical situation. And in other sense, a class itself is a course in acquiring language, in this case the languages of writing and reflection.

***

It's also true, as one reader suggested to me, that as I've collected and thought about and analyzed and thought about and articulated (again) what I see in my students' work, I've conducted a kind of research myself. That was not my original intent, but it has become a secondary purpose. For instance, when I look at the collective activities described here as reflection-in-action, I see that I've begun to understand more generally how reflection assists in development of writing. Put simply, it asks that students acquire four "kinds" of knowledge: self-knowledge; content knowledge; task knowledge; and judgment.

1. *Self-knowledge:* the knowledge that the writer has his or her own writing rituals and practices; of the fit between what the writer hoped to say and then got onto the page; of the kind of writer—eg, single-draft, multi-draft, discovery—that he or she is, or used to be; of how the topic connects personally with the writer in ways we can't see from the primary text.
2. *Knowledge of the content:* in writing any text, we learn about the thing that is our subject, and yet we rarely ask our students about what they have learned in that writing. I had a student a few years back, for instance, who wrote a fascinating account of the Salem Witch Trials in three versions: as mass hysteria; as east meets west (side of town); and as a fatal case of misogyny. I wish I had asked her what she had learned—about how the history of our country seems to have been written, about how our social/geographical/gendered place literally establishes our ethos, about what questions this learning might have raised about other historical events for her. In other words, in theory the writer learned what we read in the text, but the writer may also have learned a considerable amount that couldn't (and

shouldn't) go into the text—both specific information related to the topic and larger insights that link this topic to others. (Since this knowledge is more related to identity formation and less to the creation of a single text, it will be considered in chapter three particularly.)

3. *Task knowledge:* when we say that we are developing writers, what we often mean is that we are helping them understand the nature of writing—the role that audience and purpose play; strategies for developing a persuasive argument; ways of voicing different kinds of texts and understanding when rhetorical situations call for different voices. The assumption here is that a writer can talk about writing. Task knowledge is conveyed in a specific language—drafting, images, argument, audience—and we look for that detailed language too as a measure of task knowledge.

4. Judgment: this category doesn't fit neatly with the prior three, but it is relevant for several reasons. In the first place, it asks that writers familiarize themselves with their own work: you can't talk about your writing with any authority until you take a look at what you have. Historically, we have not asked students to look at their own writing; historically, we have looked at it for them, and we have done so in spite of our understanding that experienced writers do look at their own writing throughout composing in order to compose, and afterward; in spite of the fact that we do want students to exercise some authority over their own work. When writers do look at their own writing, they begin to see themselves as a verbal construct: taking one subject position in one rhetorical situation, taking another in a second, sometimes taking multiple subject positions within a single text.

In the second place, a request for judgment, as conceived of through reflection-in-action, requires that students like something they have done, and as Peter Elbow suggests, we have to like before we can invest ourselves. (*And we can't like until we know.*) Only after we know, and we like, can we critique—or doubt—and we can't make something better without understanding that better is needed, ie, without doubting. So I think there is a kind of sequence here that is required before judgment can be made: knowing, then liking, then critiquing.[6] And in the third place, the ability to make good judgments is one characteristic of expertise, and it is precisely this expertise in writing that we are seeking to develop in our students.

In addition to the scale that Faigley and his colleagues proposed, I'd like to suggest this one, not for summative evaluative purposes, but as another way of thinking about reflection-in-action and the kinds of knowledges it fosters:

- Knowing: Does the writer display/demonstrate familiarity with his or her texts?
- Liking: Does the writer like his or her texts for reasons that other readers would concur with? How sophisticated does the appreciation seem?
- Critiquing: Is the writer able to articulate how a text might be changed: to produce a finer draft, or another version of the text for a different rhetorical situation?
- Applying: Can the writer complete the plans outlined above?

***

Reflection-in-action helps make the classroom a place for multiple intertextuality—not only the Bakhtinian intertextuality of texts, but also the Vygotskyian intertextuality of contexts that students bring with them. In the language of curriculum, reflection-in-action brings together the lived curriculum of the students, the delivered curriculum that the teacher has designed, and the experienced curriculum of the writer. In the language of Pratt's contact zone, reflection-in-action is the place where the different languages of writing and reflection come together, the place where reflective writers develop. In the language of rhetoric, reflection requires that students invent practice, and in so doing, they invent selves.

***

In the May 1997 issue of *College Composition and Communication*, Margaret Marshall makes the argument that we readers of student texts need to take particular care in our reading of those texts. She says,

> The question for teachers, then, becomes: how do we interpret students' discourse in order to make such pedagogical decisions? To learn how to read students' decisions in their writing is not the same as learning how to recognize a comma splice, or how to teach proper documentation. Reading such decisions, becoming able to recognize students' attempts

to learn academic practices, requires practice, to be sure, but it also requires learning a set of methods or frames to use when reading student work. (245)

The reading Marshall calls for here is critical, as I'll argue more fully in chapter five. But it also positions students as non-participants in their own texts. In calling for teacher reading uninformed by student perspective, it places the reader in the garret, while it maintains the perogative of the teacher at the expense of the student. This chapter argues otherwise. It is precisely through student participation, by means of reflection-in-action, that students become fully literate: able to write, able to write about.

Failing to ask students to so participate denies both them and us.

Notes

1. Student names are pseudonyms; materials used by permission.
2. As David Jolliffe makes clear in his review of *Twelve Readers Reading*, we are always responding to students, not to texts. See "Twelve Readers Reading: Exemplary Responses, Thorny Problems," *Assessing Writing* 3.2 (1997): 221-33.
3. For examples of questions that extend the basic template, see chapter three.
4. For a detailed examination of the relationship among reading, response, and the roles they play in reflection, see chapter five.
5. Both Geoffrey Sirc and Irvin Hashimoto make the point that structured heuristics won't work for all students, a point well-taken. The point here isn't so much to argue in favor of heuristics per sé, but to suggest that certain questions do prompt a way of seeing one's work, and to suggest as well that the questions are generative. As exemplified here, questions frequently lead to insights that are not predictable, precisely because the student directs the response to the question, which is itself a function of the intertextuality brought to bear by the student. And as Sirc suggests, responses can take diverse forms, from flow charts to verbal text. The point here, then, is the questions themselves as one means of prompting reflection-in-action.
6. It's not clear yet how much of a sequence this pattern is. For instance, students could begin at the liking stage rather than at knowing. It's also the case that students can become "fixed" at one point, often in liking and be unwilling to move to critique, which seems an argument for this schema as sequence. On the other hand, it may be that these are all ways of seeing one's work, and that the sequence is recursive and/or fairly individualized.

CHAPTER THREE

Constructive Reflection

"Reflection": A seeing inside.

Yup'ik translation

After all, the goal, the hope, of composition is to change not just the awareness but the writing of students, to alter not merely what they know but how they come to know it.

Joseph Harris

IN "BETWEEN THE DRAFTS," NANCY SOMMERS TELLS THE STORY OF how she became a writer, through a kind of unconscious imitation of others' voices, through resistance, through encouragement, ultimately through force of will: *between and among and beside and even in spite of the drafts.* In thinking about what this means for our students, she says, "When we create opportunities for something to happen between the drafts, when we create writing exercises that allow students to work with sources of their own that can complicate and enrich their primary sources, they will find new ways to write scholarly essays that are exploratory, thoughtful, and reflective" (30). Reflection-in-action is one way of understanding such *writing exercises*: places and occasions where students create their own knowledges–about language, about rhetoric, about the topic of inquiry, about life. The texts of reflection-in-action we saw in chapter two—process descriptions and Talk-To's and Talk-Backs—focus on a single primary text, it's true. But it's also true that taken together, they create something else: the diverse stories of how these writers have invented, how they continue to invent, themselves. What I've come to call *constructive reflection.*

∗∗∗

The work of Donald Schon, particularly some of his latest thinking, is again germane here. As we've seen, he has talked not only about how we as teachers and students can learn from practice, but more importantly, about how in theorizing practice we also learn from it. Given that we work in a messy universe, creating and addressing problems undecipherable by means of the paradigms or mechanisms associated with technical rigor is not the same thing as not learning: quite the reverse, though the means of learning *is* different. Any messy (human) problem-solving efforts, Schon says, function dually: as a way of solving the particular and as a way of investigating the general:

> From the point of view of the logic of the experiment, the context of organizational inquiry differs from that of normal science because the inquirer here is not only a researcher but an actor in the situation—in Geoffrey Vickers's phrase, an "agent-experient." The organizational inquirer investigates puzzling phenomena in order to figure out what to *do* about them, and when she takes an action in order to fix what a causal story says has gone wrong or capitalize on what it says has gone right, she subjects that story to a critically important test. In organizational practice, therefore, the very same actions tend to function *at the same time* as exploratory, intervention, and hypothesis-testing experiments. This has significant implications for the logic of experimentation in organizational practice. (1995, 86-87)

For writers, what this means is that as we devise a particularized rhetorical situation, as we create the material of it, as we draft and share and re-draft and finally complete the task we have set for ourselves, we tacitly take on the general question: how do I write?

As we saw in chapter one, Schon labels this particular-that-is-also general "reflective transfer." Causal inquiry, he says,

> typically centers on a particular situation in a single organization, and when it is successful, it yields not covering laws but prototypical models of causal patterns that may guide inquiry in other organizational situations—prototypes that depend, for their validity, on modification and testing in "the next situation." "Reflective transfer" seems to me a good label for this kind of generalization. (97)

In other words, through reflective transfer—or what I will call constructive reflection—we create the specific practice from which we may derive principles toward *prototypical models*. In composing a text, a writer invents practice that may have within it certain understandings and strategies that accommodate themselves to another rhetorical situation. Moreover, in inventing practice that spans rhetorical situations, a writer invents him or herself, re/creating the identity of writer.

Constructive reflection provides a telling moment in the reflective classroom, first, because it works from (but is not co-identical with) reflection-in-action. In part, constructive reflection is the *cumulative effect* of reflections-in-action on multiple texts, and thus in part it can be seen as contributing to a more generalized response to a set of particulars. Thus, constructive reflection *entails* reflective transfer—that is, a writer's ability to *gather* knowledge and apply that knowledge to similar problems—in the case of writing to understand, for instance, that arguments often involve multiple perspectives, that good arguments rely on multiple and valid sources. Constructive reflection, however, also involves invention—of the self, the writer who moves from one rhetorical situation to another. The extension from reflective transfer to constructive reflection, then, is from being able to generalize across rhetorical situations to *seeing oneself so generalize*, seeing oneself interpret differently from one to the next and understanding that these generalizations acquired through reflection-in-action exert their own cumulative effects.

The *successive gathering and application* of reflective transfer contributes to more than an enhanced ability to address an issue or solve a problem. Over time, it contributes to an identity, the identity of a writer—or of a teacher. The identity of a writer and what role, if any, our teaching should play in fostering it, is a pretty important issue in writing classrooms. It's not uncommon for faculty—especially new faculty and graduate students/teaching assistants–to get stuck in the question of whether our purpose in the classroom is to help students write better *or* to develop writers—whether our purpose in responding, for instance, is to evaluate the text or reply to the writer. This isn't an *either/or* proposition, however: it's a relational one. Constructive reflection is one means to see it as relational, as *both/and*.

Schon raises a final issue related to reflective transfer: it requires skills different from those called for in reflection-in-action: "Clearly, it is one thing to be able to reflect-in-action and quite another to be able to reflect on our reflection-in-action so as to produce a good verbal description of it; and it is still another thing to be able to reflect on the resulting description." (31) Accordingly, what we are doing when we ask for multiple texts from a student, from yet another perspective, is asking that the writer articulate in words—make explicit—the choices that will construct him or her—*between and among the drafts*.

***

My colleague Laura Kaplan, a philosopher, talks about these same issues—knowing and writing and practice and identity—but from another lens, that provided by philosophy. She attends to the value of experience with an almost-Deweyan appreciation for what our own lives can teach us. We all deal with empirical questions, Kaplan says, although the ways we think about them differ:

> My husband and I have very different views about how one answers an empirical question. My husband's brand of empiricism is positivist empiricism, not surprising, of course, since he is a trained "social scientist." His understanding of empiricism is sifted through the mythology of science. Insights must be verifiable by a trained experimenter. To control for differences between experimenters, verification must be in numerical form. In other words, experiments must take place *out of the context* in which the phenomena were first considered to be important or meaningful, if insights are to be universally valid. . . .
>
> My brand of empiricism is faithful to its roots in the Greek word *empeiria*, experience. A question arose in the course of my experience, and I propose to answer it using my experience. I propose to study phenomena as they present themselves in my experience, in my natural habitat, so to speak. (23, italics added)

Further, Kaplan claims, such an approach is what the examined life calls for. Theorizing takes place, she says, in the "context of concrete experience" (21). Bringing theory and practice together means twice: first, that we "adopt theories so that they point out the gaps, insincerities and dark spaces in our ordinary self-understandings" (21); second, that we work from what she calls the "outer life" and the "inner life."

> To speak in the terms I used in an earlier essay called "Symbiotic Stories," our writing often displays an outer life as defined by the philosophical community, but hides its inner life. And such an undue emphasis on meeting the demands of outer life has its effects on the inner life. Gradually, our wonderings about the world are molded into conventional forms. If philosophy is about creating an examined life, then leaving out the life which philosophy examines seems to sabotage its aims. (24)

When the inner is excluded, the outer can be none other than alien, as a student explains:

Reflecting back upon this semester, I realize that I could have gotten so much more out of this class. From day one, I could never put this class on a first person perspective. I always felt like I was looking at these topics from the outside while the other students in the class got to explore the topics from the inside. Since I couldn't get to the inside of the topics, I basically just went through the motions of the class. (Gene)

Constructive reflection takes place in the intersection of inner and outer lives.

***

If we want students to be reflective, we will have to invite them to be so, may need to reflect with them. Reflection, like language itself, is social as well as individual. Through reflection, we *tell our stories* of learning: in the writing classroom, our stories of writing and of having written and of will write tomorrow; in other classes, other stories, often told through writing, too. This story-making involves our taking a given story, and our lived stories, and making them anew.

I suppose I think this reflection is so important because without it, we live the stories others have scripted for us: in a *most* unreflective, unhealthy way. And I think the stories we make—whether inside the classroom or out, whether externalized or not—construct us, one by one by one. Cumulatively. So I think it's important to tell lots of stories where we get to construct many selves for us to attempt, some we continue to inhabit.

***

We can ask for constructive reflection in many ways. One, early on, is simply to ask for a writer's goals. A second is to ask questions that call for such story-making, such observations deriving from particular assignments. A third is to ask more generally about what students understand themselves to be learning. And a fourth: to know that students will do this whether we ask them anything at all.

One student begins class by stipulating a goal.

My goal in this class is to earn an A.

All goals, however, are not equal, and more to the point, reflective goals can't really be set until a writer has worked in a class for a while, long enough to make sense of what the class offers. The student brings a *lived curriculum* with him or her, the writing and reading that she or he has done prior to this class, it's true, and we might think that this curriculum itself would be sufficient to enable the student to set goals early on.[1] But the intended class—the *delivered curriculum*— itself contextualizes what a student will see as possible—the *experienced curriculum*—not only through the curriculum that is to be delivered, which we see in the syllabus, the readings and the assignments, but also through the specifics of the class: in the teacher, in the students who populate the class, in their interactions and so on. A class, like writing, is social: *the social context is one intertext for the individual writer.*

Once a class is made material, students can begin to elaborate some goals.

Goals Revisited

1. I would like to write more clearly and concisely. I feel that my writing can be ambiguous. I don't always use enough details, although I know as a writer, reader and teacher that details are essential. I like to write to an audience that has some knowledge of my topic already, so I don't have to explain the intricacies, but instead get into analyzing and discussing my particular take on the topic. I don't want to repeat myself, so I don't go far enough to make sure I have been clear. I would like to broaden my writing modes. I want to write more than analysis or opinion.

2. I want to improve my transitions between paragraphs and ideas.

3. I want to write in a more creative manner. I feel like I have something to say that doesn't have an outlet in my usual writing situations (i.e., criticism, analysis, journal, editorial). I continue to wonder if I really have a story to tell.

4. I have a hard time analyzing my own writing. While there are some basic things that I know I have difficulty with, I feel that my writing is fairly consistent. I have to pay attention to those problem areas.

5. I want someone to tell me what I am doing wrong and how to be a better writer. I want to be a better writing teacher, by understanding how to improve my own writing. (Meg)

The student here begins to articulate *what she wants to learn.* Some of this seems general and overly textual and too familiar (and I'm sorry, and this isn't her fault, but I've heard it a hundred times before): *I want to improve my transitions between paragraphs and ideas.* The beginnings of other assertions read likewise. Reading *I would like to write more clearly and concisely,* I hold both my tongue and my reply: that writing is not a machine guaranteed to punch out (like widgets) *clear, concise* texts.

But wait, read this again: she *explains. I don't always use enough details, although I know as a writer, reader and teacher that details are essential. I like to write to an audience that has some knowledge of my topic already, so I don't have to explain the intricacies, but instead get into analyzing and discussing my particular take on the topic.* She sees more than isolated textual features; she sees how she both uses rhetorical features and is used by them. She *knows* what is needed, but cannot always do what this calls for; the writer identifies a *gap between knowledge and practice,* a gap she wants to explore. The writer also understands how she works, how she writes to a chosen audience so that she can avoid making the kind of text that would call forth the kind of intellectual work that she feels she cannot control, so that she doesn't have to *explain the intricacies.*

The writer *continue[s] to wonder if I really have a story to tell:* as she weaves the story of herself as writer past, as she plans her course—the one where she invents her writer future.

***

Sometimes, constructive reflection occurs as an unexpected benefit of reflection-in-action. In the midst of reflection-in-action, students work from the tacit, articulating processes and observations that move from inner to outer, that bring the language of the author into the context of the writing curriculum. Sometimes, the observations don't surprise:

> After making the changes that were suggested, I found myself going over the paper again, this time cutting some of my own thoughts that once seemed necessary. I found numerous places where I had changed the tense, not realizing what it did to the rest of the paper. I have found that keeping in the same tense is one of the most difficult tasks I face as a writer. This paper is a prime example of that. When in conversation, we do not usually remain in the same tense, however, when composing formal writings, it becomes necessary to be consistent. (Kelly)

Well, sure: that makes sense. From the same first-year writer, however, something more interesting, to me at least, something that makes me pause, think:

> Another of my writing faults was illustrated in this text; I have found that I tend to be wordy, maybe even long-winded. I was able to change this by editing out some sentences that did not enhance my plot, but

were only there—like removing non-essential chemicals from the net ionic equation.

Kelly—a science major—uses a field of science (chemistry) as a frame to understand writing. It's science as the language of translation. And it seems to make sense: the *removing* of *non-essential chem-icals* from an equation is a useful way of articulating the editing out of sentences from text—for the purposes of *enhance*[ment]. There's a sense of refinement here that appeals to me. More important, I think I see the student learning aloud, as she articulates an understanding located in her contextual frame and in her language. She uses her language to invent and describe her writing. I see her learning; I also see me learning from her.

And it happens more often than we think, once we start asking these questions about what happens *inside and outside and between and among the drafts.* And once we start attending to the responses, we see that in these responses students use their native language— that is, the language in which they think, a product of the multiple discourses in which they participate, the idiolect native to that speaker and writer. With this language, they talk about writing, nec- essarily bringing to that talk their own experiences, their own assumptions, their own discourses. Such talk is a primary means of inventing oneself as writer.

Cindy, another first-year writer, provides another example of con- structive reflection as invention. Asked about two texts on the same topic but in different genres, for example, she says, "In writing the pattern and the expository paper on WWII I saw the effects of genre. The effects were very distinct because the topic of the papers was the control." Well, of course. I hadn't seen it that way, but it's true. The topic, World War II, was the *control,* the rhetorical situation the set of variables. As Schon says, in understanding the particular, we concur- rently move to the general.

***

Sometimes the reflection-in-action focused on a single text can include questions that work explicitly toward constructive reflection, work toward what the student "takes" away from a writing task, what he or she may be able to transfer reflectively. In other words, there are some assumptions here: that students learn more about a topic than we see in any given text, that students learn about rhetoric and genre more generally by working particularly. Asking them to express what they've learned provides a formal and structured occasion to figure that out, allows us to learn with and from them, provides us with an opportunity to reply.

One student, Josey, in writing a Talk-To on an argument about banning smoking, writes only a little on the first set of reflective questions, the questions we saw in chapter two.

> I believe that this is the very best paper I have ever written. . . I got my point across to my audience by backing up my information with facts gathered from various sources that were credible. My paper showed the other side of the story and tried to find an answer that would satisfy everyone's needs.

*

> I believe that this paper is not worth the trees it is printed on. I need to give maybe a little more view of the other side. I also may need to give a little more information on where I got some of my facts from.

*

> I predict that Yancey will read my paper and like it. It shows what a danger smoking is to innocent people in a rational manner, supported by facts from reliable sources. She may agree that I need to give an extra source or two.

*

> I will agree with what she will think. I really enjoyed writing this paper and believe it is one of the better ones I have written.

This reflection-in-action isn't extraordinary: it provides me with enough of the composer's perception that we can talk about the primary text from several points of view—the nature of *argument, sources, reliable sources,* the *other side.* As my obstetrician used to say about a normal pregnancy: unremarkable.

What is remarkable is the story of learning the student tells when asked other questions: specifically,

What did you learn in the writing of this text that we cannot see there?

What did you learn about writing an argument?
"I learned," Josey says,

a lot of information about women in general and the health effects on
them especially. However, it did not pertain as much to my paper as the
effects on babies did so I decided to add it to my bank of information in
my head and drop it from the paper. I also learned how tobacco companies have found ways to add even more nicotine to their cigarettes, so
they will be even more addictive. I couldn't find a way to incorporate this
into my paper in a way that made sense, so I put it with the info on the
women and filed it away.

*

I learned that a successful argument is one that takes a lot of time and
hard work. A good deal of research must be done first, especially if you are
writing on a subject you don't have a lot of knowledge about. Once you
get some sources, you need to make sure they are credible ones. After you
pick a point to argue, you must choose information that will back up your
point. However, you must be able to back up your information by finding
it in more than one source or by using an extremely credible, unbiased
source. After you write your paper and cite your sources, you must revise
and edit until your argument is clear and concrete, yet does show the
other side.

I'm somehow aware, again, that I am witnessing learning as it
happens—which wasn't really my intent (I confess). My intent in
asking these two questions was as much to send a message as to learn.
I didn't know what I might learn, but I wanted to remind the students that in order to obtain and hold focus, writers exclude material.
In other words, I wanted students to contextualize their own work in
relation to what experienced writers do: they too should have learned
information that they could not include. And I confess (again): I was
curious about what they'd learned. Like my other questions, these
were genuine.

What I learned: that Josey has a *bank of information in my head*
where she has stored several pieces of information. She excludes this
information *about women in general and the health effects on them,*
from her text, but she includes it in what she calls her *bank.* She is
aware of this, and she can theorize the process as well as the place.
Remarkable. About argument: Josey seems to know how to proceed;
her view is, admittedly, somewhat dualistic—are there always and

only two sides to a story?—but she understands that *credible* and *plural sources* should be consulted, that an opposing perspective should be both accounted for and fairly represented. This is rhetorical knowledge, something for her to build on in her future arguments, and the application of which—a different kind of knowedge—we will or won't see in her primary text. Regardless of the success of that application, however, we know that she understands something about how to go about writing an argument. Except that I asked Josey, I wouldn't have known that.

Josey too is writing her own curriculum, one embedded within and without the drafts—by way of constructive reflection.

***

The Talk-Backs of reflection-in-action also provide a place where students may contemplate their writing practices over time, where they may discern patterns in multiple texts, where in reviewing these multiple texts they see themselves emerge as writers with practices and habits that transcend specific texts. Working in the particular, they mark and map the general. John, a history major seeking to be an English teacher, is one such writer.

> I've just finished the task of reading over the notes you made on my paper on personal voice: it was difficult at times, but no more so than my own handwriting (actually mine is probably only legible to myself).
>
> A number of your suggestions, from this past paper and others that I've written in your classes, have to do with my setting the scene, or introducing the point or idea that I'm trying to make. Sometimes I get writing and fall into the trap of thinking only for or of myself. In this paper especially, I feel that I was the primary audience and therefore didn't need to elaborate—after all, I know what I'm talking about.
>
> Some of the questions you pose (why's this important, because why, . . .) are good ones. As above, I guess I'm considering only myself (even though I know that others will be reading it), and getting caught up in what I write at the time, without really finishing the ideas on paper. I know I should be getting someone else to read them before handing it in for the last time, but. . . .
>
> I can't say that I've felt too good about any of the papers I have handed in this semester—having trouble getting focused, not allotting myself enough time to get things done. This has been frustrating but I've still got some time to straighten out.

From my perspective, the point of the Talk-Back, as discussed in chapter two, is for students to talk about a specific text, for "unpacking" purposes, for summary purposes, for inventional and revision purposes. But often students will have their own purposes. What seems to happen here is exactly that: John understands my response to his particular text *within a larger context:* the context of several of the papers he has written this term. He sees similarities among those papers that I had not remarked: *A number of your suggestions, from this past paper and others that I've written in your classes, have to do with my setting the scene, or introducing the point or idea that I'm trying to make.* And then he works to establish causality in a Schonean way: *Sometimes I get writing and fall into the trap of thinking only for or of myself.* So, he understands a problem, identifies it within this text as an instance of a larger problem, concurs with it, thinks about the causes, and plans some approaches: *considering* others besides *myself;* obtaining more response to drafts before he submits them; *allotting myself enough time to get things done.*

We talk about students participating in their own learning and about the desirability of that. We talk about reflection and how it enhances writing. Here, by means of a Talk-Back (i.e., a text focused on a real question: how do you and I read this text?) a student through reflection not only invokes a larger context—his own intertext—and participates in his own learning, but he also charts the next steps.

* * *

Constructive reflection can also be "staged." That is, we can ask students to articulate what they are learning; ask them to express the tacit; ask them to bring it to the page so that we have *a good verbal description.* In other words, as Frank Smith suggests, students will always learn. So the question is never, "Are you learning?" The question is, "*What* are you learning?" The answer, the *experienced curriculum;* the means, constructive reflection. More problematic are the questions we use to prompt *constructive reflection.* Do we want very general questions that cut across classes, do we want very specific questions that are embedded in a specific academic context, and/or do we want a mix, perhaps at different points in the term, at different points in the college career?

One sequence is designed for almost any class. Upon reflection, it looks too general to me; the set doesn't seem to take advantage of working through the specific to get to the protyptical, to use the pragmatic to make theory. But sometimes, the set seems to "work" anyway.

- What have you learned?
- How does this connect with what you already knew/know?
- Is this what you expected to learn? Why or why not?
- What else do you need to learn?
- How will you go about learning it?

Using this set as a guide, a first-year student talks about what she has learned:

> In this class so far, I've learned that writing is really more complicated than I had once thought. At one time it was completely acceptable for me to write something, give it a once over and then move on. This isn't what successful writers do, they analyze, write, rewrite, and argue with themselves and others. I have also learned about this mystical science called causality. Through trying to tame this science in a paper on WWII, I became aware that in the past I had incorrectly assigned simple cause and effect situations. This also showed that even if you believe you know something because you can regurgitate it, you may not have true comprehension if you are unable to articulate it. So in general I have become aware of the complexity of writing, and that writing can be an indication of how well you understand something.

*

> I did not expect to learn more about the process and complexity of writing, because the entire class was devoted to this subject. I felt there was probably more to writing than I was aware of because it is something that some people spend their entire lives doing.

*

> I didn't expect to learn about that whole causality mess, because I thought that the cause and effect of everything was easily defined. (Barbara)

I don't think of first-year writing as a course in the plurality of cause and effect (though I am beginning to think that I should, since causality is at the heart of rhetoric), but we do spend time looking at that, so I'm not surprised. In fact, perhaps I'm pleased, given that in general (and in life?) our perceived causes and effects seem to drive so much of our decision-making, and not always in felicitous ways. And I'm pleased because in addition to learning to compose more fluently and fully by way of *analyz[ing], writ[ing], rewrit[ing], and argu[ing] with themselves and others,* the student understands these activities, what she calls *the complexity of writing,* as *what successful writers do.*

Through constuctive reflection, she is re-creating her construct of a writer as well as becoming that writer.

***

Lara, another writer in that first-year composition class, responds to the same set of questions, but more discursively.

> It has become apparent to me in the past months that I can no longer get by with one draft of a text. In the paper about my Grandfather I wrote at the beginning of the semester, I wrote about four or five drafts. After each of these drafts I felt that I had done my absolute best and there was no way I could improve on the draft. However, after each I let various people read it and got their input, including Professor Yancey's. This helped me see how others viewed and reacted to parts of my paper. This kind of continual revising made me feel more secure about my paper and made me feel like the feelings I wanted to get across to the reader actually did.
>
> During this course I have found that I must look at my writing from different perspectives and to look for ways I can change, transfer and edit to make my paper more clear and focussed. The paper I wrote about whether World War II was a good war or not was a paper that, after writing for the first time, I found that it was confusing in some places, drawn out in others and too short in others. I was not efficiently getting across to the reader my opinions about World War II specifically. I looked over and reread my paper as another person might read it. This really helped me to see where to cut and where to move certain things. Also my group told me that some of my sentences were confusing. From this I have learned that I must give a little here and there, even though sometimes I may not want to, to make the writing more meaningful to the reader. Even though I know I must give a little, I refuse to compromise my style to the point that the identity of my paper is lost. Compromising is one of the most important lessons I have learned in this class.

I can no longer get by with one draft of a text, Lara says, sounding a theme common to these students.[2] And the students here were important to her: in her own words, they became *the reader* to whom the writing needed to become *more meaningful,* the reader who thus motivated the multiple drafts. And there were other readers as well. For the paper on Lara's grandfather's death, for instance, she'd told me that she'd taken it home to share with her parents, so I had known she'd had multiple readers. As she says, *I let various people read it and got their input, including Professor Yancey's.* All of these readers mattered, and, I think, they mattered in the way she suggests, with me on the list but only as a single reader and, given the topic, not necessarily the most influential one.

As important, through writing *for readers*—not after the fact but *as part of the process* of understanding and writing, Lara found herself becoming not just a writer, but a reader (the importance of which chapter five argues): *I looked over and reread my paper as another person might read it. This really helped me to see where to cut and where to move certain things.* In so seeing, however, Lara feels the tension between her own view and what she understands readers to expect: *I have learned that I must give a little here and there, even though sometimes I may not want to.* She has made a commitment to her own voice: *I refuse to compromise my style to the point that the identity of my paper is lost.*

In "I refuse . . ." we hear echoes of Nancy Sommers between the drafts:

> It is in the thrill of the pull between someone else's authority and our own, between submission and independence that we must discover who to define ourselves. In the uncertainty of that struggle, we have a chance of finding the voice of our own authority. (31)

In her writing, Lara takes up big questions, questions that she cares about: for one, how do I make sense of my loving grandfather's tortuous death? She shares that writing with her colleagues and with more "natural" readers of the discourse, natural in the sense that they share her interest in and commitment to the topic. They will respond. She hears what her readers say. She understands about writing, that it is always a social and negotiated act. She is willing to enact that understanding, to decide for herself what she is willing to negotiate, what she is not.

Constructive reflection, Lara reminds us, is both individual and social. To be meaningful, reflection must be *situated:* the writer creates meaning in context, in community.

*** *

And sometimes when students talk about what they've learned, even in a writing class, it's about much more than writing.

> The concept of a good or bad war also made me think. Even though there is no such thing as a totally good war or a totally bad war, I was forced to look at all the results and how they affect us today. In all reality, World War II turned out to be partially good, something I never thought I'd say. Regardless of the lives lost, the war extended open markets and offered thousands of new jobs in science and medicine. (Cindy)

*** *

One last model of constructive reflection, one that looks forward as much as backward: a set of two questions:
In this writing class, what have you learned?
How/can you use what you have learned in other contexts?
Kirsten answers. She's enrolled in an advanced writing class at the same time that she is working as a technical writer, so her answer spans contexts. And since she is asked that question on a class email listserver discussion group, she is talking in public.

> It seems like every semester I take at least one cool class and I get so pumped about the class—you know, really wanting to apply what I learned. But then I go into another class the next semester and the teacher is saying exactly the opposite of what I learned the last semester—and then I focus on the new class. It never seems to end. I'm really saying that although I think the concepts/ideas generated in this class are great, I'm just not certain I will apply them when I step into Dr. X's class because I know Dr. X wants dry, academic prose—not me parading my knowledge of voice. But then I have to wonder if I am underestimating Dr. X. Maybe s/he would really love some innovative writing, but everyone is just too scared to do it. This is an issue that I cannot easily resolve. I know that I will be more secure with my writing and my sense of voice—and that I will definitely apply in Dr. X's class (and I will **always** be concerned about my weak verbs!). Maybe that's the point— maybe I don't have to produce a mold-breaking paper, I can just become better in the form I have to write in?

*

> As far as applying this to my job—well, that's an interesting question. So often we think of technical writing as being "voiceless." But since this

class I have really begun to see the voice (and lack of objectivity) in technical writing (I am a technical writer, for those of you who don't know).
Actually practicing technical writing has been a really wonderful comple-
ment to this class because I can relate so much of what I've learned to a
field that is supposedly a sterile environment—free from all that we have
been learning in this class. You cannot separate technical writing from
expository writing or from poetry—they all involve the same process and
all have the same basic purpose—to communicate. Everything I have
learned about voice and about the multi-faceted nature of stories—all of
it applies to technical writing. For example, just today I received some
documentation from a developer, and I cut out nearly half of what he said
because it was too technical (it wasn't in the right voice). I rewrote most of
it in the voice that is appropriate for my company, and I left out a lot of it
because I didn't think it was important to the user (I was being selective
about my story telling). I really think we all do this every day, but being
more aware of it can only make us better writers and communicators. I
know no one is reading this long message (except Kathi), so see ya'.

It's a truism that the students inhabiting our classes today don't
look so much like yesterday's students (or much like us, either), literally and metaphorically. In the last fifteen years, the students on my
own campus, for instance, which, as an urban comprehensive institution, has historically been populated by the non-traditional student,
have gone from working 20 hours a week to 50. So the intertexts they
bring with them will be work-related as well as family-related, extra-
curricular in new and interesting ways.

Kirsten embodies this last observation. She talks about the experience of most students, that what they are rewarded for in one class
can be what provokes critique in the next. But she takes this observation the next step as she begins to theorize from her own practice, her
own experience: *I know that I will be more secure with my writing and
my sense of voice—and that I will definitely apply in Dr. X's class . . . .
Maybe that's the point—maybe I don't have to produce a mold-break-
ing paper, I can just become better in the form I have to write in?* As she
raises a good question, Kirsten continues to learn, and she prompts
all of us on the listserv to think aloud with her.

But because she is a technical writer, Kirsten has another story to
tell, which she does in the language of the class, by way of *selection*
and *voice* and *story: I cut out nearly half of what he said because it was
too technical (it wasn't in the right voice). I rewrote most of it in the
voice that is appropriate for my company, and I left out a lot of it*

because I didn't think it was important to the user (I was being selective about my story telling). From practice, she generalizes: *You cannot separate technical writing from expository writing or from poetry—they all involve the same process and all have the same basic purpose—to communicate.* I'm not certain I agree, but her examples are telling, and I appreciate the theory.[3]

***

When we talk about identity and constructive reflection, Kirsten comes to mind: a plural writer composing in multiple sites, able to see differences and similarities among them, able to exert agency. What this means for our classrooms, in Kenneth Gergen's view, is that "[t]here is little reason to suppress any voice. Rather, with each new vocabulary or form of expression, one approrpriates the world in a different way, sensing aspects of existence in one that are hidden or absent in another, opening capacities for relatedness in one modality that are otherwise hindered" (147).

***

I'm composing this chapter, but I've been sitting in the same chair too long, been tapping my worn keys too intensely, been drinking too much lukewarm coffee. I close the file; I logon to email, but without anticipation. It's June, and while it's not nearly as hot or as sunny as it's supposed to be in Charlotte this time of year, most of the listservs I'm on seem trapped in the stifling quiet of dog day afternoons. They're approaching listless.

Without warning, Steve Jamar, a law professor who directs a writing program at Howard University, comes on WPA-L, a listserv for writing program administrators and other writing faculty, asking a stunning question:

> Maybe it's just summer. Maybe it's the distressing quality of too many of the papers in my seminar. Maybe it's the number of D's earned in the first year legal writing course–and you need to work hard to get a D! But I've been wondering if maybe we are not going about writing all wrong. Maybe it cannot be taught out of context, out of a discipline, outside of a one-on-one tutoring setting of a supervised, significant project or of a journalistic setting.
>
> As I was having these musings, I thought I would ask the members of this group how you learned to write. (June 11, 1997)

In his own discussion, Jamar clarifies his question: "I am not talking here about when and what I was taught, but *when I learned*" (my italics). His conclusion likewise appeals:

> Perhaps there is more happening here–students do learn in groups and from classroom instruction in writing, but they learn more and most from direct, extended feedback on their own writing. This leads me to think that perhaps the things some of us fret and worry about don't really matter—what matters is not a program per sé or the content per sé, but the ability of the teacher to see the individual student's writing problem and to communicate that to the student, and the willingness of the student and ability of the student to hear and understand the feedback, and the ability of the student to abstract essential elements from that process and to transfer it to a new discipline or new setting. (June 11, 1997)

There is wisdom here, I think. If we want to know how people learn to write, we ask them. That's what Jamar does of his colleagues; that's what I've done with my students. My conclusion about how we learn to write echoes his, though I think it's more both/and: both the classroom with its opportunities for audience, as Lara demonstrates, and the *ability of the student to abstract essential elements from that process and to transfer them to a new discipline or new setting.*

While our conclusions seem alike, the road I took to mine was circuitous.

Because I was interested in portfolios, I became interested in the reflective texts that describe and narrate and explain the disparate primary texts in portfolios (as we'll see in chapter four).

Because I knew students would need to write these texts at the end of the term, I saw that my classroom would have to become hospitable to reflection *throughout the term,* not just at the end when portfolios were assembled and composed: reflection entails time and practice and time and thought. So the challenge was to consider how to link reflection to assignments: reflection-in-action.

But it also became clear to me that the discrete pieces of reflection needed something threading them even before the time when students wrote for their portfolios; that such a thread, if *woven into the curriculum,* would contribute to a writer's identity, I thought, would allow a student to invent both practice and self. Furthermore, I began to appreciate how reflection could mediate among our curricula, the lessons I thought I was delivering, the ones that students experienced, the ones they brought with them.

Constructive reflection is valuable, yes, as a kind of rehearsal for the reflective texts that "matter"—the ones inside portfolios and the reflections-in-presentation accompanying them. And constructive reflection is also valuable for itself, for what it captures *between and among and outside and inside the drafts: the writer inventing him or herself.*

Notes

1. Setting our own goals is what "graduated" writers do, of course. It may be, however, that one purpose of a writing course to help students learn to act that independently.

2. In another project, Meg Morgan and I are taking up this issue by reviewing a set of reflective essays culled from a set of exemption portfolios. What we've found so far includes: students see the first term as an elaborated exercise in revision; they have a language that they can use to talk about writing, which varies from a non-rhetorical kind of "product language" to a "rhetorically based" language; they see writing as dichotomous, with it either being "creative" or "academic"; they don't believe that the two voices or stands can be combined in a single text. See "Reflective Essays, Curriculum, Research, and the Scholarship of Administration: Notes toward Administrative Scholarly Work," forthcoming.

3. I'm hoping that the others on the listserv are listening, too, as I pose myself a set of new questions relating to the interaction between electronic communication and reflection. Is a listserv a particularly good place for reflection, as some have claimed, and if so, why and how, and how would we make the best use of it? What effect does having a class audience exert on our observations, our reflection? I argued earlier that having others to hear our stories is crucial for reflection; I still think this assertion is true. But I have to wonder when and where and how/often.

CHAPTER FOUR

Reflection-in-Presentation

What we call the beginning is often the end
And to make an end is to make a beginning.
The end is where we start from.

T. S. Eliot

An age that has become distrustful of history is still willing to read
avidly the first-person account, one . . . by the participant true to
his or her subjective response.

Robert Folkenfilk

IRONICALLY, THE REFLECTION THAT IS BEST KNOWN—WHAT I'VE called *reflection-in-presentation*—is the least well understood and the least well theorized. It's (also) the reflection that we are most familiar with, regardless of the form it takes: the introductory "Letter to the Reader" that fronts the writing portfolios used for exemption at Miami University (Black et al.); the annotations upon single pieces that accompany selections in the Missouri Western portfolio-in-the-major (Allen, Frick et al.); the final reflective essay that summarizes and interprets the exhibits appearing in the New Standards portfolios used in the K-12 context (Myers and Pearson); and the various stand-alone reflective texts that students write to conclude a course (Marshall; Perl 1997). All of these reflective texts are presentational, although as Miami University researchers Black, Daiker, Sommers, and Stygall point out, what's valued in these presentations shifts from context to context. Part of that context is the situation within which a portfolio is read. Is the course or program grounding the reflective text one that favors cultural critique, for instance, or is it oriented more to issues of voice and expression? This context will have much to do with—may even (over)determine—what is valued in the reflection-in-presentation.[1]

In this chapter we'll examine two varieties of reflection-in-presentation: 1) the reflective text that accompanies a classroom portfolio; 2) the reflective text that stands alone as a culminating document. Then, in chapter seven, we'll renew the discussion on reflection-in-presentation by examining its role in a more formal assessment context.[2]

***

In the phrase *reflection-in-presentation*, we see its dual nature: it is both a *reflection*, a "seeing inside" (to use a Yup'ik translation), and a *presentation*, a public text representing the self. Rhetorically, it is occasioned by a call to explain to someone outside the self how a practitioner—a teacher, say, or student—works to define and address problems, and/or to summarize and interpret what she or he has learned. Learning results from addressing the problems, sometimes from the materials and interactions of a course, sometimes from the teaching enterprise unproblematized. Typically reflection-in-presentation occurs in two contexts: 1) as an independent document, in a class at the end of a term as a kind of cumulative event (Marshall; Perl 1997); 2) more commonly, within a portfolio, at the end of a course or at a point of decision-making (eg, placement into a first-year course; tenure and promotion for faculty). In this sense, then, reflection-in-presentation is public and academic, and at the same time, personal and extra-curricular—an explaining *both of the self and about the self* to an outside audience.

Given the rhetorical situation of reflection-in-presentation, it can be seen as drawing on several disciplinary contexts. The first, as we might expect, is the context supplied by reflection itself: its relationship to reflection-in-action and constructive reflection. Reflection-in-presentation is very like constructive reflection in that it is cumulative, and as it works from the particular to general and back, it focuses ultimately on what William Gass calls a *shaping self* (51). It is what we ask of our students when we ask them to draw texts together for review, to discern patterns, to synthesize, even to recognize gaps and make sense of those—and then to explain what they observe and understand in a public way. In writing classes, we do this when we ask students to think about who they are as writers, when we ask them to discern patterns among subject positions they have taken, when we ask them to plot their own cumulative development as an increasing accretion of writing selves—and then to explore and explain all this in a formal presentation to an "other."

As important, reflection-in-presentation differs from reflection-in-action and from constructive reflection. For one thing, it requires different skills, as Schon explains:

> Clearly, it is one thing to be able to reflect-in-action and quite another to be able to reflect on our reflection in action so as to produce a good verbal description of it; and it is still another thing to be able to reflect on the resulting description. (31)

Reflection-in-presentation is that *good verbal description*, but with one important caveat: *as prepared for an audience.* Accordingly, it is a description that must *satisfy both the writer and the reader.*

***

We can also understand reflection-in-presentation by drawing on its similarity to two fields of work not typically associated with reflection per sé: the one, science; the other, autobiography.

In separate presentations, faculty advocate and current Carnegie Foundation President Lee Shulman and philosopher and social scientist Walter F. Fisher compare the processes employed by scientists with those employed in reflection-in-presentation. Scientists, Shulman says, use a two-stage process to make knowledge: first, they occlude the flow of work; second, they prepare that work for public presentation.[3] The interruption of work allows the scientists to review what they have accumulated, to read the data and begin to make some sense of it. The preparation for a public audience requires that the scientists (working in a Vygotskian manner) explain what they have learned. In forming that explanation for others, they explain it to themselves.

Walter Fisher makes the same case for the combination of reflection and presentation as *intertwined means of learning about, of knowing.* In discussing the invention of the double-helix, Fisher explains,

> Rigorous reasoning obviously was involved in the invention of the double-helix model, but so was reflection not guided by strict inferential rules but by alternative possibilities and choosing the most apt, persuasive ones. As the mental processes that produced the model were shaped

by choices with an audience in mind, the thinking became rhetorical. (182)

Reflection-in-presentation operates on the same principles: like Shulman's and Fisher's scientists, students and teachers interrupt their work, they review it, they prepare what they see for others. The *thinking* becomes *rhetorical*. Thus, reflection is both individual and social: in part, it is through the social that the individual comes to know.

* * *

Both because of its personal nature and because of its representation of the self, reflection-in-presentation also bears similarities to autobiography. For one thing, autobiographies focus on the past, as Robert Folkenflik points out: they "generally are narratives about the past of the writer," although the past doesn't necessarily "take precedence over the present moment or moments, which often provide the point of departure that organizes the autobiography" (15). The autobiography is, in another phrase, "retrospective consciousness" (217). But the perspective is not totally inward: like Shulman's scientists and like our teachers and students, the autobiographer looks both inward and outward:

> Autobiography promises intersubjectivity, not just intrasubjectivity. Because autobiography manipulates the prestige of the self in relation to the other, it enters the play of desire that constitutes the symbolic order. Here the self as a point of reference outside the text and the self as represented, constructed within the text, are in rightful tension. (Folkenflik 234)

The *tension*, then, occurs between the *actual* self and the *represented* self, a tension that is *rightful*, that is productive. It is perhaps, then, the kind of tension we might expect to see—even desire to see—in reflection-in-presentation.

And as important, there is more than a single self, as, as William Gass reminds us:

> the self divides, not severally into a recording self, an applauding self, a guilty self, a daydreaming self, but into a shaping self: it is the consciousness of oneself as a consciousness among all these other minds, an awareness born much later than the self it studies, and a self whose existence

was fitful, intermittent, for a long time, before it was able to throw a full beam upon the life lived and see there a pattern, as a plowed field seen from a plane reveals the geometry of the tractor's path. (51)

Any self we see within text, particularly autobiography but reflection-in-presentation as well, is multiple, is *shaped*, is constructed; is necessarily contingent, transitory, filled with *tension*.

✳✳✳

In discussing reflection-in-presentation, however, I'm working after the fact. When writing teachers first began asking for reflective text, usually in portfolios, we didn't call it reflection-in-presentation; we didn't see it in relation to other kinds of reflection; we didn't see it in relation to science or autobiography. All we really saw was a portfolio that made much more sense when it included a student's narrative or interpretive text, and we saw that, in fact, without such a text—one that came to be called reflection—portfolios were merely folders of work (Yancey; Weiser). More specifically and pretty quickly, we wanted the reflection to perform one or more tasks:

1. *create a context* for the portfolio documents so that we as reader can understand how they were created and thus should be read, either individually or as composed text;
2. *describe (and sometimes assess) the processes* that the student used in creating texts, with specific reference to processes that explain how one draft evolved from an earlier one;
3. *explain the student's goals* and how those were accomplished, by reference to texts within the portfolio;
4. *explain the curricular goals* and how well those were accomplished.

In other words, we wanted the student, at the least, to supply some context, and possibly to assess his or her work. We understood reading as *contextual*. We therefore wanted to students to participate in creating the contexts in which their texts would be read. But we weren't terribly clear about the specifics of reflection: for instance, about how reflection "worked," or about what was most important to our reading, or about what a reflective text might include, or about the form it might take.

Without knowing what it was that we were looking for, then, most of us—the teachers asking for this reflection—looked for anything and everything, working under two assumptions: 1) that students could easily have something to say that we couldn't predict; and 2) that we should therefore use directions that were as open-ended as possible. That's what we asked for, just about anything that the writer deemed relevant or interesting—about their texts, about their processes, about them as *writers*, about them as *persons*. For example, in a set of directions that has been widely adopted by colleges and universities across the country, a typical reflection-in-presentation— a comprehensive letter that introduces the portfolio—may do any number of things, including

> describe the process used in creating any one portfolio piece, discuss important pieces in creating the portfolio, explain the place of writing in your life, chronicle your development as a writer, assess the strengths and weaknesses of your writing, or combine these approaches. Your letter should provide readers with a clearer understanding of who you are as a writer and a person. (UNC Charlotte)

What we have here, of course, is a cascade of questions, one that in no way prioritizes what is expected or what is valued.[4]

Interestingly, within the same general period of time, beginning around 1988, faculty were also beginning to create portfolios, *teaching portfolios*, usually for purposes of annual review or, more likely, for promotion and tenure. These portfolios, like student portfolios, also called for reflection-in-presentation. By way of contrast, faculty were provided with both rationale and rather pointed directions. In the first American Association of Higher Education monograph on the teaching portfolio, for instance, Pat Hutchings and her colleagues talk about the rationale for reflection in ways that sound familiar:

> General reflection, divorced from evidence of actual performance, fails to capture the situated nature of teaching. Work samples [eg, syllabi, assignments, sample graded work] alone aren't intelligible. But work samples *plus* reflection make a powerful formula. The reflection is grounded by being connected to a particular instance of teaching; the work sample is made meaningful and placed in context through reflection. (9)

As with student portfolios, there is a belief that the two kinds of texts—what Anson calls the primary texts (or what Hutchings calls the *work samples*) and the secondary texts, the reflection—*together* provide a more accurate portrait of the phenomenon under scrutiny. Moreover, the view here is decidedly Schonean: the particular instance of teaching, grounded though a reflective context, makes possible some general observations about a faculty member's teaching.

But there is a telling difference here as well regarding reflection-in-presentation: while faculty are advised to write a *reflection* on every *work sample*, students are typically told to write a general, overview kind of reflection, as we've already seen. In the best known college models—those at Miami University and the University of Michigan for instance—the reflection that is asked for is an overview.[5] And in most well-known K-12 portfolio models—the Kentucky model, for instance—again, the larger view is solicited, not reflections on individual texts or work samples.

Another telling difference: while students are given wide berth in deciding what to share and how to share it and are explicitly invited to include personal information, exactly the opposite occurred with faculty. The latter are not asked, for example, to *explain the place of teaching in your life*, nor are they encouraged to *provide readers with a clearer understanding of who you are as a person*. Rather, they are told quite specifically what is expected of them; information targeted to informing readers in very specific ways about the portfolio composer's accomplishments. Hutchings advises faculty. for instance, to include two introductory documents in addition to the individual annotations:

> The first is the professional biography of the person who is preparing the portfolio. At a minimum, this could be a traditional resume. But it might also be useful to have the person write about key stages in his or her development as a teacher.
>
> The second is information about the specific environment in which the individual works . . . what the campus and department expect in terms of teaching, research and service; what specific classes the individual faculty member teaches; and the important details about these classes that affect teaching—such as course size and the characteristics, abilities, and motivations of the students. (11)

And Christine Hult, in detailing what an administrative portfolio might look like, offers similar advice:

> As with the teaching portfolio, anyone compiling an administrative portfolio should guide the evaluators through the materials by means of

self-reflective glosses on the contents. A self-reflective overview letter can highlight for readers those items of particular importance, tying documents to their underlying scholarship, for example. Thinking of the entire administrative portfolio as a persuasive document, buttressed by significant evidence (in the form of artifacts) to support the argument, will help the compiler toward a cohesive whole. (129)

Several observations are worth noting here. Does it matter that students are not asked for individual annotations while faculty are? I think it both does and doesn't. On the one hand, if reflection is built into the curriculum so that students continually are engaged in reflection-in-action and constructive reflection, then perhaps reflective individual annotations aren't as necessary; students will already have reflected upon these texts precisely because the curriculum includes *the processes of reflection.*

On the other hand, it seems a truism that writing individual annotations for a reader, as a kind of presentation, is itself an instructive endeavor precisely because, as Shulman suggests, it changes what you see; it makes the reflection *inter* as well as *intra.* Focused on a single work sample and presented to a public audience in a formal way, such a text requires a depth of insight that we want students to have, one that could contribute to the more comprehensive text as well. (This would be true regardless of whether the comprehensive text is attached to a portfolio or is an independent document.) And it seems likely that for many students, this more focused reflection might pose less of a challenge, so that we could build a sequence here: an integration of reflection into the curriculum which culminates in a final reflective document, a means of both process and product. One thing is clear, however: in the literature on reflection-in-presentation, we have two forms—the individual, the more comprehensive.

And a second point: the directions provided for the larger, comprehensive reflective text embody different models, the (student) one very open, the (faculty) one very constrained. Which is better? If the advice given to faculty is restrictive, and if we assume they are the better writers, shouldn't we emulate that in the directions we provide to students? Again I want to say *yes and no.* Much of my reading of what's called for here depends on context: as I argue in chapter seven, a high-stakes assessment situation demands clear directions. Such directions work toward providing the same opportunity to everyone by framing the task well. Moreover, in the process of articulating those directions, we clarify our own expectations, a feature that is especially important for high stakes situations, too, given that often both faculty and students are writing to and for the "unknown" reader. Providing clear, if restrictive, directions seems only prudent.

On the other hand, students—especially those who are writing reflection-in-presentation in a class for a teacher they do know—are not writing professional documents, nor is a single course typically considered a high stakes assessment.[6] Within the classroom, then, there is a certain freedom that we can use to learn about reflection-in-presentation—about how a reflection-in-presentation *shapes a self*, about what we value in such texts, about the forms and metaphors and connections students construct to shape themselves.[7]

In other words, it's a design issue. Given an appropriate context, the open design has much to offer it. And in fact, thinking of reflection only as modelled on the professional text is a mistake, I think: it's likely that we would lose the chance to learn from it what it can teach us. A comparison shows why: the constrained version of the comprehensive reflective text is constrained for a reason, to produce something predictable. From such a document, we will learn: about the writers individually, about the writers in the aggregate. But we will not learn much about reflection per sé, about the forms such a document might take, about what we value in it—precisely because in constraining response, the directions *preclude exploration that can teach*. In the classroom rhetorical situation, we know more about the contexts the students have been working in; allowing students considerably more freedom—to imagine and experiment and explore, to create reflection as a specific kind of discourse taking place in specific sites–thus seems appropriate. It is through such freedom that we all learn.

As is self-evident, however, a large caveat: we have to value and engage in such freedom cautiously. We have to remember that ultimately, teachers are responsible for helping students manage this freedom; how we go about doing that in a way that isn't hegemonic, that is respectful, is a key question. We also have to remember that we are the ones who award the A's, who valorize the truths and the selves telling those truths, who compose students in this process. We are the ones who decide which reflections-in-presentation—which pluralized narratives—will be permitted, will be seen as universal truths.

***

There are many questions to put to reflection-in-presentation. Some of them include:

How explicit should the directions for reflection-in-presentation be?

Are there specific questions that students should take up?

What form/s will be allowed (eg, a letter, a poem, an essay, a web site)?[7]

What expectations come with this "assignment?"

How will one know if it "works?"

(Have you ever written one?)

(Could you generalize about reflection generally on the basis of your own experience with it?)

(What would happen if we began to talk about it?)

***

Regardless of the model of reflection-in-presentation we prefer or enact, however, we haven't done a very good job of talking about what we value in such a text. We have scoring guides (e.g., Miami, Michigan) that talk about what's valued in a program portfolio more generally, but we haven't talked about what it is in this particular kind of discourse that "works." This is surprising: the reflective letter, for instance, has generated considerable interest and comment (eg, Sommers et al.; Schultz et al.; Conway), but as we'll see in chapter seven, mostly in terms of individual response or in terms of the kind of author a reader is likely to construct on the basis of this discourse.

What's needed is a more generic sense of what is valued in such texts, if indeed readers share certain expectations. I think we do. And perhaps the easiest way to demonstrate that we do is, ironically, to read a text that violates these expectations: by means of what Joseph Janangelo calls an "inverted exemplary narrative" (100), in this case a reflection-in-presentation.

The reason I chose this essay is because I felt it was perfect in every way. Even in the preliminary draft stage I felt confident with this essay. I only had two minor mistakes in the rough draft. The final draft was flawless. I can't find any weakness with this essay. One of the reasons it was the strongest is because it came from the heart. When I write from the heart and deal with my emotions and feelings, I truly am being honest. This story was true and is still vivid in my memory to this very day. If I would have had to make up a fictional story, it simply would not have worked. This essay was strong because it flowed well. The reason it flowed well is due to strong transition. Strong transition from paragraph to paragraph makes an essay easier to follow for the reader. "From Butterflies to Victory" is without a doubt, the strongest essay in the portfolio. The story was true and meaningful, flawless, and flowed well due to strong transition. As I said earlier, I am very proud of this essay. I wouldn't change a thing about this essay.

I want to point my initial comments toward what I think *is* working. The student has written an essay that she cares about, and she evidences some understanding of textuality, for example in her references to *strong transition*. More generally, however, the writer in this text, in this presentation to an audience, disappoints precisely because she violates expectations we bring to such a text. These violations include:

First, the writer seems unable to see text as synthetic and to use that as a basis for a discussion about the text. The essay is *perfect in every way,* she *cannot find any weakness with this essay,* and it was almost perfect from the start apparently, since the author found only *two minor mistakes in the rough draft.* Now all writers aren't multidrafters, as Muriel Harris reminds us; perhaps this writer is a single drafter. But a single drafter is capable of having the same *discussion about text* that a multi-drafter can. We don't have discussion here; we have a very limited, repetitious summary.

Second, as indicated already, the writer doesn't seem able to assess her own text. Even writers who are satisfied with a text can see—in specific terms—how it could be changed, how those hypothetical changes might work and make informed judgments about them. We don't see that here: what we do seem to see is a version of Perry's dualism, the *perfect* paper implicitly contrasted with the hypothetical imperfect (e.g., one with weak transitions).

Third, the writer doesn't seem to understand the relationship between a rhetorical situation and text. We seem to be expecting a self-assessment that is related to some notion of context, of rhetorical situation, of audience and how the needs of an audience (fictionalized or not) have something to do with the development of text, how much it satisfies them, and so on. Instead of discussing a rhetorically situated kind of judgment, the author keys on a sole criterion to evaluating text: honesty.[8] As the writer says, *One of the reasons it was the strongest is because it came from the heart.* Without a rhetorical situation that includes an audience other than self, *she has no one to satisfy but herself.* This reasoning, we have to say, is perfectly logical. It is not, however, rhetorical, nor is it reflective.

What the writer does offer textually is length, and a certain length does seem to be a value we endorse, as it is in many other kinds of texts. That length presumes, however, a kind of development, depth of insight—*reflection*—that is missing here.

I want to think about this refection-in-presentation in one additional way: developmentally. If this text were a reflection-in-action, or a constructive reflection, I'd think the text would provide some starting points for us: 1) given the generally a-rhetorical claims here (eg, *strong transition, vivid memory*), I'd want to know how some of them applied specifically to the (primary) text under discussion: 2) as I argued in chapter two, I think students have to know and like their texts before they are ready to re-work them. I'm not persuaded that this student actually knows her work: I don't see the specifics relating to the primary text that would suggest the writer's familiarity with it. Which wouldn't mean that the student doesn't like it (perhaps has even more reason to like it, ironically). In fact, this student shows signs of being what I call "stuck in like"; that is, infatuated with her own text, she cannot see how it might be changed, much less how it might be improved. Developmentally—for student, for text, for processes—I have a starting point. But we don't expect reflection-in-presentation to be developmental: we see it as one form of summative assessment, a concluding moment. We bring different expectations to it. But it's also true that in a larger sense, such a presentation can become a point of departure, perhaps most especially when it violates our expectations.

***

I'd like to point to two other inverted exemplary narratives as instructive in moving towards understanding what we value in reflection-in-presentation. The first has to do with the emphasis we in composition studies tend to place on revision. According to Elizabeth Metzger and Lizbeth Bryant, students take that emphasis and play it back to us in ways that disturb; the authors quote a student, for instance, who claims "*to have botch*[ed] *a paper so it looked like I revised*" and who then claimed that the revision was part of what she should be rewarded for (7), a version of what Irwin Weiser calls "psyching out the port prof" (299). The question: how important is revision? Do we believe in single-draft writers, as Harris suggests? Is there a single-draft reflection-in-presentation that will satisfy?

The second narrative has to do with the kinds of claims that students can make but that are generally recognized by faculty as tangential (e.g., amounts of effort and time) and as unrelated (e.g., shmoozing). Students often equate (confuse?) sufficient time spent with quality of product, and they associate effort with high grades, not entirely without reason, of course.[9] Shmooz is a more direct appeal, appearing in a text that plays back to us quite explicitly (quite manipulatively?) our own values. As Irwin Weiser explains,

> "Shmooz" . . . is the often indistinguishable evil twin of "glow," the-telling-the-teacher-what-he-wants-to-hear that students may very well write in their reflective letters . . . . I don't want to suggest that we discount or mistrust students' reflective writing; I mean that reflective letters, precisely because they do reintroduce the personal, force us to recognize the subjective nature of our readings. (301)

For readers, reflection-in-presentation, seen in this light, can be tricky to navigate. On the one hand, we create educational environments precisely so that students will be influenced in very specific and (we hope) positive ways. This *is* the nature of teaching: *it's reasonable to think that students will reflect that context back to us in their reflective texts.* On the other hand, we don't want to encourage nor reward what a cynic might characterize as obsequience or false compliance.

The question seems to be how we would know whether we were reading the product of (genuine) learning or the product of shmooz. How we answer that question depends on our own context for reading and the role we are playing. As I'll argue in chapter seven, in a high stakes assessment situation we probably want to be more directive in our requests, precisely because we don't know the student, and we don't know the context(s) the student is working in. The absence of this kind of contextual knowledge can make the task of interpreting and evaluating more difficult. (I have to pause, briefly, to note the irony here. It used to be the case that we assumed that the *less* we knew about the writer, the better a judgment we were assumed to make: hence two "blind" raters in a holistically scored essay exam. But once we began to apprehend the role of context in influencing, if not determining, meaning, we began to ask about what those contexts were, how they do affect our readings, and how we might externalize them in productive ways. Chapter five discusses this more fully.)

In the case of the classroom, however, we are talking about readers who teach their own students, who presumably do know them, and who thus can bring multiple contexts to bear in their reading, as we'll see in some detail in the next chapter. For now, it's sufficient to note that in the case of reflection-in-presentation accompanying a portfolio, the primary texts and the reflective text relativize each other, hold each other to account. In the case of independent reflective texts, the context of the teacher's experience of the class relativizes the claims in the reflection. Ultimately, of course, determining the value of the student's reflection-in- presentation requires informed, thoughtful, reflective judgment.

Textually, there are signs that reflection-in-presentation is not "working" as we'd hoped, that articulated, elaborated, complex learning is not occurring. Indicators include:

- a text that is too short
- a text that is uninformed about the composer's work or learning: the student doesn't seem to know his or her texts, his or her own knowledge, understanding
- a text where the author cannot think rhetorically or synthetically, can read neither links nor gaps
- a text that parrots the context of the class or the teacher without demonstrating the influence of either

What we also need is a set of texts that might speak to what can go right.

***

I don't think it's surprising that we've seen so little discussion about what *works* in reflection-in-presentation. It's always easier, more comfortable to critique. Critiquing is part of our teacherly identity; it's what many of us have been rewarded for our entire academic lives (Elbow and Yancey). But saying what we like, what we value: that's tricky. Having that kind of discussion requires a disclosure that parallels what is asked of the composer of the reflection-in-presentation. Even in the best of circumstances, revealing what we value in such a text makes us vulnerable in ways that discomfit (Allen, Condon, et al. 1997), so much more the case when we go public.[10]

But it is also true that without such discussion, we write and read in the dark.

***

I want to read several reflections-in-presentation as a way of thinking about what we might value in such reflection. Initially, in this exploration, I was looking for different kinds of texts that themselves work in different ways—to show a range of what can work, to show that students can *do* this kind of work. I did find that range:

two texts from writing classes,

one reflection-in-presentation from a capstone portfolio, and

one reflection-in-presentation as a cumulative independent document.

What I also found is that these texts, as disparate as they and their contexts are, show writers engaging in similar thinking processes, processes and rhetorical moves I've come to recognize as *reflective*.

***

Daphne is a returning student in an advanced writing class. Her final reflective essay, which brings the portfolio to closure, itself concludes:

> As I reflect on what I have learned in this class and what I will take with me when the class is over, I realize that the final grade was no longer the destination I was striving so hard for—what really matters is what I have learned while on this particular journey. Recently, I came across a book of poetry that I had taken as a freshman. Included in the book was the poem "The Road Not Taken" by Robert Frost. As I gathered up the written work from this class to put into my portfolio, these final lines stayed with me: *Two roads diverged in a wood, and I—/I took the one less traveled by/And that has made all the difference.* Somehow, these lines seemed to strike a cord with me. In the beginning of the semester when I started this class, my major goal was to get a good grade as well as to improve as a writer, but perhaps what I have come to realize is that the grade is not as important as the discovery of *who* I am as a writer— and that has made all the difference.

Daphne makes several moves here that I have come to understand as characteristic of reflection-in-presentation.

First, Daphne seems to answer the large question, what have you learned? Reflective writers seem to take this question up, sometimes opening with it, other times weaving it throughout the text or concluding with it. But taking this question up seems a key rhetorical move.

*Second, in answering the question, Daphne moves beyond the class;
again, reflective writers tend to draw on multiple contexts to explain what
they have learned.* (We might even contend that learning *calls for* interaction among multiple contexts.) Daphne tells us that in preparing her
portfolio, she *came across* a book of *poetry* and read Robert Frost,
whose *lines seemed to strike a cord with me.* She then uses those lines in
a Bahktinian way to talk about what she has learned: *but perhaps what I
have come to realize is that the grade is not as important as the discovery
of who I am as a writer—and that has made all the difference.* To
describe what she has learned in this class, Daphne synthesizes from
earlier experiences; she rewrites Frost to make her meaning.

*Third, Daphne invokes a metaphor, a common one, the class as jour-
ney, as another way of talking about her learning:* about how the *desti-
nation* for the journey changed, how the journey itself involved a
Frostian choice between *Two roads.* She understands that choosing
the road of learning instead of the road of grades is taking the *less
travelled* route.

***

Sharon was enrolled in a different section of the same course; and
what she learns is different.

She begins her reflection-in-presentation, an essay that concludes
the portfolio, by *presenting:* by explaining the course and addressing
her reader, someone she does not expect to be familiar with the class.
Because that reader isn't familiar with the context of the class, Sharon
explains.

> The focus of this course, Expository Writing, was on the metaphor of
> "voice." As you have seen in the writings included in the portfolio, we
> attempted to define voice, explore its uses, and "try on" new uses. We
> soon discovered that "voice" was not something to be easily defined, but
> we learned a great deal in the process of trying to attach a definition to it.
> My understanding of voice has come to be that particular approach that
> you take in writing. The voice you use, whether consciously or uncon-
> sciously, is a function of both audience and purpose.

Sharon addresses the reader directly and assumes that the reader has
reviewed *the writings included in the portfolio.* These reflect, she says,
what we attempted: *to define voice, explore its uses, and "try on" new
uses,* the *we* here suggesting a kind of communal enterprise. *The first*

context Sharon invokes, then, is that of the class. But Sharon worked individually as well, toward an *understanding* of *voice* as *a function of both audience and purpose.*

Sharon invokes another context, however: that of the writer she used to be:

> During this course, we also addressed the issue of finding our "one true voice" if it exists at all. When we began discussing this topic, I felt sure that my true voice was contained in my personal journal, but as I began to leaf through those pages that had become like friends to me, a whole new perspective dawned on me. As the tattered notebook was opened, each entry displayed a new and fresh voice. My voice in June was one of loneliness, but August's entry was positive and hopeful. The older entries show a voice of immaturity, and sound so unlike my voice today because of the local high school colloquialisms. Then there was the 1993 summer school entry. This entry was written after finishing a very flowery 18th Century novel, and my voice sounded almost exactly like the voice in the book.

Here, we see Sharon *weave multiple narratives.* One concerns her past writing lives, her past writing selves. Like Joan Didion, Sharon sees the writers she used to be; she's someone who thought of her writing voice as *true.* But unlike our writer of the *perfect essay,* Sharon is willing to learn about, get to know her work. That's another narrative: she looks at her writing in her *tattered notebook,* finds multiple "true" voices. She finds her writing sympathetic to what she feels, whether that be *loneliness* or *hope*; iconic of her adolescent context, filled with *high school colloquialisms*; resonant with her own reading—*my voice sounded almost exactly like the voice in a very flowery 18th Century novel.* At the same time, this is another narrative characteristic of reflection-in-presentation–a narrative of the course, of what she learned *inside that context.* Here, she learned what she thinks voice is; she acquired a kind of knowledge that can be applied.

And finally, Sharon answers Daphne's question, *what did I learn?*

> My conclusion, after spending more than three months in reflection, is that I don't have one true voice at all. I now believe that I have a variety of voices on hand to choose from, and can create new voices simply by trying. All that is needed to utilize a voice is to determine who your audience is, and what your purpose will be. An early architect, Sullivan, sums up my understanding of voice in his statement "form follows function." Although Sullivan was speaking in terms of architecture, this idea can be applied to voice as well. The form of voice that you choose will follow the

function that you desire your piece to serve, and without knowledge of your function, you are left without a form.

Again like Daphne, Sharon shares with us the conclusions she has drawn—in her case that *I don't have one true voice at all.* We might even say that we see here her move from a Perry-like dualism to a stance between relativistic and reflective. Although she sees voice as a function of a rhetorical situation, she has yet to consider the value of her move or the ethics of it, important issues, to be sure. Still, what she does consider is how a metaphorical reference will help her explain what she has learned, hence the connection to the architect Sullivan. But Sharon is not studying architecture, so where did she get this reference? From her peer review partner, an architecture major.

Through reflection, we learn to see through others' eyes.

***

Kate is a senior majoring in Spanish, minoring in education, and hoping to teach Spanish to secondary students. She also participates in UNC–Charlotte's honors program, which requires that students complete a final project in order to graduate with honors. Kate has chosen to compose a capstone portfolio. To satisfy the honors requirement, this portfolio must synthesize work in the honors program, which is grounded in study of peace and justice, with work in the student's major. Kate decides to use the concept of honor to perform this work: *what,* she asks throughout, *does it mean to be honorable?* Is honor merely a cultural construct, or do we see honor similarly in different cultures, specifically in Anglo cultures and Spanish cultures?

She takes this question through several sections of the portfolio: she has a comprehensive, introductory reflective essay as well as smaller reflective essays that take up questions related to her theme. Although this is a different kind of reflection-in-presentation, we will find its rhetorical moves surprisingly similar to those we have seen before.

Like the other reflective writers, *Kate begins by establishing context:*

> As I began sorting through my experiences in college, I started to think about what was truly honorable in my life so far. I've worked as a baby-sitter at the Battered Women's Shelter in Charlotte; I've given blood to the Red Cross; in High School I did such things as making Christmas cards for the elderly in Senior Citizen's homes; I've also worked with the Food Run program [a food bank effort initiated by students in the honors program] at UNC-Charlotte and done some tutoring with local schoolchildren in

the Project Hope program. In all of these cases I've noticed that the difference is begun on an individual level, but that it is a group effort that sustains. This is the way in which all groups are formed, be it a non-profit organization, a political lobbying organization, or any underground revolutionary movement. I was reminded of this as I watched the Home Box Office (HBO) original movie "The Power of One." At its end, this movie reminds us all that, "Changes can come from the power of many, but only when the many come together to form that which is invincible . . . the power of one." These ideas begin with one person, spread to many, and then the many can come together to accomplish tasks which alone one person could not accomplish. The experiences I mentioned above are some of the times when I have been part of the many.

Kate cites her own experience here to show the relationship between the *individual* and the *many*. Although she understands herself as an *individual*, she also sees that her contributions contribute to a larger effort—*The experiences I mentioned above are some of the times when I have been part of the many*—and she understands this way of seeing social action as explaining everything from *non-profits* to *underground revolutionary movements*. We see Kate here, in other words, moving from the inside (her experience) to the outside (social theory) and back (herself as contributor): connecting what might seem to be disparate activities: putting herself both personally and intellectually into this context, into this text, authorizing herself to speak. In terms of reflection-in-presentation, we see her making connections, providing context, and beginning to put that context in relation to the question, what have I learned? *To answer that, she begins to theorize about social action.*

In the next section of the reflective essay, we see Kate as reflective writer: she chooses a controversial question related to her topic of honor and develops it factually. She then relativizes the situation, showing the multiple ways it can be viewed. Finally, she shares with us her judgment on the issue. In the act of writing reflection-in-presentation, Kate becomes a reflective writer.

She begins by weaving dual narratives, the one telling us about a class she took, the other again answering the question, *what have I learned?*

If I have learned nothing else from my Honors Program classes, I know that I have taken away from them the ability to understand the different points of view. In the HONR 3701 class, *Science, Technology, and Human Values*, we had to write a paper on a controversial topic in which science and technology have come into conflict with Human Values. Since my initial introduction to it in Biology in High School, the study of Genetics has always fascinated at me. We can actually find out which chromosomes are the cause of which traits, genotypical and phenotypical. But the focus of my paper is on what happens when we mandate genetic testing on unborn children and they test positive for abnormalities, diseases, or other genetic defects which can leave a child with a quality of life lower than that which parents hope for in the life of their child(ren). Knowing about any condition before a child is born leaves the parents in a difficult position: should they terminate the pregnancy in order to save themselves the pain and save their child from the ridicule and other suffering?

Here, then, Kate takes what we know about genetics and applies it in the specific situation of *mandatory genetic testing*, and she raises (what I take to be) an impossible question: *should they terminate the pregnancy in order to save themselves the pain and save their child from the ridicule and other suffering?*

Kate then explains how this is relevant to her theme of honor; through the questions she raises, we see the complexity of the situation. The question about mandatory genetic testing is included, she says,

> because the overlying question has to do with honor. Once the child is tested, to whom does the information belong? Should there be a requirement test, and if so, should there be a requirement to reveal this information, and if so, to whom? The parents? The doctor? Should anyone else be allowed to see it, such as insurance companies? Is it reasonable to tell parents such potentially devastating news? *Are the recipients appreciative? Are we really performing a necessary service?* Or are we only trying to play God by choosing ourselves that which Nature used to sort out? Who gets to decide whether genetic testing is "beneficial"? . . . *Is there honor in forcing parents to make what might be probably the most difficult decision of their lives?*

Kate reminds us about something we are inundated with daily: information. But information brings with it implications. It's intolerable to acquire information, Kate implies, without establishing a context in which to understand it. That's the general maxim. The local: in this context, *honor* and *mandatory* are mutually exclusive.

> It is my personal opinion that there is no honor in forcing this kind of decision on anyone, yet mandatory genetic testing has done just that. If parents make the decision to have the testing done and to deal with the consequences, let *THAT* be their choice . . . . Technology has made it possible to

make genetic discoveries which were not originally intended to be made and which humanity was not and is not ready to deal with. Heaven help humanity if we ever make it mandatory to kill a fetus which carries certain chromosomes. While the idea behind genetic testing was noble in the beginning, the moral issues which parents would face make mandatory genetic screening less than honorable.

Kate both tells and shows what she has learned: facts certainly, the process of relativizing as well, the gift of seeing gaps and drawing those to our attention and playing out the consequences of neglecting those gaps, and the art of making reasoned judgments. She shares this with us in a synthetic reflection-in-presentation that draws on multiple selves: the student in the honors program, the woman who someday would be a parent herself, the informed citizen, the person who wants to be part of something larger.

In telling us what she has learned, Kate finds out herself.

***

Kevin, a sophomore, is another student in the honors program at UNC–Charlotte; he is taking an honors course in the history of science from Physics Professor Mike Corwin. Although it's a history of science course, the object isn't just for students to understand how we moved from Galileo's model of the universe to Kepler's; it's also for students to identify the model of the world they hold true and to explain how that is so. Given that UNC–Charlotte sits in the middle of the Bible Belt, and given that many of our students still consider the theory of evolution at odds with "a loving God's plan," this is a harder task than one might expect.

And making it more difficult in its own way is a change in Corwin's assignments. This term the students' tests and papers have been replaced by what Corwin has called a "reflective notebook" and a final "reflective paper," defined here as a reflection-in-presentation.

We can understand Kevin's reflection-in-presentation by sampling parts of it. He begins as the others do, thus in a way we might (by now) predict. *He weaves multiple contexts, multiple narratives*, the one beginning to answer, *what did I learn?* the other, *how did this course help me learn it?*

This semester, I have learned to think of the world and my role in it in a totally different way than I had ever thought before. Philosophy had always been something very foreign to me, until now. This semester showed me that philosophy was something that I was capable of doing if I was willing to spend the necessary time and energy. Philosophy took two primary forms in this course: one was done through class discussion, and the other was done through a reflection notebook. The reflection notebook is the focus of this paper.

Kevin begins by focusing on the materials of the course: the *discussions* and the *reflection notebook*. That's one story. He includes another narrative as well: first, *I have learned in a totally different way than I had ever thought before*; learning requires *necessary time and energy.*

This narrative, about how difficult learning can be, acts as a refrain in Kevin's reflection-in-presentation. That learning isn't easy, of course, is a common student narrative. But the fact that we have heard these narratives before doesn't make them false; it alerts us to take their measure against the text that is to come. One way of taking their measure, Walter Fisher calls "fidelity" and "coherence." He asks,

- is the account (text) faithful to what we know to be true in other accounts (reasons)? And what values are expressed?
- is the account (text) internally consistent, complete and ethical? (177-78)

These are questions we can put to Kevin's reflection-in-presentation.

***

In the next section of Kevin's reflection-in-presentation, he tells us how this notebook differed from others that he's kept, and reiterates the fact that *it was not as easy as I had hoped.* But he also begins another narrative, one that concerns objectivity and the personal and truth. In many ways, this is the key answer to the question, *what have I learned?*

At the beginning of the semester when the notebook was assigned I thought I knew how to go about writing such a notebook from my past experiences and reflections. It was not as easy as I had hoped. The notebook took time and more importantly thought to get an acceptable entry written down. I tried to make the notebook somewhat personal, but I also tried to stay as objective as possible when trying to make decisions. My goal was to re-evaluate my current understanding of the universe and particularly the world in which I live. I hoped that this evaluation would help me create a clearer picture of what has, is, and will happen in my world.

To do this, Kevin "found myself questioning beliefs I had and trying to convince myself that they were true." Put differently, Kevin wants coherence between his beliefs and what he is being taught as science: both pretend to explain the world. Kevin tries to explain his dilemma, first by summarizing a view put forward by Richard Tarnas, and then by reacting to it:

> While science is "discovering new laws," and "making new models," there is a need to fill the gaps with something. Religion is the answer. In the notebook I did not state whether I believed this position or not and I should have. I think that science is a tool used to find knowledge that can be used to develop models of the universe to help us understand the world. But a disclaimer must be made: these models will never be perfect. The knowledge we do not find through science leaves gaps in our world views. These gaps are filled with beliefs in religion.

There will always be gaps, Kevin believes: science will never create the comprehensive model. Which takes us to evolution, one of the topics addressed in the course.

> Evolution has always been a topic for debate in many circles. It is hard to argue that it has not occurred to some extent over time, but it is also hard to convince me that simple chemical elements some how become ordered and transform into life. It is much easier for me to believe that God was the one who set the universe in motion and made the laws that govern it today.

Again, we see *ease* as narrative, pitted against *hard*: again this reflection-in-presentation tells the story of difficult learning. Or: *learning involves multiple contexts, isn't easy, can't be neatly summarized, isn't always satisfying precisely because it can bring different knowledges and belief systems into conflict.* (Not a bad lesson.) Evolution as a test case, Kevin says, looks persuasive: *It is hard to argue that it has not occurred to some extent over time.* At the same time it's unconvincing: *it is also hard to convince me that simple chemical elements some how become ordered and transform into life.* It may be easier—and more comforting—to believe the one: Kevin seems stalemated. At the same time, we also see Kevin working toward a relativist stance, beyond the dualistic.

Kevin turns to his conclusion by rewriting his performance in the course; the rewrite is based on an *assessment* of how he learns, how he could have learned.

> If I could have done anything differently I probably would have started questioning my present beliefs much sooner and then maybe I could have developed a cosmology that better estimates the world. Some aspects of my world view have been questioned, though. The biggest of these questions I feel concerns absolutes. Is there a Truth, or only truths? . . . Even though I do not believe in Absolute Truth, I believe in God because it is a reasonable solution to the remaining questions I have about life. I am willing to live a contradiction as long as it serves my purpose to give meaning to life.

Kevin has learned: about himself, about the need for a coherent *cosmology*, about *Truth* and *truths* and willingness *to live a contradiction as long as it serves my purpose to give meaning to life*. Like Lara, whom we saw in chapter three, Kevin has determined where he is ready to compromise and where not. His reflection-in-presentation presents a plural self, one who understands a scientific model of the world, who can plot that against his personal model of the world, and plot again against one informed by religion and a belief in God. He brings material together by locating it in his own learning as he tells us how he learned. In Fisher's terms, the reflection-in-presentation exhibits both fidelity and coherence: it is student discourse consistent with other student discourses, working both inside and out; it is consistent in method, material, and tenor.

It is, in sum, instructive, for Kevin and for us: the reflection of a student struggling to learn, learning by telling us of that struggle, showing us how we *live contradictions* when they are *purpose*[ful].

＊＊＊

As I work toward completing this project, I'm asked about what a reader sees as the personal dimension of reflection-in-presentation: isn't it just another form of "personal" writing? Since I've linked it to autobiography, of course, I have invited this question. But I also think that a false dichotomy—between the personal and the academic—is suggested by the question. In my view, all writing has a personal element to it, certainly, and this is likewise true for reflection-in-presentation, as we've seen. Precisely because reflection-in-presentation is performative, in Erving Goffman's sense of the word, however, it's necessarily social: audience-oriented in very specific ways that remove it from the sphere of the exclusively personal (if there is such a thing). In *The Presentation of Self in Everyday Life*, Goffman explains the range of roles that performers, like our students, may take on *for others* and of the effects such role-taking can have, particularly in a context involving evaluation:

> At one extreme, one finds that the performer can be fully taken in by his own act; he can be sincerely convinced that the impression of reality that he stages is the real reality. . . .
>
> At the other extreme, we find that the performer may not be taken in at all by his own routine. This possibility is understandable, since no one is in quite so good an observational position to see through the act as the person who puts it on. (19)

Most students, I think, inhabit the middle ground of this range. We ask them to take up certain questions, we reward certain kinds of response, and at some level, many—if not all of them—understand, as Goffman puts it, that we ask them to put on masks that (we hope) bear some relationship to the ways they do or might see themselves:

> In a sense, and in so far as this mask represents the conception we have formed of ourselves—the role we are striving to live up to—this mask is our truer self, the self we would like to be. In the end, our conception of our role becomes second nature and an integral part of our personality. (20-21)

Complicating this dilemma can be the self-doubt of the performer:

> While we can expect to find natural movement back and forth between cynicism and sincerity, still we must not rule out the kind of transitional point that can be sustained on the strength of a little self-illusion. We find that the individual may attempt to induce the audience to judge him and the situation in a particular way, and he may seek this judgment as an ultimate end in itself, and yet he may not believe that he deserves the valuation of self which he asks for or that the impression of reality which he fosters is valid. (21)

This, then, explains in part why and how teaching is an ethical act, *why asking students to reflect for others can exert a powerful shaping effect*. But because classrooms do invite certain kinds of behaviors, it's dangerous ground as well; it's easy (perhaps most especially for the well-intentioned) to make mistakes, to insist on our ways of seeing, to demand that students revise our way, reflect in our language, play back to us our insights and understandings. When we consider reflection in this light, we are reminded about the value of a reflection-in-presentation like Kevin's, one infused not with the unity of a projected teacher's singular mask, but rather with the struggles of the multiple *contradictions* of his own life. But in order that such reflections be performed, we teachers have to accept and value and reward them.

In other words, because it works both inside *and* outside, reflection-in-presentation is personal, but it's social as well. Because it takes place in an evaluative setting, reflection-in-presentation invites performance. This problematizes our evaluation, but chiefly because it makes issues within our evaluative practices more obvious. On the plus side, this means that we can identify these issues, can talk about them, can try to fashion ways of working with them that are reasonable and responsible and ethical and reflective. Classroom evaluation has never excluded the personal; reflection-in-presentation simply makes the personal more obvious. More to the point, if there is a relationship between/among knowing/learning/the personal, as we currently believe there is, then it makes that relationship more salient and thus it works toward greater learning—*which is the point of education in the first place.*

So both—reflection and evaluation, especially when brought together—make something of a Pandora's Box, it's true. But as these boxes go, this one's an improvement on what we are accustomed to.

***

What I've done here is to read these reflections-in-presentation in a Schonean way. I've focused on individual texts, reading them closely, interpreting them within multiple frameworks. I've also read across these texts in an effort to read the general as I make sense of the particular. In the patterns across these texts are the common threads defining reflection-in-presentation.

As we've seen, such reflection can take several forms: the individual annotation, the comprehensive text. It allows the individual to work in a social context to make meaning. As autobiography, it is *inter* as well as *intra.* As presentation, it is *rhetorical.*

Within the classroom, the text representing reflection-in-presentation, whether in a writing class or another class, whether attached to a portfolio or written as an independent document, typically makes certain rhetorical moves. These include

- introducing the text by invoking a context of experience and/or a context of the class
- speaking of past selves as a way of understanding the current self
- using metaphor as a means of exploring relationships
- assessing one's work or learning
- invoking other contexts voluntarily as a means of understanding and explaining
- looking toward gaps and making connections, as two means of synthesizing and relativizing and reflecting
- answering the question, what have I learned? with as much emphasis on the I as on the learned

Another way to think about these features is to say that these are the kinds of rhetorical moves we expect, ones we value. If that's so, then we have another narrative against which reflection-in-presentation can be plotted.

Notes

1. A key feature is genre: this will discussed in chapter seven.
2. Technically, if a portfolio is used for summative evaluation, it should be governed by the same good assessment principles and practices regardless of the context in which it is produced or evaluated. But as a matter of practice, the contexts widely differ: the classroom, for instance, with a teacher reading the portfolios of students she or he *knows*, as opposed to a program portfolio that has multiple readers, none of whom knows the student at all. In fact, as in the case of the Miami University placement portfolios and the Michigan entrance portfolios, the student may not even have matriculated in the school hosting the readers. Such contexts make for very different opportunities and dangers.
3. In this research process, scientists are not composing a reflection-in-presentation; they are seeking to know. There is an intervening step, however, that Shulman skips over, the reading and interpreting of data. Since this too is a key move, it requires far more attention than we've given it. For a fuller illustration of how this can work in a writing classroom, see also chapter six.
4. See chapter seven for a fuller discussion of the relationship between directions and reflection-in-presentation.

5.   The University of Michigan actually started with individual annotations as well as the overview, but moved to include only the latter.

6.   For reasons not to model undergraduate work in reflection-in-presentation on the work of professionals, see Yancey in *Situating Portfolios*.

7.   Lillian Bridwell-Bowles discusses alternate modalities of reflection in *CCC*, Sandra Murphy has discussed the kinds of formats and illustrations that students have developed for reflection-in-presentation, and Louise Phelps speaks of a graduate student writing a dissertation that develops a genre specifically for reflective text.

8.   It could well be that the student here is simply reflecting values we have inscribed, like honesty: see Faigley's "Judging Writing, Judging Selves," for a critique of this view.

9.   See, for example, Sadker and Sadker.

10.   See, for instance, Allen et al in *Situating Portfolios*. Laurel Black made the same case for faculty course portfolios in her presentation at the 1997 NCTE conference on reflection.

CHAPTER FIVE

Reflective Reading,
Reflective Responding

But the fictions of language may in fact be reality, or at least the only reality we can know. And what we like to think of as living in harmony with reality may be simply a knack for multiplying fictions, for accommodating new versions of experience to older ones so that we may impose a personal if always tentative unity on the inexplicable richness of our imagination.

Leo Barsani

Instead of coming before practice, then, theory comes out of practice—theory helps us explain what we are already doing.

Joseph Harris

SOMEWHAT SURPRISINGLY, GIVEN THE TEACHING, READING, AND writing that English faculty do for a living, we don't talk very much about a *philosophy of reading student work*, or a *philosophy of responding to student work*, or even a *philosophy of evaluating student work*.[1] Too infrequently do *we* make a Schonean reflective transfer from our own *reading practices* of non-student texts—be they texts in the mainstream media, in professional journals, or in a volume of poetry—to our reading of student work. Too infrequently do we apply what we understand, about multiple kinds of responses to and dialogues about our own writing and reading, to our classrooms, where we claim, at least, that we want conversations and excitement and passion about learning.

If these observations are accurate, it seems fair to conclude that when it comes to reading and writing, we faculty seem to operate in two different worlds: the classroom world and the "real" world. When it comes times to read and respond in the classroom world, we ultimately invoke a transmission model of education: papers turned in, papers turned back. In the "real" world (or worlds, really, since admittedly, they are plural), the texts we read and write are seen to provide something else entirely, what we like to talk about as a *site for negotiation* or an *occasion for learning*: a chance to exchange ideas, to compare notes, to do the thinking game with each other, against each other.

Suppose, however, that we paused to reflect upon this observation and its implications regarding *differences*—differences between theory and practice; differences between practice in one setting and practice in another; differences between purposes and authority and expectations and assumptions and how they are relativized according to *location*. More specifically:

> Suppose that we reflected upon what we currently understand about reading and responding to student texts: what might we find?
>
> Suppose that we reflected upon the kinds of dialogues—even difficult discussions—we have about our own texts, our own work, and introduced those *kinds* of dialogues to students?
>
> Suppose that we really believed in and enacted text as site of negotiation: what questions might we ask?
>
> Suppose that we received answers to the questions we posed: what might we do with them?

This chapter takes up these questions and considers them theoretically, specifically and reflectively: first, by way of a quick review of literature on reading and response; second, by way of seeing how methods of (multiple) response can invoke text as site of negotiation. In taking up these questions, this chapter re-visits the conceptual work developed in chapter two on reflection-in-action. As claimed there, reflection is both individual and social. In the classroom particularly, the individual writer reflects, as often as not in reply to questions a teacher has posed. Fair enough. What then?

How do we read these reflections? As independent documents? As companions to the "primary" text? How, then, do we respond to this set of texts?

*

Sandra Murphy and Mary Ann Smith tell a quick story that illustrates many of the expectations that surround the reading and evaluating of students texts. One afternoon, an English teacher slumping out of school with a set of student texts in his arms meets a colleague who asks him to go for a beer.

"Can't," says the English teacher. "I have all these papers to correct."

"How do you know there's anything wrong with them?" the colleague asks. (49)

This story in some ways is *the* story of reading and responding to student work. On the one hand, as readers, we are not expected to read so much as we are expected to find error and *correct* it. (And by extension, our courses are expected to perform the same function: eradicate a student's tendency to create error; innoculate the student against making error permanently.) We, on the other hand, are complicitous since—if truth be told—we also expect to find error of some sort: rhetorical, grammatical, stylistic. We might react to error differently than our colleagues, to be sure: Mike Rose and Glynda Hull, for instance, have demonstrated how important identifying and interpreting error can be in helping a writer develop. Still, it's not text as site of negotiation so much as text as site of error. And finally, on a third hand, students expect to have their texts returned with errors marked, and sometimes they expect those errors corrected. This context, one dominated by "error," has informed the reading of student work for some time.

Another influential context governing student work is that of *preferred response* to student texts: what forms it should take, how students respond, what effects it might produce. We have research reports like those of Nancy Sommers (1981) and more recently, Summer Smith (1997), which conclude with an over-riding recommendation: make comments that are specific to the text. At the same time, we have research reports, like that of Robert Connors and Andrea Lunsford, suggesting that we teachers *don't* enact these recommendations; according to this report, we provide a-rhetorical, often cryptic comments. To see a spectrum of what Ronald Lunsford and Richard Straub call "response styles" ranging from directive to (preferred, they say) non-directive, we can go to their study of *Twelve Readers Reading*, which is both a report on the responding styles of twelve well-regarded compositionists (including, for instance, Peter Elbow, Chris Anson, and Anne Gere) and a set of recommendations for creating "facilitative" response.

What's interesting about these multiple, generic contexts governing the reading of and responding to student work, from (yet) another perspective, isn't only the expectations that various participants in the educational process bring to student texts, nor their sense that all students will respond similarly (if not identically) to response styles, although both of these issues merit further consideration. It's how these *separate* processes—of reading, of interpreting, of evaluating, of responding—have been conflated into a single activity, and of what we lose when we allow such conflation. Understanding them as different processes is thus one point of departure for reflective reading and responding.

How, we might ask, do teachers read student texts? How do students read texts, their own and others? How do teachers respond to student texts? And how might teachers and students *work together* to read, respond and understand student texts?

***

Some assumptions grounding this argument: Reading helps shape response. A teacher's response can never be better than the reading that grounds it. A teacher can only be as good as her reading of text and her response to it. Reading and response also ground any summative evaluation of text. The act of reading, then, is both prior to and central to developing good writers *and* good writing.

And it's not either/or, developing a good writer or developing good writing. It's both/and.

***

To review current thinking regarding how faculty read student texts, we can go to two major primary sources: 1) theory and 2) experience.[2]

Two theorists plot recent understandings about the kinds of readings of student text we engage in: Alan Purves and Louise Phelps. In making their analyses, it's worth noting, both work "backward"— from their work in assessment. Precisely because assessment—what and how we test and measure—is emblematic of so much else, it acts as a kind of prism, showing us how text is always *mercurially perceived*, as Susan Miller argues:

> The example of the examination might be replaced with examples of literary, public, or distinctly private writings. But this sort of writing is apt for consideration here because it can stand in relation to all of the textual features recognized in the disciplines of rhetoric, literature, and composition. Examination answers seem to be the most ephemeral of texts, but in some measure, literary theory and criticism may in time result from considering this sort of writing event. The examination is a piece of writing

in self-consciously public space, as Foucault's analysis of it in *Discipline and Punish* showed. Its student writer is required to "speak for" a received and supportable, not a private, view. But the exam is also always a personal event, and its writing and reading are always privately significant. While stable in itself, then, this sort of text is mercurially perceived. (49)

As my students in chapter one noted when I collected their first formal writing assignment, *a text is by definition a test.*

* * *

Drawing on his work in writing assessment in international contexts, Alan Purves in 1984 published "The Teacher as Reader: An Anatomy," in which he explains that the ways we read texts are connected to our purposes for reading, purposes like "read and enjoy" and "read and judge" (290). Purves specifies eight reading roles that classroom teachers can play, categorized under four over-riding purposes:

- *read and respond,* the reader playing the role of common reader
- *read and judge,* the reader playing the roles of proofreader, editor, reviewer, and gatekeeper
- *receive and analyze,* the reader playing the roles of critic and anthropologist/linguist/psychologist
- *receive and improve,* the reader playing the role of diagnostician/therapist (261).

On the basis of this analysis, Purves makes three observations. First, he observes that since teachers adopt multiple roles when reading student texts, a text will receive more than one "reading" from a single reader. Second, Purves encourages teachers to continue to read in these multiple ways but also to apprise students that they will be doing so; we need to communicate, he implies, about *how* we read these texts as well as about what we read in/to them. Finally, Purves recommends that we *learn more about* how we read student texts.

Louise Wetherbee Phelps approaches the question of how we read student texts through the lens of hermeneutics. Like Purves, Phelps categorizes the ways we can read, but she does so by locating not roles that readers play, but by specifying the "attitudes" that construct the reading. Also like Purves, Phelps finds that analysis, in this case of four attitudes, separates reading processes that in practice overlap and intermix. Specifically, she identifies four such attitudinal—textual relationships:

- *evaluative attitude, closed text* [e.g., holistically scored examinations]
- *formative attitude, evolving text* [e.g., a draft that may be revised]
- *developmental attitude, portfolio of work* [e.g., text as a part of the "life text" a writer produces, which requires the writer's own perceptions of problems and possibilities and a search for reader/writer "shared images" of textual meanings]
- *contextual attitude, text as context* [e.g., text as "embedded in and interpenetrating many other discourses," including "teacher's assignments," "commentary on drafts," and the sources that a text incorporates] (1989, 59)

Attitude, then, frames the *way* we read, thus the kind of response we provide. Phelps also calls for investigation into how readers understand reader responses:

> One conclusion I drew from this work [the study of response] is that I was not paying enough attention to student writers' views of what teachers were doing and saying. What is going here is not simply one-way reading, but a whole circle of reciprocal and interlocking interpretations: teachers of texts and students and situations; students of assignments and commentaries and class discussions and conferences; writers of their own writing and so on. (64)

Reading, as Phelps argues, isn't *one-way*: in the presumed reading of a text, we read multiple contexts. How we interpret influences what we interpret; both work together to establish how we respond.

***

We also have several kinds of experience regarding how we read student texts, and how we read and *negotiate* our own texts. Educator Patricia Carini, for instance, has developed what she's called a "reflective conversation" method of reading student texts. As described in "Dear Sister Bess," this communal method of reading includes several basic components: reading a text aloud with others; attempting to describe it with those others; and then moving to draw inferences about student work as well as the author of the text. The result is a kind of multi-vocal reading process, not unlike a readers theatre performance of text in its own way, that makes audible and thus visible the motivations, intents, potential, and effects of a particular text. Such a multi-vocal reading is located in difference, of course; it makes plain the *multiple* ways we read text.

Since the advent of portfolios, with their multiple texts and multiple kinds of texts, we've also seen several studies of how sets of texts are read and interpreted, as chapter seven details. Most of those studies, however, haven't looked so much at how we read as they have at how we rate, or score, texts. Still, that body of literature enables us to draw two conclusions. First, as represented by members of Portnet (Allen, Condon et al)—a group of faculty across the country who have exchanged and read portfolios from each other's campuses—we bring multiple, often local assumptions with us to student texts. In other words, *what Phelps posits theoretically, Portnet finds experientially:* a rhetoric of reading interacts with a rhetoric of writing in *a whole circle of reciprocal and interlocking interpretations.* Thus, for example, in recalling how she read an honors portfolio, Portnet member Cheryl Forbes recalls:

> For every question about my own rhetorical reading choices, then, I asked two about the writer's rhetorical choices. Why did she—we all assumed it was a she—choose *her* particular order, why the reflective letter at the end? What language showed that she had changed her mind about world population or the United States's use of resources? What kind of relationship with her professor and her text did her responses reveal? Why did she move between personal and distanced discourse? What tensions did her revisions reveal? . . . I couldn't go to the writer and ask her these questions, any more than I can stop mid-sentence and shout a word to Joan Didion or Cynthia Ozik. I could only ask my colleagues. I could only ask, "Does my asking make sense?" (374-375)

Our readings, then, provoke questions that go to multiple contexts—*relationships, discourses, tensions.* Of course, this Portnet reading was multiple: by definition, Portnet is plural. It includes several readers of the same text—in its way, it's a kind of externalization of the multiple single-reader recommended by Purves—and this issue, that of multiple readers, is the second that the portfolio literature has raised.

A recent article by Robert Broad illustrates the issue of multiple readership, especially when a *consensus score* is the aim of the reading. In "Reciprocal Authorities in Communal Writing Assessment: Constructing Textual Value within a New Politics of Inquiry," Broad reports on his ethnography of portfolio readings and of the sources of authority within a pluralistic reading, what he calls a collaborative rating model. He identifies three kinds of authority: first, *administrative authority,* whose roots lie in the history of the program as well as in disciplinary knowledge and power, represented by one reader; second, *teachers' authority,* a kind of insider knowledge deriving from classroom experiences and interactions with the students whose work is being reviewed, represented by a second reader; and third, *outsider authority,* that wielded by a third reader, an outside reader/evaluator whose readings appear disinterested but informed. It is, Broad suggests, in the *interaction* among these kinds of authority that we create rich textual readings and ratings. The interaction of a rich reading seems to be, then, what all these models of reading take as their premise. In its own way, a plural reading might be thought of as a *triangulated reading,* one whose fullness is created through multiple perspectives. (And interestingly, such a reading parallels the move toward triangulating the writer through "reading" him or her textually, also through multiple texts.)

A key question, then: short of asking all teachers to read all student texts communally—as in the Carini model of reflective conversation, the Portnet model of plural reading, or the programmatic model of collaborative reading and rating—is there another way to include both insider and outsider perspectives so as to provide for rich readings? Might students, through reflection-in-action, play the role of insider? In this rhetorical situation—the situation of reading and understanding and interpreting student text—aren't we the outsiders and they the (consummate) insiders?

***

The query regarding the value of asking students to read their own texts and share those readings with us complements, of course, the argument regarding reflection-in-action presented in chapter two. In that chapter, as in the following two chapters discussing constructive reflection and reflection-in-presentation, I asserted that students could help us read—not as part of a research project, but routinely, as readers from whom we could learn something. Such a concept isn't new, but it is radical, predicated on a dialogic understanding of meaning-making. Kenneth Gergen outlines that understanding, one he claims marks a coming paradigmatic shift in education as we know it:

Traditional educational practices are built around improving the minds of single individuals. Sustained by modernist assumptions, teachers and professors take the role of authorities in a given subject, their task to fill the students' minds with knowledge of their specialty. The postmodernist, however, would view academic subjects as forms of discourse peculiar to communities (biologists, economists, etc.) engaged in different activities. Students themselves are experts within the discourses of their own particular subcultures—languages that help them to maintain their life styles and adapt to the world as they construct it. Thus, education should not be a matter of replacing "poor" with "superior" knowledge, but should be a dialogue, in which all subcultures may benefit from the discourses of their neighbors. Teachers would invite students into modes of dialogue as participants rather than pawns, as collaborative interlocutors instead of slates to be filled. (250)

To a certain extent, this shift is already in process: as *participants*, students are asked to read not just for us, but *with* us. Just how they might do that—by attending to text, by highlighting what seems significant to them, by assuming different rhetorical stances as readers—is increasingly the object of discussion, as we see in a spate of recent articles in *Journal of Advanced Composition*, *College English*, and *Teaching English in the Two Year College*: Nancy Morrow's "The Role of Reading in the Composition Classroom," for instance, and Mariolina Salvatori's "Conversations with Texts: Reading in the Teaching of Composition," as well as Jeff Sommers's "Portfolios in Literature Courses: A Case Study." Largely in these discussions, however, students are asked to read literary discourse. Morrow also talks about students reading each other's drafts, and Sommers asks students to account for their reading processes in much the same way he has earlier asked them to account for their writing processes (see chapter two). What students are not *yet* asked to do is to read their own text—as *collaborative interlocutors*; as we see in chapter two, that is one purpose of reflection-in-action.

But reflection-in-action is itself contextualized—by a writer's intertexts, by the classroom context, and (not least) by the response we provide to that reflection. Students articulate their understandings, and we respond: our response shapes later iterations of reflection-in-action; it shapes new iterations of reflection-in-action on other texts; it shapes constructive reflection; and it can contribute to reflection-in-presentation. That students *can* read their own texts is, I think clear; documenting such a claim was, in part, the purpose of the earlier chapters. So now: *within this rhetorical situation* how do we respond to these readings?

***

Like the research on composing processes, the ways that faculty respond to student text has now and again sparked considerable interest, then gone dormant, only to return again, often in other dress. A review of the conventional wisdom regarding response, however, reveals several coherent themes and raises several still-unanswered questions, some of them fundamental to the task.

To begin, consider the context. What is the rhetorical situation governing response to student writing? Faculty are the rhetors, reading the text (as we've just seen), but—as the opening to chapter two illustrates, *reading it according to what?* David Jolliffe suggests a first (almost default) context: the assignment created by the faculty member to which the student writes, with the reader inquiring about the *fit between assignment and student text.* Such a reading, Jolliffe suggests, can produce deleterious effects: "I wonder the degree to which a teacher's focus on fulfilling the assignment makes writing a composition seem more like being examined (and the writer feel more like a patient) rather than an act of construing meaning (in which the writer feels more like an agent)" (221-231).

Peter Smagorinsky suggests a second context that is no doubt invoked at the same time, the *interpersonal context* that carries over from the classroom:

> A teacher and student have a relationship of some sort that affects a reading of response to writing. Is the teacher arrogant, distant? Warm and caring? Sarcastic and bitter? Supportive? Scathing? How do these traits interact with those of individual students and the social groups to which they belong? Surely, these interpersonal characteristics make a difference in the ways in which teachers couch their responses, and in which students read them. (215)

A third context is provided by *what we hope for:* what we hope to communicate to our students, based on what we understand about how students *read* our comments. As detailed in chapter two, and as observed by Purves and Phelps, we know far too little about how students do understand our meanings—though the Talk-Back of reflection-in-action is one vehicle for doing just this.

Nonetheless, we have advice regarding response, based on the research that exists. Nancy Sommers's advice is by now canonical: provide as clear and specific comments to the writer as you can. More recent work on the same topic, as evidenced in Smith's "The Genre of the End Comment: Conventions in Teacher Responses to Student Writing," reiterates essentially the same advice, some 16 years later: "Perhaps most importantly, the teacher could personalize the comment by referring to specifics of the paper's comment, and by including a reader response genre to emphasize the teacher's position as reader and the effect of the paper on readers" (265). Student interviews conducted at Harvard earlier this decade on how students understand teacher response, based on students' experiences in many different kinds of classrooms (i.e., not composition classrooms particularly), lead to advice that dovetails neatly with the advice above (Bushey, cited in Light). Its summary targets two primary problem-areas with teacher response.

> Two specific obstacles impede students' writing improvement: 1) misinterpretation of teachers' comments on their essays, and 2) lack of specific strategies for revising essays. Students whose writing improves the most overcome both of these obstacles by implementing specific actions suggested by their teachers" (Light, 39).

There certainly seems to be a clear message here.

But other researchers call that message into question. Lisa Delpit, for example, writes in *Other People's Children* about cultural differences in communication style and how those can lead to differing interpretations of the same guidance. As glossed by Smagorinsky, Delpit's contention seems commonsensical: "there's a tendency among mainstream whites to prefer *indirect* ways of conveying their wishes to others, and a tendency among blacks to prefer *direct* ways of communication" (216). Consequently, the same advice, something like "You might address those questions in your next draft," can cut two completely different ways: it reads one way to the student who says, "ok, I'll try that," *and* differently to the student who says "'I might address them?? But I might not? But what are you saying I should do?' To Delpit," as Smagorinsky remarks, "both types of responses are controlling, but differ in the degree to which they anticipate and explicate the reader's expectations" (217).

Other interpretations of the rhetorical situation of response are less politically charged, but every bit as complicated and troubling. Consider, for instance, the purely idiosyncratic kinds of readings that students can give our responses, and multiply that by the numbers of students in a class. To illustrate such misinterpretations, as well as the implausibility of a response that could be *universally* facilitative, Jean Chandler shares some telling anecdotes.

> An American student told me he was frustrated by his teacher's frequent comment that his papers were wordy when he had written exactly the number of words the assignment called for! Yet another student felt that her teacher didn't like either her or her writing; she said he had called it "theatrical." She developed this perception because the teacher had once suggested that the tone of a particular word was a "tad too dramatic." (273)

Based on this experience, Chandler draws a by-now familiar conclusion: "What is needed is more research about how individual students 'hear' and understand the comments a teacher makes on their writing before we can make judgments about how facilitative the teacher response is likely to be" (274). One means of doing this, of course, is to work within reflection-in-action, to ask students to create texts like Talk-To's and Talk-Backs, to make visible and audible those *understand*[ings]. However, another dimension of this rhetorical situation concerns the readings and the responses we provide—to the primary texts and to the reflection-in-action texts associated with them—and how they interact with each other.

Or: reflective reading and reflective responding.

∗∗∗

Three student texts illustrate how reflective reading and responding might work within a classroom:

- an informal text with response
- a reflection-in-action and response to it
- a formal text with a Talk-To, a constructive reflection, a link to reflection-in-presentation

In this last set of texts, particularly, we will see *layers of reflection,* the *reflective intertexts* in which the primary text is embedded.

First, the informal text. For homework, students in a methods class are asked to profile two kinds of students they should anticipate teaching: "the ideal student"and "the student from hell." What features or behaviors or attitudes define each of these students? The purpose here is multi-fold: to ask the students to anticipate what their prospective students will be like; to define for themselves "the ideal student" and "the student from hell," through a process of recording and reflecting on the page; to make their assumptions about students visible.[3]

As a homework assignment, this task produces an informal text, so I don't want to respond to it as fully nor as formally as I might to an "official" assignment, but I do want to provide some audience, some response, some of my own thinking. I want the students to see what I like, to know that I think an observation is astute, to understand that after two decades I still struggle with some of these definitions and ways of understanding others. In other words, my response is both very focused and very limited, though also deliberately so: it's keyed first to what I like or find intriguing; and second, but as important, to questions that I think might broaden, re-contextualize, enrich what's already there.

The following text, from Jill, exemplifies what I mean here. The text appears, first, as it was presented to me: unmarked. Just below that text, I've repeated the text, but *as marked*, that is, as highlighted in yellow (digitally represented in gray here) accompanied by some few questions and quick verbal responses.

How do I read the text? *How do you read the text?*

Middle School Students

Thinking back to all of the middle school students I have witnessed in classrooms or just hanging out at the mall. I believe that my ideal middle school student probably does not exist. I picture my ideal student with normal body proportions—no long skinny arms and legs or giant hands and feet with which to stumble over. They have perfectly creamy skin, love their hair, height, and body weight. My ideal student, boy or girl, would totally have their act together—mature, responsible, caring, a natural leader. This student is intelligent, socially responsible, and feels very comfortable with who they are and where they fit in society. They have strong parental support and are not embarrassed by their parents mere existence. My ideal student loves school, loves learning, and excels at everything they attempt to accomplish. Oh, what a wonderful world.

However wonderful all that would be, I do not live in a fantasy world. I am sure I will undoubtedly have my share of students from hell. These students were put on earth to make my life a living hell. They suffer from "schoolitis." Not only do they hate school but they also passionately hate me because I'm a teacher, books, reading, and anything else that comes in contact with school. When I try to develop a relationship with these students they just push me away and act repulsed by the thought. they sleep all day in class, ignore instructions, and refuse to do any class work much less homework. They have no friends—except maybe another bully with which to terrorize other kids. They also have bad parents that just don't care about them, no self-esteem, poor social skills, and they feel as if the whole world is against them. Even though I am sure these kids wreak havoc on teachers it is these kids I would most like to reach.

I'm of several minds when reading this text. I agree: the ideal never exists, but positing the ideal is a useful exercise. I'm surprised at the physical description of the ideal student—I don't think that I think in those terms—but the logic of it makes sense, and perhaps I *should* think more in those terms. I appreciate the way the writer has situated the ideal student—as one with strong parental support. You bet: that context matters, too.

But I have to say, I'm disturbed, too: by the flat characterization of the opposite student, by the portrayal of a student who passionately hates me because I'm a teacher, books, reading, and anything else that comes in contact with school, by the sense that the teacher and student are somehow implacable foes. Still, this is the author's view, she is entitled to it, and it does provide us with *a text for negotiation.* And wait: the author then goes on to situate this student too: to note that this student has no friends—except maybe another bully with which to terrorize other kids. They have bad parents that just don't care about them, no self-esteem, poor social skills, and they feel as if the whole world is against them.

Yes, that seems likely.

In other words, I read the text; I highlight the text, looking for major points, for insight, for points of contention.

As you can see.

Middle School Students

Thinking back to all of the middle school students I have witnessed in classrooms or just hanging out at the mall. I believe that my ideal middle school student probably does not exist. I picture my ideal student with normal body proportions—no long skinny arms and legs or giant hands and feet with which to stumble over. They have perfectly creamy skin, love their hair, height, and body weight. My ideal student, boy or girl, would totally have their act together—mature, responsible, caring, a natural leader. This student is intelligent, socially responsible, and feels very comfortable with who they are and where they fit in society. They have strong parental support and are not embarrassed by their parents mere existence. My ideal student loves school, loves learning, and excels at everything they attempt to accomplish. Oh, what a wonderful world.

However wonderful all that would be, I do not live in a fantasy world. I am sure I will undoubtedly have my share of students from hell. These students were put on earth to make my life a living hell. They suffer from "schoolitis." Not only do they hate school but they also passionately hate me because I'm a teacher, books, reading, and anything else that comes in contact with school. When I try to develop a relationship with these students they just push me away and act repulsed by the thought. They sleep all day in class, ignore instructions, and refuse to do any class work much less homework. They have no friends—except maybe another bully with which to terrorize other kids. They also have bad parents that just don't care about them, no self-esteem, poor social skills, and they feel as if the whole world is against them. Even though I am sure these kids wreak havoc on teachers it is these kids I would most like to reach.

In addition to highlighting salient points in this text, I raise some few points that I hope we can think about. Accordingly, I circle *parents* and *no friends*, asking by inference—*important?*—how important these factors are. By drawing both of them to the word important, I'm trying to suggest a pattern, a linkage. I want to move beyond symptoms of the problem to get at what might be causes. But I want only to suggest.

My other query here—*why is this? what have* we *done to them to induce them to feel this way*—intends, again, to complicate the reading of the student here. Often, this kind of student has few friends and/or absentee parents, true enough–but incomplete. There's more to the picture: what we have contributed to the problem–because of a teacher who soured him or her; because of years of being told that the student is inadequate; because the student needs standing up and moving around to learn, and *we* make him or her sit down—in rows. As agents of the school, we too are part of the context. That's my view, at least, but it may not be Jill's. The question is intended to find out.

At the conclusion of this text, Jill expresses her wish to work with the students from hell. I'm surprised—hence the *aha!* As I had read the text initially, with highlighter in hand, I thought she was moving toward wishing that only ideal students would inhabit her classes— and I wasn't reacting very favorably, if truth be told. Of course, I *don't* know that this is what Jill was saying at all: perhaps I read the text this way because I'd had a bad day myself, or perhaps I was influenced by the student text I had read just before Jill's (where this attitude was expressed), or perhaps I just expect (project?) this attitude because it's all too common—or then again, perhaps Jill *was* thinking this at one point. Who knows?

Which is the point. The method of reflective reading described here prevents me from pretending to know in this sense, from rushing to judgment, from foreclosing on the text, from deciding before I finish reading the text what it means. It focuses me instead on identifying what in the text contributes to my meaning-making. After I've identified that, I can react—and begin to negotiate.

This, then, is one means of reflective reading and response.

***

Second: a reflection-in-action. In a graduate class on contemporary rhetoric, I am collecting a set of exploratory essays. One student, Mary, has focused on the relationship between and among the poet Audre Lorde, the philosopher Richard Weaver, and rhetoric. As a companion to the primary text, Mary completes the following questions, in a reflection-in-action.

- Believe that the paper is strong
- Doubt that it's very good
- Project Yancey's take on the paper
- Identify what the author learned that doesn't appear in the text

Mary complies:

I believe this paper is pretty well organized and focused on Lorde, Weaver, and rhetoric. It relates their philosophies, showing places where they could correlate and deviate. It gives a neat twist to rhetoric, by relating it to power.

I doubt . . . hmmm . . . maybe this paper could have gone more into Lorde's poem, but I tired to take the main points and emphasize what I interpreted her rhetoric to be, not the poem's content itself. Maybe I could have stressed more that I was interpreting Lorde, than just stating everything as Lorde's take. However, my title indicates this, and I didn't want to get into explaining intentionality within the paper, b/c that would be a long discussion (including Plato's intentionality, Weaver's take on it, and Weaver's intentionality—a whole new paper). Is my conclusion focused enough?

Kathy's take/questions: better organized than last paper . . . Is she relating Lorde well to Weaver? . . . more handleable topic . . . Is it focused well?

What I learned/left out (for the sake of focus) more on power and how/*why* it relates to rhetoric (a whole other paper topic) Lorde's and Weaver's background motivation . . . although they have different perspectives, their approaches resemble one another. . . but at the same time cause them to emphasize different aspects of these similar philosophies . . . more on why they interpreted rhetoric similar in areas/why diff in others . . .

Two key questions, then: *How do I read this kind of text? How do I respond to it?*

I read:

In the *believe* section, Mary says that in this text, she takes rhetorical concepts and applies them to two figures, Weaver and Lorde; they are similar (they correlate) and different (they deviate.) Rhetoric, she sees, is related to power and rhetoric.

In the *doubt* section, Mary really plays out what other texts she might have written: one that focused more exclusively on Lorde's poetry qua poetry, for instance. Perhaps, she says, she should have emphasized the fact that she was interpreting, though she hastens to say that she does indicate this, and that had she undertaken the topic of intentionality as well, that would be a long discussion—and she provides the topics that would belong to it. In other words, she establishes her authority here by considering the kinds of reactions that a reader might have to her text, and explains in the process why she made the choices we see in it. She concludes with a question: Is my conclusion focused enough?

In the *predict* section, we see again a concern with focus: Is it focused well? Focus has now been mentioned in each section: Mary seems to be moving to the prototypic from the specifics of this text, so this is something that I want to respond to. There seems to be a presumed connection between the fact that the paper is more handle-lable and its focus, and there is a query as to the relationship between Lorde and Weaver.

In the *identify* section, Mary again sees what's possible: a text on power and how/*why* it relates to rhetoric, perhaps some commentary on Lorde's and Weaver's background motivation. I think: yes, she did learn information that doesn't appear in the text (and that's good), and yes, she sensibly excluded that information. She's learning the content of the course, and she's connecting it to her own interests. She's learning the *art* of rhetoric; she's learning what to leave in, what to leave out.

I respond:

My goal in responding to this reflection-in-action is primarily to *concur with her judgment.* Along the margins of the reflection-in-action, I mark *yes, yes,* and *yes* again. When she says that she could have

stressed more that I was interpreting Lorde,	I say *sure.*

When she says that this text is

better organized than the last,	I say, *oh yes.*
Is my conclusion focused enough?	*Yes—very nice job.*

Which doesn't mean that *everything* is working. In fact, she's focused so tightly in the text that it's almost closed. I want more elaboration: Responding, then, to the query,

Is my conclusion focused enough?	I say, *Yes, I did want some fuller explanations in part, and I made some stylistic suggestions. See what you think?*

The places where I want the fuller explanations are marked on the primary text, as are the stylistic suggestions.

It hasn't taken me very long to read this reflection-in-action; it doesn't take me very long to reply to it. My response does take the form of a reply; this reflection-in-action allows the writer to establish a dialogue between us that *provides for additional kinds of conversations about texts and text-making*, in this case,

about this text relative to what might have been;

about possibility relative to shape/ing;

about the art of rhetoric that she is developing;

about this text relative to others Mary has written in this course;

about this text as exemplar of the well-focused text.

Mary is learning to read her own text (and her own learning) well. In my response, I indicate where I *concur* with that judgment; I indicate where I demur.

***

Third: an assignment in a first-year writing class, some reflections-in-action (including a Talk-To and a Talk-Back), a constructive reflection, a reflection-in-presentation: the *reflective intertexts* of an assignment and the assignment itself.

Students have been asked to talk about World War II: was it a "good" war? an "honorable" war? a "just" war? What do these terms mean when they are applied to this particular war? These questions, however, only provide the parameters of the assignment: students are asked to create their own statement of purpose, *their own rhetorical situation* within which they will work. Some of the students look at gender issues, some at violence (with particular reference to the atom bomb: should it have been dropped?), some at the role that African Americans played in the war. Jesse has *her own way into the topic* as well: she wants to look at how people of different generations view this war, specifically how three generations of Jews view it.

Her essay, and it's a long one:

To ask if World War II was a good, just or honorable war we must question one of the largest groups effected by this war: the Jewish community. They were victims. They were the ones selected for total annihilation only because they were Jewish. In today's society the Jewish community (referring to ethnicity more than religion) consists of three or four generations. There are the survivors (first generation), their children (second generation) and their grandchildren (third generation). The viewpoints of World War II between these three generations differentiate greatly.

In order to look at these generations' viewpoints we must first define the elements we are looking for. Webster's Dictionary defines good as satisfactory; honorable as deserving honor (a symbol of distinction); and just as morally right. Although these words seem to be very similar they each have a distinct meaning and interpretation.

The first generation, or the survivors, have the most profound effect on our interpretation of what World War II was all about. It is these people that give us the firsthand information, vivid images and more. They make what happened become a reality just by living. They are our direct link to World War II.

It is appropriate to say that this generation views World War II as good and just. They see it as good because they were more than satisfied with the outcome of this war since it meant life for them. Of course they think that it was morally right, or just, to invade Germany because once again this is what saved them. Whether it is was honorable is another question. There is nothing honorable about what they had to endure. There is nothing honorable about the Holocaust.

The survivors of World War II have a common conflict. Some of them are reluctant to talk about what they have been through. Remembering the Holocaust is painful, horrifying, and sickening. These people want to put this behind them. On the other hand there are those survivors that are very willing to share their experiences with others. These people believe that by sharing their stories they are personalizing history. This usually makes lessons more profound and meaningful.

The education of others is an extreme concern to most survivors. They often speak in classes, conventions, and other educational events. This benefits both the students and the survivors. The students are given the opportunity to put a face on the people they have read about. The survivors are given the acknowledgment that what they endured has a great value. These people also join museum committees and other such organizations in order to increase the possibilities of getting the importance of their survival across to everyone. Since most of the Holocaust survivors are aging rapidly the fear of losing their stories is evident. There are several projects in progress where these people's testimonies are being recorded on video so that the world of tomorrow can benefit from today.

The second generation looks at World War II in a different way. They see it as good because they are satisfied with the outcomes. They do realize that they could possibly not have been given the chances of existence if it had ended differently. This generation also believes that World

War II was an honorable war because they want to honor their parents and the people who saved them. It is the moral issue that this generation questions. Rather than looking at the rescue of their parents as just, they look at the events that occurred and ask if they were morally right. The evil images portrayed give a strong argument that this was not morally right.

The second generation is removed from the war. It is a part of their history and therefore there are many interpretations. Tracing their family tree to see that it goes no further than their parents is a wake up call to the reality and importance of this history. This motivates this generation to also participate in the development of educational programs. They too want others to learn about the Holocaust in order to ensure that this may never happen again.

There is a conflict in this generation too. Time has passed since the war, allowing people to carefully evaluate the events and put blame on others. Since this generation consists of the sons and daughters of survivors, the conflict occurs when they meet the children of the Nazi survivors to whom the blame has been placed. The feelings of these two groups vary. They range from cold-heartedness to a sympathetic understanding. There have been several conventions and conferences held to improve relations between these groups of people. To bring these two groups to an understanding has proven to be a great challenge. There is too much pain and hatred clouding their minds.

It seems that the less connected a person is to a past event the less importance that person places on that event. Even when there is a slight link or connection, the third generation seems to be very disconnected with the events of their past. Their view of World War II is that it was a good war. They are satisfied with the outcome so therefore it is good. They question whether it was an honorable or just war. The third generation does honor their family and those who saved them, but they do not think the war is honorable. This generation also looks at the events of the war to judge that it was morally wrong.

The third generation has the most insights of the war. They are provided with the most researched information. There are many interpretations of the facts. Looking at this information allows them to make their judgments.

The third generation of the present-day Jewish community seems to be very distant from their connection to this war. They are taught many interpretations of the events, focusing a lot of attention on the Holocaust. Facts are drilled into their brains, causing the importance of learning about this event to be lost. It becomes just another chapter in their history books, rather than an event that teaches us important lessons about mankind.

As I mentioned before, both the first and second generations focus a lot on the importance, significance and understanding of the Holocaust; from how precious our lives are to how much we can learn from human behavior. They have developed many ways in which the third generation can experience the Holocaust rather than just read about it.

One of the most profound creations is the Holocaust Museum in Washington D.C. This museum gives an intense and vivid display of the horrors by virtually placing you there. They have a large collection of personal items such as clothing, eating utensils and toys. This intensifies a person's empathy. Pictures and videos help to further humanize the Holocaust. The overall effect this museum has made on those who have been through it is astonishing. Another recent development that has allowed the third generation to experience the Holocaust is a movie titled "Schindler's List". Created by the famous director, Stephen Speilberg, this movie provokes emotions and triggers discussions. Speilberg made this movie to educate others. In fact he has given every high school in American a free copy to use for educational purposes. There are texts published that shows teachers how to effectively teach "Schindler's List". From my own experience I believe this format is highly effective.

A third development in the education of the Holocaust is a program called "Facing History and Ourselves". This program uses Holocaust education as a way to teach about institutionalized hatred, bigotry and racism. Their goal is "to move students gradually from literary and historical examples of genocide back to present-day experiences of intolerance and racism." Students gain critical perspectives and develop new reasoning by going back and forth from the past to the present. I have also experienced this program. Because of this experience I feel that I gained a better understanding and a more profound interpretation of the lessons of the Holocaust. I believe my feelings resemble those of the second generation, but with a stronger compassion for the first generation.

The first and second generations have worked together to paint a clear picture of the Holocaust for the third generation. Their efforts have created new programs and museums that are allowing this generation to experience history. It is through this progress that these generations have been brought together. They have strengthened the historic connections among these generations.

By tracing three generations of the present-day Jewish community we can see the differences in viewpoints, the conflicts they face and the origin of their opinions. The source of their information is the backbone of their viewpoint. That is why the first and second generations have emphasized the importance of the way the third generation is taught and the content of what they are taught. They realize that they must teach this generation the lessons of the Holocaust in a way that will ensure that history will not be repeated.

How do I *read* this text? As this chapter argues, we read the same text multiply; we can point students in all kinds of directions.

What I read: I see this as Jesse's way to connect with World War II, *to find an insider route to an outsider topic.*

What I read: a fairly interesting account of the ways different generations of Jews, quite understandably, view the war. I'm not Jewish myself, but I'm aware that there is some generational difference, and I've had good friends who've sent their children to go through the educational experiences Jesse mentions. So, on one level, the text interests me: it teaches me a little more about inter-generational Jewish response to World War II.

What I read: It's also true that a number of the assertions here could be called into question. Were Jews the only victims of the war? (No, there were others.) Is there a single Jewish community? (Not even in Israel.) The survivors are reluctant to talk but do provide talks? (Probably: but the contradiction here needs to be accounted for, I think.) You get the idea: there are several assertions that want reconsideration and/or qualifying.

What I read: I see this text the way I see many student texts, I think, *because I am a teacher*: as (the proverbial) textual work-in-progress. I want to ask Jesse to clean up her text, to clarify points (*I'm lost*, I say), to tighten connections, to eliminate some of what I see as needless repetition, to return at the end to the point: which is? Also, I want the citations here: I don't doubt that she's done her homework, but I'd like to know what that homework was.

What I read: a student who is trying to understand why her elders feel similarly and differently about the war, who is grappling with her own, more detached reaction.

And these readings are confirmed in her reflections-in-actions:

When asked what she was hoping to do, she replies with both a *believe* statement and a *doubt statement* together:

I was aiming to show people the differences and similarities in the viewpoints of World War II from the eyes of the three generations of the present-day Jewish community. I believe I did this to the best of my ability. I showed their viewpoints, discussed the conflicts that exist within their generation and mentioned the origin of their viewpoints. I have some added information that kind of steers away from my main goal in this paper. This information about the educational processes that have been developed by the first and second generations for the third generation is interesting and informative. It shows how the three generations are not only recognizing their connection but they are building on it as well. I think I deserve a B for this paper.

When Jesse says,

It shows how the three generations
are not only recognizing their
connection but they are building
on it as well.

I reply,
Bring this into the paper?

And earlier in the same reflection, Jesse expresses the same concern regarding the educational information, the information that makes her an insider:

There was not enough information
on my original topic to just write about
it so I had to expand on the educational
aspects.

I reply,
*I think it works ok. I've
raised some points I hope
you'll consider—especially
my question at the end.
Exploring it would make for
a good conclusion.*

At the end of the paper, Jesse claims:

That is why the first and second
generations have emphasized the
importance of the way the third generation
is taught and the content of what they are

taught. They realize that they must teach
this generation the lessons of the Holocaust
in a way that will ensure that history
will not be repeated.

> And I reply:
> *It's a particular view of*
> *history, yes? Would you say*
> *that the war is honorable if*
> *its survivors ensure that*
> *such genocide never*
> *happens again? Or can*
> *honor never be used in this*
> *connection?*

I do think that this is a particular view of history. That doesn't make it any less valuable; it simply reminds us that all histories (all truths?) are *situated*. Jesse may disagree; I'm interested to know. And the other question: I've laid out two alternatives, but of course there are others. And as I say, I don't know the answer to this question. I'd like to know what Jesse thinks, since she seems to know more about this than I.

Text as site of negotiation.

***

If this were merely a story, then I could now present Jesse's revision, complete with thoughtful answers to the questions I presented to her. But Jesse worked within a portfolio system that allowed her to focus her revisions on two of four texts, and she chose not to revise this paper. As Tom Hilgers suggests, the decision not to revise is a valid decision. Still, I gather from some of her other reflections that she continues to think about the issues raised here—which in some ways is all I really wanted. I really didn't want answers, though I'm not sure that I signalled that intent well.

When asked about the most interesting question we've discussed in class, Jesse replies,

The most interesting question we've discussed is what makes a war justifiable.

When asked what she *knows* as a result of writing this text and what she *understands*, Jesse says,

This paper gives a vivid display of what I know. I am part of the third generation of the present-day Jewish community. I know how this generation feels, what they think and how they form their opinions. I also know what kind of influence the generations before me are trying to portray. I have experienced some of the new educational programs that I discussed in my paper. I know what kind of effect they have.

Being part of the third generation, I've had some insight on how the generations before me feel about World War II. By doing this paper I have a better understanding of why they feel this way. I also understand why the generations differ and the reasons behind the conflicts that occur within these generations. Why they stress the importance of learning about this part of our history is another understanding that I have come to.

What I think:

Jesse is still struggling with the issues here: the relationship between and among the generations; the (invisible topic of the) atrocities of the war; her (implied) questioning about the educational experiences; the ways we justify war.

In her reflection-in-presentation, Jesse narrates some of what she learned in this assignment, some two months later: she's still struggling.

My thoughts, feelings, and knowledge was being exposed to unexplored areas. It was one thing one thing to ask what the basic facts of World War II were, but it is entirely different to question the source and its credibility. Or to question what we should and should not include as basic facts [such as the start of the war, which is one date for the Polish, another for the Americans]. The difficulties intensified when we had to make interpretations of these facts. This caused us to go beyond our circle of opinions . . . . I thought we had reached the limit when we did a group paper on whether we thought World War II was a "good" war. Once again I was pushed to go further. I had to go into areas I had not even thought to contemplate. No longer was I just questioning if it was a "good" war or not. Now I had to ask whether it was "just" and/or "honorable" as well. I had to take it even further by focusing my viewpoint to the present day Jewish community. Never in my life had I written such a thorough, challenging, and focused paper. This opened my eyes and I began to question my abilities.

Sometimes when we learn, we see what's possible. It can be intimidating. And it can take more than a semester to complete that learning. Particularly when the question is profound: *when is war justifiable?*

***

How do I respond? In two ways.

First, as indicated in my illustrations above, I *reply*. Although writing-as-conversation has taken on the status of a defining trope within composition studies, we haven't played the metaphor out very well.[4] We haven't seen, for instance, 1) that reply-as-mode is a logical extension of the metaphor of text-as-conversation; and 2) that if we were to understand response-as-reply, we might have an entirely different conversation altogether—text as occasion for reply, and multiple texts as a cascading succession of replies. *Reply* places writers and readers quite differently than does respond or mark or grade—or correct.

Second, I try to be *responsive*, and I count on reflective intertexts to help me with that—on each individual text, and on the cumulative set of texts. I think I'm more indirect than I might be. I worry about being the indirect teacher Lisa Delpit talks about; I worry about being too direct, about making my questions their questions. I count on the reflection to compensate for both tendencies, and to provide a regular and safe *place for negotiation*—about the primary text, about the processes that go into it—and, simultaneously, to make another provision: for a site for invention and revision of the primary text—as we see here, as we saw in chapter two. As a respondent, I'm learning about the power of the visual in this effort, especially for students who are incubated in visual media:

about how **highlighting** student texts, for instance, shows them how I weave thoughts together in my reading (much as I do in all my readings)

about how *formatting*, as I did with Mary's prose here, can provide a visualization of the dialogue I want to have with students about their texts, their ideas, their sense of themselves as writers

about how asking students to pose questions sets up a kind of formatting conducive to talk, to dialogue, to negotiation–to *reply* about how with and through those questions we can craft a reply–what I an beginning to think of as an appropriate *differentiated response*–to students and their texts.

Ultimately, of course, I agree with all those who have said that we need to learn more about how students read our writing and how we read their writing and how the readings and writings intersect: *how they work together to create new meaning.*
Reflection provides one vehicle to do just that.

Notes

1.   There are obvious exceptions to this claim: Peter Elbow's article on the value of liking a student's text and the more recent *Twelve Readers Reading*, among others.
2.   We could also review our own work to see how it changes as a function of the kind of readings and responses it produces. Chapter one makes the point. In fact, the draft of that chapter sent out for peer review included a very quick survey of composing process research; both reviewers suggested that I expand this: hence, the more elaborated version. A second example: in that chapter, I was more explicit about the issue of agency raised by Afhild Ingberg. This is a key point, the complete answer to which continues to elude me.
3.   One thing I have learned in teaching this kind of class is that one teacher's ideal student is the next teacher's student from hell; although that isn't the primary purpose of this exercise, it will make those differences among us apparent as well.
4.   Susan Miller, of course, argues against a rhetoric based on the oral: see her *Rescuing the Subject.*

Reflection and the Writing Course

We begin with history. Archeology is the study of the past. The practice of archeology is a reflection of the present.

Sherman Apt Russel

We must learn to ask not only what can we see, what have we taught, but also what questions have we failed to ask, what literacy practices have we not made visible to ourselves and our students, what still exists in the domain of the unmarked?

Margaret Marshall

HOW HAVE I TAUGHT? HOW DO I UNDERSTAND MY OWN TEACHING? when I say that a writing class—a first-year writing class at my comprehensive urban university—went well, that the students learned, that I think they're becoming good writers (some of them, at least), what do I mean? And how would I know that such assertions were true? *Could I theorize more generally about such a course*—about the components needed to foster the development of such students? What makes me think that I have anything new to add to what we already know? Or: what might I add to what we *do* know if I could theorize about the development of these writers?

Short of treating students like rats in a lab or like plants in a rooting medium, we won't know the answers to these questions—if by the word *know* we mean the product of a monological process characterized by a scientific, technical rigor that is predictive in nature. As is self-evident, since students aren't rats or plants, we *can't* know in that way. As what Susan Brookhart calls a "misapplication of the scientific 'paradigm' to a social problem" (3), such knowing is too singular, too reductive, ultimately too inhuman. Put differently, life and the people who populate it are too rich and too complex for such a knowing.

Which doesn't get us off the hook: we do have a need to know what works, especially when we are working with people, perhaps more especially when we are working with people-who-are-our-students.

As teachers, as people who design *curriculum-for-students*, we need to be able to identify causes of desired effects *so that we can repeat them deliberately and purposefully*. Too often we design curriculum as though it were an independent agent, or as though it operated in some vacuum or in some institutional context that wasn't inhabited. Curriculum, however, is designed for students, typically for specific students who embody specific needs; it's a *curriculum-for-students*. As important, precisely because it is a *curriculum-for-students*, its effects will be like the students themselves: plural, contradictory, on occasion baffling. Thus, it is that a course can both "work"—can succeed—*and* not at the same time. As a teacher, as someone who designs curriculum, I need to know what works, if it works for all students or just for some, what doesn't work, and in all these cases, why. Theoretically, and pragmatically too, if I can sort these workings out, I can take this knowing and weave it into something larger, perhaps into a theory of composition curriculum.

Through reflection—the reflective texts produced by some first-year college writers, and my reflection upon them—this chapter hopes to demonstrate how to read our practices as it weaves just such a theory.

* * *

One way to know how a student, a class, and a curriculum work (together, that is) is to see our own teaching and learning *practices* as a source of knowledge, a metaphorical text that can be systematically observed, questioned, understood, generalized about, refuted—in a phrase, *reflected upon*. In understanding our practice this way, we assign ourselves a role, that of the causal inquirer, someone who focuses on a particular situation in a single organization in order to understand what and how it works, not in terms of scientific laws but in prototypic models of behavior. As we've seen, this is what Schon calls reflective transfer.

Reflective transfer, the procedure that enables us to learn from and thus enhance our practice requires four steps: that we

1. observe and examine our own practice
2. make hypotheses about successes and failures there, as well as the reasons for each

3. shape the next iteration of similar experience according to what we have learned, when

4. we begin the cycle again

In a writing course, such reflective transfer has a specific application: to help us understand the processes by which students learn, the assignments that motivate and structure such learning, the responses that invite insight, the tasks that invite the inside as well as the outside to come together. Another way of thinking about this course is to frame it in terms of the familiar and the unfamiliar, as David Schwalm explains:

> I think it really is important to move away from the juxtapositioning of "personal narrative" and "text-based" writing and think more about the underlying distinction between writing about the familiar and the unfamiliar. We cannot simply dismiss the possibility that chronological and spatial structures are "easier" (at a workaday level) than "invented" structures of logic and the rhetorical loci. We can't dismiss that fact that writing about a shared reality imposes constraints on the writer that writing about one's interior life does not. But the distinction between familiar and unfamiliar is much more important. (For example, so-called "personal writing" really gets hard when the writer is making a serious effort to explore alien territory of interior life and to capture it in language that makes the exploration meaningful to readers: an instance of dealing with the unfamiliar in the personal.) And what we often mean when we say that students should be able to read or write about "college level" topics, what we really mean is "unfamiliar" topics. Thinking of writing courses as a strategy for helping students read and write about the unfamiliar is really useful. It doesn't, for example, mean that they can't do personal writing. It does mean that we have to up the ante on personal writing so that it becomes genuinely exploratory and requires a relationship between the personal and the public. . . . And it calls for a recognition of what sort of a burden we are placing on a student who must write an analytical essay about some topic or text that is new him or her . . . . This is what Bazerman recognized: these tasks have to be "staged" for students so that they have opportunities to become familiar with language and concepts before they have to manipulate them with skill and grace in an analytical essay or research paper. (November 9, 1997)

Seen this way, our curriculum in writing isn't either/or—about a debate or choice between the academic and the personal, between the narrative and the analytical; it's an exercise in moving from the familiar to the unfamiliar, from seeing one in terms of the other to seeing it anew. That's what I've tried to do in this course. In general, it's a course in textual immersion, I think. It includes four formal writing assignments: a narrative, an exposition, a text based on sources, and an argument that also includes resources. It includes multiple kinds of invention strategies: from cubing to free writing, and from topoi to clustering. It includes work in reading: in reading from sources, summarizing those, interpreting them, evaluating them. It includes some work across genres, as when students are asked, first, to summarize the major causes and events of World War II, then to approach it from the perspective of someone experiencing it. It includes some work in document design and the use of visual rhetoric. It includes various kinds of reflection—reflection-in-action, constructive reflection, and reflection-in-presentation—in different genres, some formal, some informal. It includes group work and peer sharing, and reflection on both. Finally, students are asked to develop an analytical narrative about themselves as learners, to answer the question "What have you learned?" in a way that draws on the familiar to explain the unfamiliar. That's what I've planned, at least.

How did this version of the course work? How was what I planned *experienced*? To answer that, I'll call upon reflection—the students' and my own—and put them into dialogue, to see how they fit and don't, to theorize about the effects of the course on the students. As in other contexts, then, reflection here is necessarily collaborative. I plan and "deliver" the curriculum, but my students will "experience" the curriculum, often quite differently. The points of intersection among both—the *delivered* and the *experienced* curricula—are the places where learning and teaching occur. It is, in fact, only through their articulation of their experience and my review of that articulation in light of my intent that I begin to understand the phenomenon that we are calling the writing class.

* * *

In this reflection, I want to consider, first, how a specific class invention exercise worked in assisting students: a simple activity, really, intended to help students develop a scene that could be used in their narratives. As I consider the effects of that activity, I also begin to consider whether it had any other kinds of effects—and to undertake that question, I turn to some other texts as well, in particular to student accounts of what they think they are learning. For a focus for this reflection, I look at the class from the perspective of three students. For two of them, the activity and the course worked, *though it worked in different ways,* and their experiences raise different kinds of questions. In some ways, they had the same course, in some ways not. For the third student, the course did not work; and his experience raises the most difficult, the most troubling, and the most interesting questions.

***

The students in this first-year writing class are working on their narratives, drafting until the bell rings. We're in a computer classroom, so I can see on the monitors how the texts are developing, and mostly, that's *not* too well. The drafts displayed on the terminals before me are vague and general and detail-less and perhaps (in some cases, I fear) even pointless. Mostly, they are very, very familiar. What to do? *Try something else.*

For the next class, I bring in a narrative written by a former student who writes of a five-minute trash run he made as a soldier in Haiti. The text works in two scenes: before the trash run at his desk, when he's safe but bored; at the filthy, fly-ridden, food-stained trash bin, where starving Haitians grab for every scrap of waste. It's a powerful read. My students and I read the text together; we highlight the details of the scenes, visually and verbally; we talk about the effects of the details on us. Then I say: Let's do this ourselves. Compose two texts: first, specify the general context for your narrative (which you should already know); second, zoom in on a scene, a vignette, that *locates* that narrative. Now, please. Computers hum; students think, struggle, imagine. Compose.

How/Does this assignment work?

Josey starts: the context for "my story is at a major fire in a warehouse. Flames are visible for half a mile away at this four alarm fire. There are three engine companies at this fire." Then, the vignette:

> The dilapidated warehouse sits on the corner of Main Street and Second Street. . . . The now yellowed, cracked cement bricks that have witnessed many disasters, both natural and man-made, during its decade of standing are now participants in their own right as black, putrid smoke puffs out from its hiding place. Rows upon rows of windows, some paneless, others just broken, let us look into the fury we are fixing to face. Vivid red

and yellow flames erotically dance out from the broken windows, thankful for the oxygen to help them flourish. The hungry crackling of golden flames devouring the old, wooden roof unnerves me as I get out of the firetruck.

I begin to *see* the warehouse and its *paneless, broken windows*, with *flames danc*[ing] *erotically* from them. The fire assumes a form, takes an intent. Not a bad beginning, I say. Be careful not to overwrite, I say. Move back and forth between saturation and selection, I say. But keep this up, I say.

Ann writes of her work as a teacher's assistant in a class for autistic boys. As she explains, "I had just come into class. This was only my second week. The administration has warned me that my boys might not even remember my name or care that I was there." Then, the vignette:

> The classroom is so well organized. Everything in it's place. The school bus is on a shelf that has a picture of a school bus on it. The shelves all have specific pictures on them for each item that belongs there. I am afraid to move anything around for fear that the teachers will not like me and make me leave. So, instead of making a mistake, I take a seat. The chairs are so tiny. My knees are touching my chin. . . . I do not remember being small enough to fit into these chairs. As I look around I am overwhelmed by color and by the things my boys [the students she comes to love] have made. They told me that the children were not capable of producing useable objects but I see kites, fish, cups, ties, hand prints in all colors, and smiles that say that making ten copies of different pictures was worth the three dollars it cost.

Working within the present tense allows Ann to remember that which is not familiar: *My knees are touching my chin. . . . I do not remember being small enough to fit into these chairs.* She also relativizes and evaluates what she observes: spending small change on *copies* so as to humanize the room is a good thing. This scene-setting works for her as well, and/but differently than it did for Josey. Josey focused on the physical details of the scene, Ann on what and how those details mean. I like each.

Does the exercise in invention "work?" Well, I like it. I like the strategy, like the two-part sequence, the context and then the focused scene, the way students zoom in on a scene, the particularization that emerges. I like the specifics that are generated, like being able to watch students, Zoellner-like, as they write this scene in class so that I can comment *as* they write[1], can point to a detail and ask for more, can point them back to something they missed. (*They are learning to write by writing,* I think.) I like encouraging writers to work in the present tense, like how that seems to help them *connect* what they observe with what they feel, to help them connect the familiar with the unfamiliar. I like the way that this activity seems to provide *another means of seeing,* another way of knowing (are those the same thing?).

And: I think the quality of the final drafts is good, better than what I'm accustomed to; almost all of them include these scenes, or part of them. In general, the narratives are focused, are detailed, include scenes—and not too many of them, either.

***

That's one opinion: mine. The students may have another. If asked, what would they tell me, or you? I ask, in a constructive reflection called a Learning Summary (similar to the ones we've seen earlier).

In this writing course, what have you learned?

They write for five minutes; they seem to *know* what they think they have learned. Then, another question:

Is this what you expected to learn?

Five minutes to reply. Ah: what they expected is what they've had before, and most of them say that this class—because of the writing *in* class, because of group work, because of reflection—is different. I believe it.

About writing, what else do you need to learn?

Another five minutes, and

How will you go about learning that?

When asked, in November of the fall term, six weeks after the assignment was submitted, *what she has learned in this course,* Josey replies:

This class, through the various activities, such as group writing, helped to show me my strengths and helped me to maximize them. I saw that I could write very well from experience. The details that I gave in my papers that were about something I had done or seen were very vivid. This could be seen in the narrative paper I wrote about a female fire-fighter.

. . .

I just expected this to be a class where the teacher would throw a topic at us and say "Here write a narrative. It's due Monday." Then we would be responsible for the paper all ourselves outside of class and we would work on something totally different inside of class. We actually learned the process of writing the paper—from brainstorming, info collecting, prewriting, rough draft, editing, editing, and editing, and then a copy we would turn in. I don't think that all of us had ever had someone go through that with us.

. . .

I have not learned the craft of making my papers sound professional.

. . .

I may need to practice revising my papers and maybe see some papers an editor has revised so I can see what mistakes I am making in my revising.

So, Josey understands the course through the lens of strength and enhancing that. She is *maximiz*[ing] her *strengths*, which she exemplifies by particular reference to the evidence within the narrative—its *vivid details*. She also says that she needs to learn the *craft* of writing; she wants her papers to sound *professional*, and she wants to see how an *editor* reacts to text so that she can understand how to revise better. Revising, she seems to understand, is like composing: it's a process that could be enhanced as well. Josey is preparing to leave the class; she knows what she has accomplished; she understands the kinds of things she might do next and some of the resources that she can call upon.

Question: Josey seems to be developing a certain kind of identity, *writer as professional.* Is that an appropriate identity for first-year composition? If so, what can I do to make curricular provision for it?

***

Ann also claims to have learned much: "I have learned alot of different things." (To be expected, I think. Like what, I wonder.)

She starts with the electronic: "I learned how to use the e-mail system and how to surf the web. I cannot be criticized for being computer illiterate anymore." (In the criticism, I'll bet, there's a story, but she doesn't share it. Also, as I wince, I'm thinking, please say you learned more/other than surfing the web.) She does.

> The information and feedback sessions with our group have helped me organize my thoughts a lot. . . . I have also begun to realize that it is possible to write a paper that can convey emotions and feelings as well as with words. I love trying to draw pictures with my words. It is cool. . . . Papers have never really been my strongest point. I am much better at talking. I still cannot figure out how I can explain what is inside without seeing the person's reaction. That way I know the person really understands. This was my basic problem with the first paper. I think I accomplished a little of the sharing of emotion. I think I got some of what I wanted to across. That is what I learned. Between you and my group the words and feelings were beaten out of me.

. . .

> I thought this class was going to be very hard and that we would have to write a lot of papers. I also thought that the professor would just rip apart a paper and not give a definite explanation why. Here we are led through the steps and are helped at every step if we need it. We can and do get that help from you and our classmates. There was no assuming that we knew how. You taught us how, even if for some it was a review. . . . I learned how to tell someone how I feel, give a point of view and check on my sources.

. . .

> I loved writing the narrative. It words and sentences and ideas made sense and were not forced. It was a story that wanted to be told. . . . The paper on WWII was ok but it was a research report. It was not something I could put my heart into. It was research and some thought put down on paper. The narrative was better. I could visualize the choices and see what my decision meant to someone else.

Like Josey, Ann learns to write *and* learns about writing, but these are different learnings than they were for Josey. Josey thinks of herself as a pretty good writer, one who can *maximize her own strengths*, who (as she says her reflection-in-presentation) wants to develop the confidence that she associates with *strength*. Unlike Josey, Ann doesn't particularly like writing, but she likes the narrative topic she chooses to write about, her *boys*. She's learning to *draw pictures with her words* and finds that *cool. She likes the information and feedback sessions with our group*, perhaps because she can talk through her paper with her colleagues—and she likes to talk, understands how to use *the person's reaction* to see if she or he *really understands*—in another kind of reflective transfer, perhaps. She is learning to anticipate how her readers will react—*I could visualize the choices and see what my decision meant to someone else*—and how to use that to create writing that is reading. The repetition of the visual metaphor is telling, I think: she likes *drawing pictures with words*, and she has learned to *visualize choices*. Mostly, she's learning what she needs to learn from the course, which bears similarity to, but which isn't identical to, what Josey has learned.

Question: How can I respond to Ann's need for the visual? Our students are visual beings in ways we are not; I need to find some ways to build that way of understanding into the course so that it can be used as a means of reflective transfer.

Question: How, I wonder, can I help Ann understand that research can be just as personally rewarding as narrative? More specifically, what assignments can I create that will foster such an understanding, that will combine the familiar with the unfamiliar, the inside with the outside? And how will I know if they work?

***

But this scene-setting, this narrative assignment, this group work—*this course*—doesn't work for everyone, and it doesn't work for Zack, for sure.

We're working on detailing the scenes, and I see Zack writing, quite diligently. His context, he says, "is eleven boy scouts, including leaders, wandering aimlessly through the mountains one late autumn afternoon." In other words, they are lost. (This narrative has potential, I think.)

Zack begins the vignette by describing the camp area:

> Our scout masters had set up camp with us in the woods about 100 yards just off the base of the mountain. The camp was the same as any camp.

We had all of our green eureka tents on one side of the camp. These tents were not very big considering that only two people slept in each tent. The kitchen was located under a blue tarp on the other side of camp. Our kitchen consisted of a couple of big, black propane stoves, a small wooden table, for preparing food, and three white ice chests full of food. Between our kitchen and our tents is a ring of stones where our campfire is built.

Since Zack identifies the camp as the *same as any camp*, I should see something wrong and I should inquire (but I don't see the signs of trouble, and I don't inquire): either he is writing to people whose understanding of camps matches his exactly, or all camps are alike. In either case, we are in trouble, I think, because if either of these is true, Zack doesn't need to set the scene. Which is exactly what he doesn't:

We went out for a hike about 1:00 on Saturday afternoon. Of the eighteen people that were camping with us, eleven of us went hiking. This included eight teenagers and three scout leaders. We hiked for a while up the mountains on a small trail that twisted up and around the huge mountain. After a while we realized that the trail had disappeared, and that we were now just pushing our way through thick grass and shrubs. About 4:00 we realized that we were lost, but we kept on walking anyway. This was a very big mistake because we would be unable to find a lot of firewood in the darkness that was to follow.

I'm eager to hear about this story, but *I want the story*. What that means to me is that I want the answers to so many questions: Which mountain? How many tents? Are all camps the same? Could you tell us about about the hike? Where did you think you were going? So, trying to be helpful, I suggest a strategy and a focus: Can you use present tense, I ask Zack, to tell us about the moment you realized you were lost? Share this moment with us, I ask.

But Zack doesn't do this—not as we work in this class, nor later in the rough draft he brings to class to share with his peers. They read as I do. Without knowing it, they make the same observations that I do. One says, "the paper overall is very good. The description is great. It does lack however some details. Maybe he should include more about how he or the group *felt* at specific times during their experience." And another:

The story is very interesting. It is not very often that people who are supposed to know where they are going tell others that they are lost. The details are good but he needs to add a few more. Zack may want to tell us more about the actual trail or lack of one. It would also be nice to know how the scouts felt or what they were thinking: were they scared, or were they thinking it was an adventure?

We—my students and I—often read alike. That's one premise of peer review: that multiple readers will read similarly and will advise writers as to what else they might do with a draft. Put differently, through peer revision the social context of writing becomes visible. Of course, I also hope that, made visible, the advice will be seriously considered, even used, by the writers. In this case, although we readers are *all* asking for more details—really, for more narrative—he does not respond to the requests. The final draft is virtually identical to the rough draft. The only added detail: that the campers ate hot dogs for lunch, before leaving on the hike. The single detail disappoints, and not even so much because of its singularity, but rather because it seems added in for its own sake, rather like filling a quota. The text isn't descriptive enough? Add a descriptive word or two. Here, the detail: it's not telling; it's not purposeful.

To return to the initial question, then: How/Does the scene-setting activity work for Zack? Not at all. The peer sharing? Equally unproductive, at least according to the terms I've stipulated. *Perhaps Zack doesn't understand what we want.* I follow this line of reasoning: I go to his Talk-To to see how Zack reads his own text. It's a contradiction in terms. On the one hand, he says, "I also use a great deal of descriptive words in my paper." On the other hand, he also says, "this paper could probably have more detail in order to give the reader a clearer description of the actual woods and mountain. It may also leave out some parts that I could have added to make the story more life-like or interesting." Zack's concept of description takes two forms: first, description as *descriptive words*; second, description as vehicle to convey something to a reader, as device to *give the reader a clearer description.* He is willing to do the first, to add a word or two, unwilling to add description that would connect to a *reader.* Why?

In his Talk-Back, Zack summarizes my reading of his paper and provides yet another clue: "Yancey seemed to make a lot of recommendations to how that I could possibly make my paper better. The main thing would be that I need more details. She says that I could have elaborated more on the fire and especially my feelings throughout the ordeal." Yes, that is what I said. Does he agree? "I agree with some of the recommendations about detail in certain places. I also agree with the grammatical errors and commas that I have misplaced. In some places I do not think that I need to add more detail because I would be overloading certain points. I think that this tends to make a dull paper."

***

How am I to understand this exchange—or lack thereof—with Zack? Because that's part of the problem: these texts could lead one to think that we are having an exchange, when my sense of this is that we are *maintaining a form without substance.*

Again, Donald Schon can help. He talks about the importance of the student-teacher relationship and of how the "stance" one brings to learning and to that relationship can determine what (and if something) is learned. Schon's contention is that the studio master— the teacher—asks the student to engage in "reflective imitation." This demands, he says, a willingness to do as the studio master is doing and, at the, "same time, reflect on what one does. Consciously entering into the master's way of designing, the student adds to her range of possible performance and extends her freedom of choice" (121).

And it's true: I'm not a design master, and this isn't a design studio, but I *do* want Zack to try, at least, to write the narrative *my* way, with details that would make it, as even he says, *more life-like or interesting.* My sense is that if he could write it this way, he would indeed *extend his range of performance* and thus his *freedom of choice.* He exercises another kind of freedom; he chooses not. (We cannot demand agency.) Such a situation is what Schon calls a *learning bind*; no learning can take place there, Schon says, and his causal analysis is instructive. In a learning bind, the learner becomes a *counterlearner* or an *overlearner.*

> When student and studio master are in a learning bind, so that some of the essential elements of designing are frozen in miscommunication, and neither student nor studio master is able to initiate reflection on that process, then any of several unsatisfactory outcomes is likely. The student may become a *counterlearner,* . . . refusing to suspend disbelief or to enter into her teachers' views of designing—except to "give them what they want." Or the student may *overlearn* the studio master's message, construing it as a set of expert procedures to be followed mechanistically in each situation. She may take as a general rule, for example, what the studio master conceives only as a limited illustration of a complex idea. Such a student may develop a closed-system vocabulary, in which she can state

the studio master's principles while performing in a manner incongruent with them and remaining unaware of that fact. (155)

Ironically, I think Zack is doing both here. He's more than willing to be an overlearner when it comes to *the grammatical errors and commas that I have misplaced*, when it comes to adding *descriptive words*. When it comes to grammar, the teacher here wields an expertise located in what Zack, like most students, sees as *a closed-system vocabulary*. He will apply this *vocabulary* mindlessly, will add in a descriptive word or two. But *rhetorically*, Zack is a *counterlearner*, unwilling to try the narrative any other way, certainly not my way, unwilling to add the details that his other readers request, wary of *overload*[ing] the text to *dull*[ness].

The labels *overlearner* and *counterlearner* help me make sense of Zack' refusal, but they also provide a point of departure. Go beyond them, I tell myself, inquire into the *reasons* for them, especially for Zack's counterlearning.

One: apparently, he trusts his own reading experience to be universal. He dislikes a detailed text; therefore, his readers will, too. (He's a dualistic reader.)

Two: he is unwilling to include the feelings that have to account for why he remembers this hike in the first place. He is asked by one colleague about how he *feel*[s], by another about whether or not he is *scared*, and he acknowledges that this is what I'm looking for, also.

Three: his group doesn't "work" for him the way that the groups work for Josey and Ann, both of whom (along with the other writers we've met, like Lara) voluntarily remark on how helpful the groups are; they see writing as social; readers become real. It's not that Zack's group could not help him, at least in terms of making good suggestions; it's that he is a learning bind with them as well, *a counterlearner with them*, too.

Four: I wonder if there isn't an implied bargain or contract or understanding that Zack is working from. He is a counterlearner: he will not give up what he knows and what he understands—to respond to his readers. But in return, he is more than willing to give ground as an overlearner, someone who will comply when it comes to rules, which are dual: right or wrong. *Does Zack need writing to be rule-governed? (What is the relation between Schon's overlearning and Perry's dualism?)*

This isn't the last time that I have a Zack for a student: what will I do when I meet another and we are writing narrative again, for instance? I need to learn from my own practice what other questions I could raise, what activities I could prompt with the next Zack, that perhaps could move us beyond this impasse. Such as:

Ask the student to think more reflectively about his own reading practices and preferences. What does he read, for instance, that includes details (like accounts of sports events, for instance), and why/does he need those details? *Is* his reading experience universal? How familiar is he with narrative of this sort, anyway? Is this a genre problem in that he doesn't understand the conventions of the genre, and/or something else? *If writing is reading, then reflecting on reading is a good place to start.*

In a narrative like this, ask the student to project how others expect that he'll feel (in this case, e.g., as he gets lost), and then confirm whether that is accurate or not. Perhaps moving the feelings to the subjunctive mood will make it easier to deal with them.

Ask the student to write two versions of the text, one for him, one for us; specify two quite different audiences and use that as a key variable in the rhetorical situation. Include a specific question regarding the two texts on the Talk-To: Are they in fact the same text, or two texts accounting for the same event? *In other words, make the counterlearning an occasion to think rhetorically, to move to the prototypical from the specific.*

As background material, perhaps develop two narratives for class discussion, one like Zack's that excludes details and a revised narrative that includes them, and use those as models for textual development.

***

I think if we don't develop specific strategies for helping students move beyond the impasses presented in counterlearning and over-learning—as they apply in a specific instance—that students are likely to simply stay stuck in these modes, possibly for the rest of the term. That's what happened to Zack, at least, as his Learning Summary suggests. Asked what he has learned so far, he replies:

> So far I have learned a great deal in this class. I now know that writing is a lot more complex than just sitting down and letting everything flow. That is ok, but there is so many more things that writing deals with. I know how to write an exposition and narrative also. The difference between

valid sources and invalid sources is also very clear to me after the first couple of months in this class. I know that you cannot believe every piece of information that you see on TV or read in a magazine.

This is, Zack, says, what he expected to learn. (Does this expectation matter? Was he willing to learn only what fit comfortably within his expectation?) When asked what else he wants to learn, Zack replies:

I would like to learn a way to make my writing more complex without really changing the meaning. I think that I can do this by substituting some of my repetitious words with good synonyms for these words. In my opinion, this would make my writing better. I know there are other things I can do to improve my writing, but these are the major points.

These replies read to me like his passage on adding descriptive words to the narrative: writing as a construct may be more *complex* to Zack, but he can't tell us how so, except that he wants the complexity without *really changing the meaning*. Which suggests that we aren't talking about the same complexity at all. He lists the kinds of disconnected things he can do, the fragments of very general understandings he has acquired. It doesn't read as "learning as process"; it's "learning as list." In Schon's terms, Zack is *stat[ing] the studio master's principles while performing in a manner incongruent with them and remaining unaware of that fact.* Or, in another Schonean frame, Zack is hoping to develop a writing that is technical, predictable, formulaic, controlled; he doesn't yet understand, or perhaps cannot accept, that writing does not operate according to rules, but according to conventions.

* * *

My claim has also been that teaching this course reflectively is a knowledge-making enterprise, that we can theorize from practice. If that's so, what have I learned?

That I can use reflection to help me understand the courses I teach. I began to ask for reflection because I thought that it would help writers develop. But it's also true that I can read this reflection in multiple ways. *In reading these reflective texts, in putting them in dialogue with the primary texts, I begin to understand intertextually how students experience the curriculum that I think I'm delivering.* As I indicate below, I can begin to chart patterns, can identify disruptions, can consider what such a course needs to do to provide the kind of experience I want to foster.

That stronger writers, like Ann and Josey, find value in the role that their colleagues played in helping them develop drafts and in becoming writers. It is true that in this version of the course I had emphasized group work in a new way. I'd asked students to engage in some reflection prior to sharing their drafts: specifically, in writing, to

summarize their text; and

predict how their colleagues would read it.

After they shared their texts, writers reflected again:

were you correct in your prediction? How so/not?

what advice did your colleagues give you?

will you take it?

what else do you need to do in your draft before submission?

In other words, by means of reflection, I *situated* the sharing of their texts. Through reflection, I tried to make the context of the peer review also visible, also something tangible that we could read and think about. And then I referred to this work when I responded to students; in that way, I also tried to make it count. I tried to ensure that our writing was social.

That groups can fail for reasons and in ways we don't fully understand yet. I think the major concern that faculty raise about peer review is that peers won't read well and therefore won't offer good advice—often put in terms of futility (e.g., "the blind leading the blind"). Perhaps: that's not what I've seen here. Zack received good advice. But he wouldn't take it. In Schon's terms, Zack was a counterlearner; *counterlearning happens with peers as well as between teacher and student,* and given the collaborative nature of a class like this, we might expect such counterlearning. The resistance isn't where we usually assign it, at least not here: it's *not* an issue of authority between teacher and student. *Rather it's an issue of authority for the student over his or her own process, his or her understanding of textuality and what goes into it.* (What else do we have to learn about resistance?)

That in any writing course, we will have counterlearners and overlearners, even in the same writer, perhaps often in the same writer. Is this so? Is my theory of Zack's implied contract accurate? Would it help to bring some of this language—counterlearning and overlearning—into the classroom? Of course, that's after we identify the students in potential learning binds, which we need to do. One way to begin is to act on the signs we see in a primary text, then go to reflective texts for confirmation. We also need to see more examples of counterlearning and overlearning and identify the motivations for each, so that we can speak to those. One key to this, I think, is to use the Schonean idea of working from the particular to the prototypic in a new way. In Schon's view of practice, getting to the prototypic only comes through the specific. By this logic, if the specific does not work, the writer cannot move to generality. Practice is not enhanced, and there is nothing to reflectively transfer. Perhaps writers like Zack should work in a curriculum-within-a-curriculum. What, after all, was the point in having Zack "move on" to the next assignment? Admittedly, there is no necessary rhetorical link from one assignment to the next; the ability to write narrative well will not assure success on the next task, particularly given its expository nature. But return to Schwalm's point: Zack is a writer who is unwilling to make the familiar strange: perhaps working within the same genre—whatever that genre is—for an extended period of time will allow Zack to develop enough practice and confidence within *that* specific rhetorical situation that he can create something generalizable, practices and understandings that he can carry on with him. If this makes sense, it means that we have to devise new ways to work with writers like Zack; we may need to revise our model of curriculum for such writers. He's not a basic writer in the conventional sense, but he is altogether too common. As site of error, his texts evidence very few surface or syntactical problems. As site of negotiation, they do not suffice. Perhaps that very understanding of text—*as site of negotiation*—is the place to begin work with Zack.

That writers bring with them a model of writing and of writing classrooms; some models are productive and others are not. Interestingly, the stronger writers—Josey and Ann—found that one understanding they acquired was how process-based writing is, how social it is, how their colleagues could help them. In other words, writing better entailed *learning about* writing. And what we see, in part, in the Learning Summaries is Ann's and Josey's revision of their models of writing, revisions that correspond with the work of their primary texts. It's this same learning about writing, however, that we do *not* see in Zack; he expects to find a mechanistic activity, and he remains commmited to that model of writing throughout. How can we help writers let go of expectations that aren't appropriate, that in fact are counterproductive? Should such a model revision be an explicit goal of a composition course?

That in many ways a writing course is an exercise in identity formation, and growth in identity is one sign that the course is working. Josey says that she wants to become more professional as a writer: I want to explore what that means, but I take it as a good sign. She has a model not just of writing, but a model of a writer as well: one who works at writing as a *craft*, who changes her *revising* in response to an *editor*. Ann wants to become an academic writer who can infuse the outside with the inside, who can use her social skills and her ability to visualize to talk to a reader: she begins to see how to reach a reader. They want different identities, both appropriate. Isn't this the aim of a writing course, to help students understand what it means to write, and to move, as does Josey, to becoming an Author? Since this issue is, I think, at the heart of Zack's problem—i.e., his impoverished sense of what a writer is—shouldn't this be another place we begin our work?

* * *

When reflection "works," it raises as many questions as it answers, perhaps more. It works from the particular to the general without ever leaving the particular. It works by asking that we articulate the tacit, that we frame our observations multiply, that we look for a coherence that patterns without disguising or discoloring or misrepresenting. This means that we don't look only at the students who've done well; it means that we learn, and *perhaps we learn the most from those who don't succeed in our courses.* It means that we learn together.

Through reflection we learn what we know now, and we begin to understand what we need to learn next.

CHAPTER SEVEN

Reflection and Assessment

Tests create that which they purport to measure by transforming the person.

F. Allan Hanson

For all of us there are shadows between the ideal and the reality.

Bob Marrs

REFLECTION-IN-PRESENTATION IS, OF COURSE, A KEY COMPONENT OF portfolios, as it can be of cumulative reflective essays, and increasingly it is being included as the second text in holistically scored impromptu essays.[1] In other words, *reflection-in-presentation is becoming a more regularized component of assessment practice.* When linked to programs, to high-stakes situations, to situations clearly in the public domain where scrutiny and accountability are the coin of the realm, reflection-in-presentation tends to raise issues that we normally associate with a formal writing assessment: one characterized by formal operations and technical rigor. These issues—how we should evaluate a student's work, and why we should include reflection in such an evaluation—can, in fact, be real issues in the classroom also. But some of them—like how external raters evaluate reflection and portfolios—are specific to the context of programatic assessment.

As we shall see, *the function of reflection in an assessment context isn't entirely clear.*

***

Although we in the writing profession seem to value reflection, I'm not sure that we are entirely clear about why—about why we think it's valuable, about why it is that we ask for reflection in portfolios or even as final assignments. Put chronologically, I think we had the cart before the horse: we asked for reflection not in advance of assessing students' work, for some theoretical reason associated with evaluation or even curriculum, but very pragmatically and *after the fact*—after we had sets of texts known as portfolios that seemed to need something else to help them hang together, some meta-commentary, some introduction, some cohering threads. Or: some of what has come to be called *reflection*. Not that reflection hasn't worked in these after-the-fact ways, serving good purposes in providing a context for these texts, whether as introduction to the portfolio, or as description of a writer's process against which a final draft can be understood, or as some synthesis of what a student has learned. It has: at setting this context and providing this additional information, reflection can be said to "work."

But this assertion just raises the question: what *work* is it that we want such final reflections, such reflection-in-presentation, to accomplish? In this rhetorical situation, the situation of high stakes assessment?

***

One assumption motivating the inclusion of reflection in assessment as well as its inclusion as a final culminating assignment is that an engaged learner is likely to perform better, which is the point of education; another assumption is that, as F. Allan Hanson points out in *Testing Testing*, the test we construct will construct in turn the person taking the test. Accordingly, if we construct a test—in this case, an assignment or final text—requiring a reflective stance and reflective activities that foster that stance, *students are more likely to become reflective.* In the language of assessment, students, by means of a reflection, are asked to locate their own work—through contextualizing it, for example, or interpreting it. Reflection is thought to enhance the *validity* of the assessment—that is, the likelihood that the assessment will measure what it purports to measure—precisely because it *requires* that students narrate, analyze, and evaluate their own learning and their own texts and thus *connect the assessment to their own learning.*

It is no understatement, therefore, to claim that portfolio assessment is different in kind from earlier tests, and (that even in cases where portfolios are not the vehicle of assessment) to claim likewise that when reflection-in-presentation is included, the assessment works differently.

Another assumption here seems to be that what we assess should in some explicit way derive from classroom practice, and that the student is capable of exerting considerable authority in determining how that practice contextualized his or her writing development and achievement. Thus, reflection acts as another means of understanding the "fit" between the writer and the contexts in which the writer has been composing. In a class or workshop where a writer composes on topics of interest, where he or she receives praise and helpful critique, the fit is said to be good, and the student is likely to do "well."

But there are other assumptions too. In part, I think what we are assessing—in portfolios, in impromptu essays combined with reflection-in-presentation, in stand-alone reflective texts—has to do with two possibilities. On the one hand, as we've seen in earlier chapters, we could say that we are looking at a writer's authority, as constructed through his or her ability to self-assess, to understand when and how he or she performs well and when and how otherwise. In this case, we seem to be assessing *two (related) performances: the writing performance and the reflecting/self-assessing performance.* Given what we know about the helpfulness, indeed the necessity of self-evaluation as a means of development in writing, this makes sense, of course. Still, these performances are not co-identical. Or is one embedded in, entailed by the other?

On the other hand, as we've also seen in earlier chapters, it might be that what we are assessing, when we look at reflection, isn't performance so much as *knowledge: self-knowledge about one's writing behavior, but also knowledge about what it may take to be a writer,* since that is one context for our own self-assessment. In other words, what we seem to reward here isn't just a sense that the writer understands his or her writing strategies and processes, but also and as important that these are appropriate, given (our understanding of) the way writers behave. The writer's authority seems appropriate, given the contents of the portfolio; the composer does have the self-knowledge claimed in the reflective text, and that self-knowledge is consonant with that writing practice.

What is it that we do reward in reflection, by the way? And what issues are related to that?

***

The short answer: no one really knows what we reward in reflection. We've looked at it in the context of portfolios, and we—teacher scholars like Michael Allen and Jeff Sommers and Jane Frick and George Meese and Robert Marrs and Gail Stygall and Laurel Black and Lucille Schultz and Russell Durst and Marjorie Roemer—have talked about it in that context, but not in any definitive way. There are ways to frame such a question, however:

What do such texts look like?

When in portfolios, where should such texts be placed?

How do we read them?

What are the dangers in such texts, from an assessment perspective?

Is a reflective text ever inadequate, and how would we know that?

***

Even within program portfolios, reflective texts take various forms. At George Mason University, for instance, portfolio is the option for exempting the junior-level WAC course, but the reflective text in that portfolio is itself a *timed writing* that focuses on process:

> Refer to two pieces included in your portfolio. Write about each. Explain your motivation to write the piece; describe your process of collecting information (sources used, problems encountered in the research); describe your process of drafting and revising, including for example, your favorite tricks for getting started, for organizing your work, for understanding your audience, for getting feedback on your writing as it progresses. (Thaiss and Zawicki, 95)

Senior writing majors at Missouri Western State College compose a different kind of portfolio, one that is used to certify them for graduation, with a different kind of reflective text. It includes individual annotations on each exhibit (and exhibits include texts from literature and technical writing classes as well as a resume), and a "self-reflective essay" that

> Clearly explains to raters how the student has developed as a writer/scholar/expert in the major emphasis; how major courses have affected the student's thinking/writing strategies; how the portfolio represents what the student has learned; why the portfolio is evidence of the student's ability to begin a career or complete graduate work; what academic problems the student has experienced, how the student has dealt with them, and what the student plans to do for continued improvement. (Allen, Frick et al. 80)

But the most popular model of reflection in vehicles used for summative assessment purposes—*the reflective letter*—is embodied in the best-known programs, those at Miami University and at the University of Michigan. Miami's program is also used for exemption, but for first-year writers, and students submitting a portfolio are told to write the now-ubiquitous reflective letter (the one providing the model discussed in chapter four).

> This [reflective, introductory] letter, addressed to Miami University writing teachers, introduces you and your portfolio. It may describe the process used in creating any one portfolio piece, discuss important pieces in creating the portfolio, explain the place of writing in your life, chronicle your development as a writer, assess the strengths and weaknesses of your writing, or combine these approaches. Your letter should provide readers with a clearer understanding of who you are as a writer and a person. (Sommers et al. 10-11)

Likewise, the Michigan program, which requires portfolios of all entering students, stipulates the reflective text in very similar terms:

> A reflective piece that discusses the work in your portfolio. We would like to know what the assignment for each piece was. We also want to know why you selected these particular pieces for your portfolio, what you like about each piece, what process you used in writing each piece, and what you learned from writing each one. Although we encourage you to send your most recent work, we are interested in hearing about your development as a writer over time. The most useful reflective pieces offer thoughtful self-evaluation. They are usually at least two pages, and we encourage you to write as much as five pages [from a total of 15-25 pages]. (www.lsa.umich.edu/ecb/)

In each case, the directions point the students toward disclosure of the self—toward *who you are as a writer and a person*, the intent here beneficent. As explained in chapter four, one intent is to allow the students to share whatever it is that *they think* is relevant, the corollary thinking that we as assessment-designers can't always anticipate what those observations may be. Thus, the very open directions. Another intent is to allow students to display not a single, unified self, but multiple selves, which is more likely if the prompt for reflection provides less scripting for a unified response.

The idea, then, as James Berlin and Pat Belanoff have suggested, is that through portfolios and their reflective introductions we see writers anew, as multi-selved experts of their own knowledge and their own texts, by an agency made possible only through textual diversity and multiple communities. Berlin talks about the writer as assuming multiple subject positions, Belanoff about multi-vocality;

both are talking about a writer who can compose to different purposes on different occasions for different audiences in different genres. Within the portfolio, and within these newer, hybrid forms of
assessment, writing—like the self—is social, is situated, is appropriately postmodern.

***

Portfolio practice is not without its critique, however, the most
salient of which addresses not the multi-texts in portfolios, but the
reflective text per sé, and thus is particularly relevant here. Most
impressive among the critiques to date is that provided by Charles
Schuster. He details four problems with portfolios when they are
used for large-scale assessment: 1) students using texts written elsewhere in their course portfolios; 2) teachers over-collaborating with
their students; 3) teachers fictionalizing students, based on their
readings of the reflective letter; 4) mediating among readers. Two of
these concerns are directly pertinent to reflection and its role in
assessment: the fictionalizing that Schuster claims is fostered by the
letter, and the reading experiences of raters.

Schuster contends that fictionalizing is particularly invited in the
reflective text since it identifies the *writer* (not just the writing), personalizing and particularizing him or her, often as a *function* of the
kinds of directions given to the student—in fact, as a function of the
kinds of directions we've just seen. More to the point, when faced
with that text, he says, we as readers have a "strong tendency to create
a portrait of the writer," a practice at odds with the (non-fictional-
ized) purpose of assessment.

> In effect, fictionalizing student authors moves readers away from normed
> criteria, replacing careful evaluation with reader response. . . .
> Presumptions concerning personality, intention, behavior and the like
> skew readings or turn assessment into novel reading. . . . Such fictionaliz-
> ing serves a useful purpose within a classroom; by doing so, instructors
> individualize and humanize their students, or at the very least, create nar-
> rative explanations and justifications for student work. Writing assess-
> ment, however, demands that we exclusively evaluate what the student
> has produced on the page in the portfolio. Fictionalizing in this context
> can only obscure judgment. (319)

Schuster's point here is well-taken; it provides a keen point of departure for considering our own practice, particularly in light of what we

know about reading practices and about student learning, as well as about writing assessment.

But first: a few caveats. Fictionalizing, as Schuster himself suggests, can play a useful role: in the classroom, it is through the power of fictionalizing ourselves into roles otherwise foreign that we become that which we might not. Students become writers in part precisely because they can fictionalize and imagine and rehearse their way into such a role (just as prospective teachers imagine themselves into a faculty role). So the fictionalizing that is useful in the classroom takes various forms, on the parts of both teachers and students. As Schuster suggests, then, fictionalizing per sé isn't the problem. If it is a problem, it's only so at certain times.

The assumption grounding this argument, however, seems to be that when we read single texts, we don't fictionalize, that we somehow read in a non-fictional, "truthful" way. The limited evidence available, however, suggests just the opposite: that texts routinely invite us to create a portrait of a writer. This was the point of Faigley's complaint, for instance, in "Judging Writing, Judging Selves": that what faculty were praising in the texts they valued was the very ethos *they* were constructing (or projecting) in their reading process. It's the point that Francis Sullivan makes when he talks about the cultural capital that "successful" students evidence even in highly controlled college placement essays. His research shows that essays that look otherwise the same linguistically are awarded different ratings based on the kinds of supporting evidence they provide, the higher-scoring essays citing traditional literary references, the lower-scoring essays references to popular culture. His conclusion: the "successful" writer, not unlike the student at Harvard in the late nineteenth century (Berlin, 1990), appears as one of us; the writer is fictionalized as one of us.

Of course, as Schuster quite rightly suggests, portfolios *don't* present an exception to this observation—and worse (from his perspective) there is some evidence beyond that on his own campus that the portfolio reflective text qua text invites such fictionalizing. The Miami University researchers, for instance, concur, at least to the extent that they are aware of how much readers are drawn to the self in the reflective text:

> One reader noted, 'I found the reflective letter to often be the most interesting part of the packet, not only because of what it revealed of the individual but because of what it showed about the writer's attitude towards their own work. What a fascinating range of boastfulness, self-effacement, wit, and

rambling.' Another commented, 'The reflective letter fascinates me. It appears to be the place where the student establishes his/her authority as a writer; positions the reader and the writer.' A third rather echoes the second: 'I liked those reflective letters and narratives which situated the writer and his or her writings best.' (Sommers et al. 11)

Rather than being concerned about the personal influencing the assessment in a negative way, however, the Miami researchers draw opposite conclusions: 1) that it is this inclusion of the personal in the portfolio that readers respond to favorably; and 2) that it thus *enhances* the reading process. Researchers at the University of Cincinnati have drawn the same conclusion and pushed it further: their work suggests that readers create not only a *persona* of the author, but also a portrait of the author working in the classroom context. They see this "narrativizing tendency" on the part of readers as inevitable:

> This narrativizing tendency constitutes one of our primary ways of understanding, one of our primary ways of making sense of the world, and is an essential strategy in comprehension. As far as portfolio evaluation is concerned, rather than say that narrativizing is right or wrong, perhaps we should start by admitting its inevitability, and by advising teachers to be aware of this tendency and not overvalue the stories we create.

The question, then, seems not to be so much how to eliminate fictionalizing from the assessment process, if indeed this tendency is inevitable, but rather to consider how our reading and our judgment are affected by the inclusion of the personal as highlighted in the reflective text. Although we cannot—and should not, perhaps— eliminate fictionalizing, the decisions we make routinely—about the genre it takes, for instance—can emphasize or diminish this tendency. More specifically, there are four frames through which such fictionalizing can be mediated:

1. according to which genres we ask that reflection take
2. according to where we place the reflective text within a portfolio
3. according to which reading/scoring process we endorse when we evaluate reflective texts and portfolios
4. according to what kinds of expectations we have, which in turn should themselves be expressed in the directions that we provide for reflective texts

***

The genre we permit for reflection-in-presentation has everything to do with the truths that students will speak. In chapter four, I implied that the classroom could be used as a kind of staging ground where we could explore the relationships between reflection and genre. In the case of high stakes assessment, however, we don't have the freedom to explore—hence the need to articulate our own expectations.

The most popular genre for reflection-in-presentation in the assessment context, I think, is still the letter. We could ask, however, that the reflection discourse take a different form. For most students, the letter as genre is *personal,* so that when they work in this genre, their inclination is to see it as a highly personal text. Such a view is echoed by the open directions that seem all-too-characteristic for reflective texts. What would happen if we asked for a "reflective essay" rather than letter? How might that change both our texts and our readings?

Any genre always excludes more than it includes. The introductory letter, as we've seen, is marked by several features: it welcomes a kind of personal address to the reader; it overviews the portfolio contents, which the reader presumably has not yet read; it provides a place to tell various kinds of stories, particularly about the writer developing (often from writing occasions long since passed); and it sets a context for the reader and thus may considerably influence the reading of the rest of the portfolio. The reflective essay, on the other hand, typically comes at another point in the reading process—after the "evidence" of primary (and perhaps secondary) texts has been presented. If only because it's an essay, it's typically *understood* as more analytical and interpretive in nature, as less chatty and relaxed, as more typically academic and formal, as more single-voiced and single-pointed. In terms of gender, the letter seems more oriented to the feminine, to the writer whose textual identity has historically been composed of personal writings like diaries and journals and letters, whose sense of self is located between and among relationships, as biographers of women, like Linda Wagner-Martin, will attest. An essay, by contrast, seems more objective, more school-like, more oriented to the texts themselves and to the institutions framing them. Given these observations, which genre should we assign our students? Asked differently, which discursive site is more hospitable to reflection?

One response is to envision the essay more capaciously than I've done here, to see it more as a kind of Spellmeyerian site of exploration rather than of argument, to use it for consideration as well as for assertion, for associational thinking as much as for thrust and parry, for connecting as well as prioritizing, to do with the essay what Wendy Bishop did in a *CCC* interchange with David Bartholomae and Peter Elbow: work around and between and among the issues they raised to get at the issues she was interested in, in collage-like, associational, multi-vocal modes. Such an essay genre would allow the kinds of insights characteristic in the introductory letter, would resist the control exercised by a unitary governing mind.

A second suggestion is entailed in Berlin's observation about why we value education in the first place:

> The point of education in a democracy is to discover as many ways of seeing as possible, not to rest secure in the perspective we find easiest and most comfortable or the perspective of those currently in power. (66)

If this is indeed our aim in education, and if genre (as Kenneth Burke earlier argued) is a way of not seeing as much as it is of seeing, then perhaps we ought to ask our students to do both kinds of reflection-in-presentation: the one that sets the stage for our reading and the after-one that interprets the contexts and develops evidentiary claims for an over-riding argument, not agonistically, but reflectively.

If the point, ultimately, of reflection is to encourage reflective writers, and if we expect those writers to work in various genres, then it might make sense to ask for more than one kind of reflective text, whether they be independent documents or within portfolios.

***

Reflective texts conventionally are placed first in the program portfolio; one might say they're used as the definitive reflection-in-presentation here. In the position of first text, they of course are often called upon to perform a variety of functions, as we've seen, from introducing the writer and/or the portfolio to contextualizing the contents by describing each assignment to describing the processes that went into the assignments and so on. Regardless of the number of functions it is serving, however, the reflective text will exert disproportionate influence in the reading process simply by virtue of its placement as first item in the set of collected texts.

We could devise other responses to these rhetorical needs, of course.

We might assign the introductory function to a different text, say a straightforward introduction or preface, or even to an annotated Table of Contents. This would enable the reflective text to do less introductory kind of work, more synthesizing reflective work. The reflective text, in other words, would be less multi-purpose, less multi-generic. The net effect of this change, however, might well be to heighten the image of self dominating the reflective text since the writing/writer would provide its sole focus.

If, however, we want the fictionalizing diminished, then perhaps separating this text from the introductory text and placing this reflective text at the end of the collected texts would make more sense. Presumably, a reader would encounter the reflection after having read the primary texts first, and thus having already constructed an image of the writer from those texts, and if you follow Schuster's logic, such a portrait—ie, that constructed from the primary texts— is more trustworthy than the reflective discourse. Perhaps more important, the reflective text in this model would simply act as another piece of corroborating evidence for the set of texts *en toto* instead of setting the stage and (over)influencing the set.

In other words, if the reflective text were placed at the end of the reading process, the tendency would be for it to either *confirm or disconfirm* what has already been constructed. As one portfolio reader on my campus put it:

> I think it is important for the reflection to come at the end for both reader and writer. As a reader, I expect to read the essays first and then the writer's own assessment of the samples contained in the portfolio. The student's own explanation at the end helps me to evaluate what I have just finished reading. As the student compiles the portfolio, he/she begins to reflect on the contents. The reflective essay is the last step, so the progression makes sense. I think the questions asked for the reflection, as they are now, help me learn more about the writer (i.e. how the person views himself or herself as a writer). One purpose of this reading, as I understand it, is to determine if the student understands what makes good writing. I think a student who is able to evaluate his/her own writing demonstrates the necessary maturity. (Anonymous Reader)

Here the rationale is, indeed, that the reflective text provides additional information, information that may be pivotal, but *pivotal after the fact of the other texts.* As important, perhaps, the reader here makes the important point that asking the student to place the reflection last in the set repeats a kind of *progression: The reflective essay is the last step, so the progression makes sense.* Put differently, the arrangement of the texts (product) recapitulates the processes used to create them, and in this arrangement we have marked the writing performance off from the reflecting performance without dividing them totally.

And this—the relationship between the writing performance and the reflecting performance—is, I think, a key issue. It may be that what Schuster is getting at here is not fictionalizing so much, but at what may be an *inappropriate conflation of writing performance and reflecting performance.* If we ask for the reflection first, then the texts we read secondarily—which are typically considered to be the primary texts, of course—are called upon not so much as an independent measure of a student's writing, but as evidence in support of the student's claims in the reflective text. But one of the truths we currently hold to be self-evident about writing assessment is that no single variable, no single text is adequate. If all the texts in the portfolio become grist for the mill of the student's reflection, then have we reduced those texts to a single variable? And how much more have we induced a need in the student to fictionalize, to tell us what we want to hear?

Of course, another large assumption undergirds these speculations: that placement of text necessarily leads to a certain sequence in the reading of those texts. We're assuming that readers will read these texts in the order in which they occur in a portfolio. But this isn't necessarily the case. Jeff Sommers, for instance, makes the point that regardless of where a reflection shows up in a portfolio, he finds it so important to his understanding that he reads it first (Allen, Frick et al.). Typically, except in classroom situations, readers don't feel that they can read hypertextually. How would they read if we allowed them to read as they would?

***

As observed earlier, we need to think a little more precisely about what purposes we want the reflection to serve so that we would sculpt our directions for reflective texts toward those ends. The directions that we've reviewed appear to welcome virtually all observations, to assume that all responses are equally valuable. But, of course, all responses aren't equal; the writer who tells us that *the story was true and meaningful, flawless, and flowed well due to strong transition* (our perfect writer, from chapter four) is in trouble once the word *flawless* is voiced. We do privilege some reflective texts more than others, though we haven't talked as we might about how and why.

I return, then, to the central questions linking reflection and summative assessment: what are we looking for? Are we interested in students' judgments about their own work and how they arrived at those? Are we interested in their understanding and application of writing process? Are we interested in the relationship between their judgments and our judgments about their texts? Are we, ultimately, interested in how they make sense of the world? Are we interested in something else altogether?

Like others across the country, when we on my own campus needed directions for a portfolio exemption program, we too borrowed from those developed by the Miami program. You'll recognize the directions:

1994 Directions

This letter, addressed to UNC Charlotte writing teachers, introduces you and your portfolio. It may describe the process used in creating any one portfolio piece, discuss important pieces in creating the portfolio, explain the place of writing in your life, chronicle your development as a writer, assess the strengths and weaknesses of your writing, or combine these approaches. Your letter should provide readers with a clearer understanding of who you are as a writer and a person. (UNCC handout)

We weren't, however, very satisfied with the reflection this prompted. Too often, it looked like this:

Reflective Essay

As with all my writings, my first step was to choose a topic. From there I gathered the materials pertinent to the topic and outlined my papers. My next step was to write a rough draft and have someone to proofread for suggestions. I then corrected mistakes and altered my paper to make it accurate, readable, and informative.

Two of these pieces required no research or bibliography, only my imagination. The two unresearched papers differed, because one was written on an assigned topic, while the other was a subject of my choice.

My main strength as a writer is my ability to revise and edit as needed. While on the other hand, my weaknesses lie in the area of sentence structure and paragraph formation.

After completing this portfolio, I see myself as a writer who continues to improve with each paper. I view myself as someone who is able to convey my thoughts in writing, in different styles when given the opportunity. (Anon.)

Now, it may be that this writer would have composed a reflection that looked like this—*task generic rather than task-specific, unelaborated and general and vague and clipped*—regardless of the prompt we designed. At the same time, we have to say: *the writer here does what we ask.* If this is so, and if the text is disappointing, perhaps we should try again. Especially when the reflective texts that are less disappointing still seem shy of the mark.

Reflective Essay

As I looked back over my portfolio, I was able to see the progress that I have made as a writer. In this essay I will assess my strengths and weaknesses as a writer and discuss the processes that I used when writing the pieces in this portfolio.

One strength of mine as evidenced by the first two pieces in my portfolio is that I effectively organized the essays to get my point across. Another strength that I displayed in my two essays is that I cited specific sources to support information that I was trying to communicate to the reader. A creative method that I used in my first selection was to incorporate a different voice, the voice of Al Maisto [a psychology professor on campus], into my paper to show someone else's perspective on my topic. My third selection demonstrates my ability to go from a serious, informative style of writing to an imaginative and figurative style.

One weakness of mine as evidenced by the selections in this portfolio is that I do not write strong introductions and conclusions. A goal of mine that I am currently working on in English 1101 is to write stronger introductions and conclusions. Even though I feel that my essays were well organized, I need to improve my transitions between paragraphs. In addition, something else that I showed in these pieces is redundancy. I have the tendency to repeat my ideas throughout the paper. As shown in the second essay, I also put my opinion into papers that are supposed to be objective.

A different process was used in writing each piece in this portfolio. In preparing the first composition, I read a selection in our English text, *Conversations,* and participated in a class discussion of the topic. Then I brainstormed ideas for an essay. I wrote a rough draft and let a peer read it in class and give me suggestions. Next, I revised the paper and turned it in to our instructor as a second draft. After I received the paper back from the instructor, I read her comments and revised it for a final draft.

The processes that I used for the next essay included reviewing my text and notes for the class. I then wrote down ideas and planned how I was going to respond to the questions that I was supposed to answer when writing the paper. My first draft was also my final draft since it was a mid-term exam and I did not have a sufficient amount of time to revise it.

My third piece involved reading different short stories and writings by Edgar Allen Poe. I had to figure out how to imitate his style and plan out the paper. Then I wrote a draft which I revised into my final piece.

After putting this portfolio together, I have realized that I am not as weak of a writer as I once thought myself to be. There is always room for improvement in my writing, though, which I was able to see by accessing by weaknesses. This portfolio has also enabled me to see which processes in my writing seemed to be the most helpful such as responding to suggestions from peers and instructors. (Anon.)

This writer also does what we ask: processes are described, as she alerts us; judgments about her written texts are rendered. But this text, which typifies the best of what we saw, didn't satisfy. We saw topics addressed, almost as independent variables; we didn't see synthesis; we didn't see *gaps* or *insincerities*; we didn't see a writer. And yes, we were looking for a writer, one who could *talk about.*

And perhaps our disappointment's not so surprising. After all, what we have here in desire is an unarticulated kind of text, a text that we will no doubt recognize once we see it, but that we are reluctant to prescribe (prematurely). The problem is that while it may feel premature to us, it's post maturity for the student who has to write one. If, on the other hand, we thought of reflection more as an assessment vehicle—that is, as an essay or even letter assignment with assessment value—then we might be more careful, more specific, more judicious in our directions. As Ruth and Murphy have demonstrated, failing to be clear and focused are two of the major errors that one can make when designing a writing prompt, which is what the assignment for reflection is.

So, dissatisfied with our own directions as much as with the results, we worked in a Schonean way to construct causal explanations: students who weren't so smart, for instance; or students who weren't so reflective; as likely, students who hadn't practiced reflection in any variety, so who found the discourse alien. But we also thought that we, or our directions, were part of the problem. So we went back to the drawing board and approached the directions from two perspectives, using our own reading of the current texts to help us understand what didn't satisfy and thus what is was that might satisfy. The first problem seemed simple enough: depth, which you couldn't obtain without sufficient length. As one reader explained,

> I wonder if we want to think about stressing this component [a suggested length for the reflective text]. For instance, a portfolio w/ a one-paragraph reflection cannot be given credit? Maybe I'm being too black & white here—maybe this is not realistic. But I do agree that this is such an important piece of writing & is revealing on many levels. So if a student is unable to generate a reasonably-sized reflection. (Anon.)

Length is a relative variable, too: what are we looking for?

We also decided that of all the questions we could ask, we were most interested in three:

1995 Directions

1. Of the texts in your portfolio, which is best and why?
2. Of the texts in your portfolio, which is weakest, and why?
3. What might you do to improve either or both of them?

In response to these questions, we decided that we'd ask for 750 words; that's about three pages, and that length, we thought, would provide enough space to develop some elaboration, some depth. In the language of assessment, we began to operationalize, to define, what we meant by length. And we provided a rationale for our questions: we thought that these three questions asked students to engage in reflection linked to reflective discourse: the processes evoked by the questions were congruent with the kind of text we had in mind. Writers make comparative judgments about texts for good reasons; we wanted to hear those. Writers think about revising in the language of revision; we wanted to hear about that. We weren't looking for agreement with our judgment; we understand that reasonable, informed people will disagree. We were interested in seeing what *reasonable* and *informed* in this reflective context looked like. And we were interested in how the descriptions of improvement *corresponded* with the primary texts we had before us. We were, then, interested in seeing a "triangulated writer," a writer textualized in multiplicity, made material in the writer's own diverse discourses.

Closing Essay

The strongest piece of writing in the portfolio is the first essay, "Crunch". In many ways, "Crunch" represents the peak of all I have learned in the past two semesters of English. As a senior in high school, I took Advanced Writing, a class very similar to English 1101. In this class, we wrote many personal essays similar to "Crunch"; however, I was never able to find a balance between writing honestly and keeping the reader's interest. I struggled to break out of the typical clichés, and appeals to the reader's emotions. In English 1101 this year, we have done a lot of free-writing and writing as quickly as we can for a set amount of time. Using parts of these free-writings has allowed me to write with greater honesty and accuracy. When I was given the assignment to write a personal event essay in English, I brainstormed for awhile to find a topic and finally chose one from a free-writing activity conducted in class. My topic was an accident in which I was involved with my volleyball team last year. Writing the paper was difficult for me because it brought back a lot of bad memories and forced me to think about and analyze what happened. Throughout my paper, I struggled to always write honestly, and in the end, I succeeded. The honesty and accuracy included in "Crunch" is the reason why it is the strongest piece of writing in the portfolio.

The weakest piece of writing in the portfolio is the COA Application essay. This essay lacks a strong central focus, and it includes a lot of opinion without support. Under the pressure of an approaching deadline, I wrote this essay quickly and without much thought. I had become so frustrated with the length of the application that my only concern was to finish it, not to make it perfect.

The COA Application essay could be improved in many ways, and the result would probably be very different from its current state. First of all, I would take the time to choose a specific angle for the essay. When I wrote the essay, I tried to include too many things instead of focusing on one or two central ideas. Though this method works for giving an overall view of the book, it turns the essay into more of a book report than a critical essay. Second, I would use more source material to support my angle. As a reader, I find it difficult to fully understand and appreciate a writer's argument if his writing does not include some type of support other than opinion. I would not only use the passages from the book, *On the Road*, to support my angle, but I would also try to incorporate material from professional reviews of the book to see the entire picture. Finally, I would go over the essay with a fine-tooth comb to spot weaknesses in grammar, sentence structure, word choice, and clarity. A piece of writing, no matter how brilliant and revolutionary, is ineffective if the reader can not understand it or becomes bored with it. Thus, it is always important to think of the audience and to tailor the writing to the audience's needs. After all of these improvements, the essay could become one of the strongest pieces in the portfolio. (Anon.)

This reflective text may not be brilliant, but it *is* closer to what we were anticipating. The writer seems to understand something about rhetorical problems like *find*[ing] *a balance between writing honestly and keeping the reader's interest* and differences in genre: *Though this method works for giving an overall view of the book, it turns the essay into more of a book report than a critical essay.* There is task-specific description of how the writer would revise, the logic of the plan and the assumptions underlying it are generally persuasive, and the plans themselves are laid with a kind of control that makes one think the author could carry it off. The writer seems pretty dualistic, though: *honesty* in writing, which is identified as the supreme value, is pitted against what the audience will accept. (She's not, however, claiming honesty as contributing to a perfect writing, it's worth noting.) More generally, the reflection is clearly tailored to the prompt; though we have more writer here, and though that seems a good thing, we still are missing synthesis.

We're closer, but we're not there yet. *We're closer to understanding where* there *is*.

***

These questions—what we want in reflection and what happens when it works—have also been taken up by at least one more group whose discussions shed another kind of light on them: Portnet, whom we met in chapter five, have read them together and have thought together—most of this online—about programatic portfolios, about the role of reflection-in-presentation in an assessment context. (See, for instance, Allen; Allen et al. in *Situating Portfolios*; and Allen, Frick, Sommers, and Yancey.) In response to what it is that we *expect* of reflection, George Meese, for instance, seems to place reflection within the genre of the capacious essay identified earlier: as a text that both satisfies a writer's need to make sense of something while at the same time *transacting* with a reader. In other words, Meese focuses particularly on the dual purpose reflection serves, for both writer and reader.

> I recall that I addressed these multiple purposes of reflection in my chapter about "Suzanne's Journal" in Toby Fulwiler's *The Journal Book*, but not exactly in the same terms we are using here. I think all our portfolio "systems" seek to have students demonstrate their awareness of how they have placed their readers and then worked language to have their readers appreciate the author's thinking, etc. What gets really interesting for me is how some writers are capable of letting me behind the conventions of overtly purposeful transaction, to see moments of knowledge-making (almost) directly. (Email January 10, 1997)

Reflection-in-presentation is a transaction, of course, but Meese's point is that when it works, it's also an opportunity for the writer to learn about his or her writing, knowledge, understanding.

Another Portnet colleague, Robert Marrs, agrees. At his campus, Coe College, Marrs has staged such a moment for reflection in an impromptu writing situation intended to place students in the appropriate writing-intensive course. The students are told:

> 1. Relax. Take a few minutes to read the two essays you wrote for the first two assignments [a memoir and a response to a reading]. Write a commentary on these compositions and the thinking/composing processes you used for reading the assignments and writing your essays. Consider such issues as the following:
>
> -How would you describe your two compositions? How do they compare with each other? How do they compare with the writing you have done in school or on your own?
>
> -If you were revising either piece, what would you change? Be specific. Identify what passages you would change and explain why. Also identify what you feel are your strongest passages in the two essays.
>
> 2. In a second set of responses, explain how you see yourself as a writer. Consider the following questions:

- How would you describe your typical writing style or styles?

- What kinds of writing do you do best? What kinds of writing do you try to avoid?

- What additional information and experiences from your background would help the faculty reading your papers gain a clearer understanding of your ideas and your skills as a reader and writer? Can you identify any significant beliefs, insights, or experiences that may have influenced your writing in these essays? You might discuss previous reading or courses you have taken, television or movies you have watched, traveling you have done, people you have met, etc. . . . .

- What do you consider your strengths as a writer? Your weaknesses? Are you satisfied with your current writing skills? Explain. (Email January 14, 1997)

Now, on the one hand, these directions seem very like the ones provided by Miami and Michigan: lots of questions, and seemingly worse, intended to produce a quick rather than leisurely response, given the timed nature of the writing situation. But, it seems to me at least, that some telling differences can be noted.

One difference: students are asked, for example, to address the two texts they have just written. Of course, they have only the two texts that they have just composed (rather than the three or more primary texts we often find in a portfolio), but it's also true that this assignment is comparatively narrow: the task—comparing the two texts—is clear. And as Marrs comments, this task is deliberately set:

> One of the major reasons why we ask for two 'essays' is because one of the most productive questions in our reflection prompt has been the question about comparing the two texts. We often learn a lot about how well the writer understood the differences between the two prompts and the two kinds of texts they produced . . . . Perhaps with the two essay format we have been unconsciously attempting to create that 'self-contradiction' and tension that Rich [Haswell] discussed. Putting the student in a state of conflict and then witness the response? Is Perry's developmental model applicable, trying to locate the students who want situations reduced to neat right/wrong choices? (Email January 14, 1997)

The idea, then, is to ask the student to make a judgment that is clearly delineated, a judgment that is assumed to be the work of a writer, and that may identify students who are still dualistic, a sign of where their work together might begin.

A second difference: students are asked to identify passages, not whole texts. Now that may seem like an obvious thing to do in a reflective text that is to include some discussion of revision, but given the novelty of this kind of discourse, it's not clear that anything about it is obvious. So the specificity of the direction here recommends itself.

A third difference: students are asked sets of questions, almost like a heuristic. In other words, the questions themselves aren't disconnected, almost/seemingly random, but sequenced, from narrow to larger, from description to comparison to larger, more abstract comparison:

How would you describe your two compositions?

How do they compare with each other?

How do they compare with the writing you have done in school or on your own?

The intent here, as Marrs explains, is to invite the students to look for discontinuities, for gaps, in their own texts, in their own practices.

Reflective prompts can invite students to compare the present text with the text they would like to have written if they had more time. A key term for me is 'gaps': can the student recognize breaks or inadequacies or fissures in the text—places where the writing is incomplete, unfinished. The reflection need not be eloquently written—at this stage I do not care about paragraphs or transitions or much beyond the sentence. I'm simply looking for evidence that the student knows that something is missing. (Email January 14, 1997)

In this explanation of intent, we have as well articulation of expectation, something operationalizing what we expect to see: a response sensitive to a *gap* or to *fissures, places where the writing is incomplete, unfinished.*

A fourth difference is that while the writers are asked to provide a self-portrait, that text is a separate response from the first, and as Marrs comments, this too is a deliberate choice:

A reflection can invite the writer to give a broad self-portrait as a writer (thus the second set of questions). One goal is to provide another point of reference for helping the reader find the writer. Someone commented earlier about our tendency, when faced with difficulties in evaluation, to try to 'image' the writer. According to my simplistic algebra, the more 'diverse' points of references, the more angles of perspective on the writer, the better chance of inferring who is behind the words. But again, I am wondering about the relevance of Rich's comment on self-contradiction: are we looking for contradictions or continuities between the analysis of specific text and the portrait of the self as writer?

We return again, then, to the *correspondences,* the *discontinuities,* the *gaps* that occur between and among different texts, between intent and execution, between writer composed and writer imagined. We move toward what it is that reflection does when it works.

We also see here within a single assessment exercise all three varieties of reflection: *reflection-in-action* on the composings of two texts (question one); *constructive reflection* on who the writer is (question two); presented in the form of *reflection-in-presentation.*

***

In this chapter, two tensions arise that I've addressed, but not fully. First, can (all) students really do this work? How does the notion of students' "native languages" fit here? And second, given the research I've cited, aren't we really replicating ourselves? I think the answers to both questions, in terms of place, lie within the realm of assessment; in terms of time, with the future.

I start with the most difficult question: can all students do this work? Not if we don't ask them. Not if we decide in advance that they cannot. I think: yes. But let's think (again) about how, first in the classroom. Start with native languages: to learn about native languages, we have to ask, and we have to listen. What are the students' native languages? How do they learn? What do they already know, and how is it changed by what we want them to learn? Students can tell us, but we do have to ask. Here, in this volume, we start to see some native languages in chapter eight, where students talk about their own literacies. We see some in the earlier chapters, where students talk about how and what they are learning—through *plot* and *imagery* and *ionic equations* and *variables* and *compromise* and *war* and *honor* and *identity.* The classroom, upon reflection, *is,* to coin a phrase, a *Bahktinian parlor.* But it only functions as parlor if we participate *as participant,* not as leader or expert. This means that we cannot immediately "translate" what we hear into our routine frames of reference. We have to try to create new frames of reference congruent with the native languages.

In terms of discourse, we have to become more pluralistic, have to move beyond the typical, beyond what I think of as the writing canon. In sum, we need to work with students to develop new forms of textual production—and then we must value those new forms, and that too will take new frames of reference. Ironically, while in the last 25 years we have moved away from *reading* only canonical texts composed by "authors," as Susan Miller calls them, most of us haven't changed our practices when it comes to assigning and valuing anything other than canonical classroom texts. The debate between Elbow (1995) and Bartholomae (1995), in this context, can be seen as merely a dispute about which canon will dominate. But if genre is a way of excluding—of *not* knowing—as well as of knowing, as Burke maintains, then it behooves us to assign not only the multiple writings that compose the postmodern self, but multiple *kinds* of writings—everything from Winston Weathers's Grammar B to homepages for the web, everything from Wendy Bishop's creative non-fiction to Geoffrey Sirc's celebration of the Sex Pistols. As expressed by Derek Owens, such multiplicity provides the core of what we should be doing in writing:

> We cannot on the one hand invite the students and colleagues of a linguistic community to think differently about a given philosophy or idea if at the same time we confine them to preselected, inflexible discourses hostile to changing ways of making knowledge with language. It's not a pejorative relativism we need to acknowledge, the dismissal of all ideology based on the fact that none are superior or inferior to one another, but a constructive relativism, one tolerant of shifts, conflicting traditions, and opposing imaginations. (230-231)

What does this mean?

That we ask students to work within poetic and rhetoric and expand them both and bring them back together.

That we allow students to play with the texts produced and encoded by new technologies.

That we ask student to represent and express the multiplicity that they are, in text.

And that we value them. When we say that institutions don't value those texts, who are the institutions? (*Aren't we those institutions?*) Why don't they value these languages? And what might we learn from those languages? As to the construction (of writers) that assessment enacts, of course: that's the point that F. Allen Hanson makes in *Testing Testing*. Likewise, it's the rationale for much of the innovative in current assessment theory and practice: put simply, as Grant Wiggins suggests, since what we ask for is what we will get, we ought to ask for something worth having. And if indeed, as Francis Sullivan and others have suggested, we are only replicating ourselves, we ought to take a long hard look at what that means.

I don't think it's a given that we replicate ourselves, and indeed if reflection as discussed here is generative at all, we won't be: that in part is its promise.

***

In an assessment context, reflection-in-presentation can play a key role. Through the public representation of self, students learn for themselves in ways not otherwise possible: students are triangulated. From an assessment perspective, this increases the validity of the assessment. But there are key issues that govern the use of such reflection:

the ways we construct students in text, and the role that narra-tivizing should be allowed to play in this context

the questions we ask

the genres we permit

the placement of the reflection-in-presentation

the ways in which we read it, including sequence, and what effect that exerts on our evaluation

our expectations for it

In any assessment that includes reflection, then, these issues should be addressed first. As I suggested in the narrative about my own campus, in doing so we have a better sense of what we expect. We can use such an articulation as a frame for interpreting what our request produces, and for discerning places and ways to change our practice.

And it is also the case, I think, that if we want to know more about these issues, we might begin to take these questions to the objects of our study and assessment: our students.

Note

1.   For example, IUPUI, Morehead State, and Coe College all routinely ask now for some reflective text to accompany more conventional timed essays.

CHAPTER EIGHT

Literacy and the Curriculum

Why do you teachers always seek to foreground what we don't know?[1]

Anonymous Student

How teachers interpret the beings who populate their classrooms shapes what they let happen in those classrooms.

Judith Halden-Sullivan

HOW DO WE USE REFLECTION TO HELP US UNDERSTAND THE CURRICULUM that we think we offer to students? And what is that curriculum? The curriculum in English studies, we seem to agree, focuses on literacy: reading and writing and thinking, presenting all those in multiple kinds of text.

Literacy provides a lens through which we can consider how reflection and curriculum work together.

***

One year out of Virginia Tech, certified as a Language Arts and Social Studies teacher for grades 6-12 and 15 credits into an MA in English, I am working in a south central Pennsylvania factory that manufactures mobile homes. Yep, trailers. I'm a sales rep, wholesale, trying to persuade mobile home dealers who know considerably more than I about what we're calling boxcars that they should carry "my" product. It's unbelievable (and not funny, as it might sound here), especially to me who is living through it (for how long, I wonder). But there it is. With no training in the design or construction of such homes, no *bona fides* in the world of sales or marketing, and no experience living in such an abode, I am set loose with everything they think I need to succeed: a line of mobile homes to sell and deliver; a territory ranging from Maine to North Carolina; a phone;

and a factory to build them—a factory that will go silent if I don't persuade. This, I discover pretty quickly, is not *merely* a rhetorical problem.

It's a recession year, and plenty of days I don't make sales; neither do the other sales reps, all men. The factory: it's corpse-like quiet. The guys in the plant (and they are all guys; Betty Freidan hasn't made it to Chambersburg yet), the ones with Playboy calendars and quick smirks as I walk by, they go without a day's pay each time we shut down. The quiet—when there's no hammering, no shouting men at each other, no Loretta Lynn picking the guitar and belting out their lives—deepens as the hands on the clock rotate; by 5 o'clock, I can't run away fast enough.

I'm strangely quiet myself. Although I've done much of my growing up only two hours away in the suburbs of Washington, D. C, I'm beginning to understand that the mountains separating Chambersburg from DC may as well demarcate parallel universes. At the center of these universes are competing notions of a literacy that I have always understood as monologic.

In the world of the suburb, literacy—of the dominant discourse, mainstream variety—is both essential and unconscious. It is so much a part of who we are that we don't think about it; we simply use it, rely upon it, assume it for others. As a displaced teacher still looking for a classroom, I want to help students acquire what I take for granted: the skills and knowledge of a literacy that I associate with salvation of all kinds, economic, certainly, but more—cultural, social, spiritual.

But, now, in this factory where I have more education than any of the other 40-some employees, I'm discovering a world that I'm not prepared for: a world where people do fine without high school diplomas; where the logic and language of an assembly line are more salient than the logic and language of written prose; where successfully hunted deer are measured in something called points; where even when sales *are* made and orders for trailers are there to be filled, men *don't show up*—it's the first day of hunting season, they say: something more important to do. Whatever counts as literacy here—and it's a lot, from a kind of seasonal rhythm they find constructive but that I don't recognize to the knowledge required to hunt a deer, then turn it into something we'd want to eat, to the history of this place and its people—it's not my suburban textbook literacy. I'm not sure anymore that I do have a literacy to teach—in this context, anyway.

Literacy itself, as I'm astonished to discover, is highly contextual.

***

Current researchers and theorists, from Patricia Bizzell to Cheryl Geisler to Cynthia Selfe, take literacy as what it is that we teach in our writing classes. It's writing writ large: reading and writing, synthesizing and critiquing, arguing and essaying, emailing and hypertexting. But "what we teach" is a slippery phrase indeed. As I have argued elsewhere, while we want our students to interrogate their assumptions and understandings, I don't think we do a very good job of articulating and interrogating our own assumptions about teaching, particularly about the teaching of literacy.

Partly, this mis/understanding of what we do is a function of the paradigm that still governs our teaching. In that paradigm, we're caught in a vise. On the one hand, we understand ourselves as teachers who are responsible for bringing together our expertise and an agenda for the benefit of students. And on the other hand, many of us try to make that agenda what we call student-centered, but it's student-centered in a narrow rather than wide sense. The activities *seem* to call for active learning, but the learning is still focused on the agenda we bring to the class. It's methodologically active, materially static. The agenda, of course, varies: one current model centers on a critical literacy through which we want to foster resistance in students to the culture at large (e.g., Berlin); another aims to help students develop a personal voice (e.g., Elbow). Regardless of the model, however, we maintain this paradox: we want students actively engaged in the curriculum we bring to them, but we want this curriculum to stay within the parameters we have set; we want it to be the one we design and deliver. This, then, is what we usually mean when we say curriculum: what we bring to students and yet that which it is we want them to animate.

At the same time, we have a disquieting awareness that what the students experience in any course may be different from what we intend: even as they sit in a classroom, students may not be receiving the curriculum we think we deliver. Rather, they may be engaging in quite another curriculum, what some call a *de facto* curriculum, what I call an experienced curriculum. This is the second curriculum: the class or course that students receive. It's analogous to the experience of attending a professional conference: there is the announced theme, which, like the delivered curriculum, governs the kind of sessions offered and the keynotes; and then there is the experienced conference—what a participant actually encounters as she or he attends and engages it. Sometimes, of course, the experienced conference matches the announced conference, but more often, there is some slippage, and sometimes there seems to be no commonality between the conferences.

In the classroom, we likewise have the announced—the *delivered*—that corresponds, or not, to the *experienced* or received. In each curriculum, students will learn, as Frank Smith points out. What it is that students do learn: that's the second curriculum, the experienced curriculum. Thus, when we think that classes have gone well, what we seem to be saying is that we think we have managed, perhaps serendipitously, a *good fit between the delivered curriculum and the experienced curriculum:* they've become co-identical. More often, there is some tension between the two curricula, which is to be expected, given the diverse quality of our students, and which can be a good thing. It is at the point of such tension, after all, that one sees the delivered in terms of experienced and thus seeks to interpret the one in terms of the other. Such work can produce the most valuable insights of a course.[2]

Finally, there is a third curriculum: the lived curriculum that students bring with them to any course. This provides the context through which the course will be understood, experienced, received, interpreted. Not surprisingly, then, it has everything to do with the tension between delivered and experienced curricula; it provides yet another source of tension. Jennie Nelson works toward this idea in her study of the understanding of school writing that students bring with them to the writing classroom. She puts it this way:

> Specifically, I argue that . . . an image of our students as uninitiated outsiders fails to recognize that students are already long-standing members of the culture of school and are highly literate about how classrooms work. This image fails to account for the powerful legacy of school experiences that students bring with them every time they step into the classroom and undertake a writing assignment. (411)

Nelson's point is true enough: what we reward in school, as she demonstrates, is as often as not absent in official documents. The fact that a professor asks for personal voice, for instance, sometimes masks a more genuine expectation for voiceless academic writing, as the subjects of Nelson's study discover. I'd like to enlarge this notion of what students bring with them to each class, however, since more than their knowledge of school literacy is involved; it's also their cumulative knowledge about literacy in the culture at large. This knowledge is the third curriculum: the *lived curriculum*. In a purely academic, technical sense, of course, it's not a curriculum at all. It's not a specific unit designed for a specific audience, delivered by a particular agent, and certified by the state: as curriculum. But as a phenomenon, the lived curriculum is the embodiment of all that a student has experienced, both in school and out, as a literate human being. As such, my use of the term curriculum here is not unlike Anne Gere's sense in her work on the "extracurriculum." She, of course, examines the non-school curriculum that takes place at kitchen tables and in rented rooms; my use here incorporates these non-academic contexts as well as the cumulative effect of the more formal curriculum we find in school.

What this curriculum is, particularly as it relates to literacy—how students have understood the very idea of literacy, how they conceive of themselves as literate human beings, what kinds of literacies they understand themselves to have some expertise in, and how they function in different contexts—is central to our understanding of our own students and thus of our classes, for three reasons. In the first place, the fact that students have an experienced curriculum reminds us that they are not, as we so frequently assume, tabulae rasae—merely blank slates waiting for us to help them "invent" the university. Second, since they bring with them what they identify as their own literate practices, it behooves us to investigate what those are and how they might be used to enrich our classrooms. As Bizzell argues, a constructivist notion of literacy is necessarily dynamic: "Rhetoricians' own world views will be influenced to the extent that they assimilate the community's knowledge to their own discourse" (526). Without asking for such community knowledge, we operate in a vacuum. As important, and as Bizzell suggests, without including it, our own world views and our own literacies don't change, don't accommodate the new that continuously creates and re-creates a living literacy. And third, including students' literate practices in our curricula provides a place from which they can speak, an opportunity for them to exercise an authority that comes with and from knowledge worth having, a knowledge that is at the heart of literacy. Put simply, it allows us to *foreground that which they do know and to ask them share it with us.*

This lived curriculum, like the experienced, is problematic to the extent that it is invisible. As a kind of contextual curriculum, it allows and precludes in ways we don't fully understand or appreciate—unless of course we begin to ask about it. When we ask that it be articulated, we begin to understand how the *delivered* curriculum will be received; we begin to include the students and their knowledge in our agenda.

What follows is a story of such asking, of the reflection that accompanied it, and of the learning it produced.

* * *

The first day of class, I'm in a shiny new computer classroom in a new building, which isn't quite so fortuitous as it sounds. The department chair and the dean haven't decided yet which of them will supply paper to the printer, nor have they considered floppy disks. So we begin the course, "Writing and Rhetoric," in a windowless room, Gateway 2000s a-humming, applying pencil to paper.

The students—all 22 of them, not a one over the age of 19, though at least one of them is a parent—arrive, lots of them from North Carolina, but several from other states as well: New Jersey and Florida and Virginia. Ethnically, they are diverse, with lots of blacks and whites and browns; one student announces her Creole heritage as a distinguishing feature. Most are first-generation college students, although several tell stories of brothers and sisters in college. Dispositionally, they are cautiously eager, all except for the two high school football teammates from a mill town just north of Charlotte. I see them looking for the game; trying to scope it out so that they can make an end run around me as soon as possible.

The first homework assignment, due on the second day of class, asks the students to bring in an object that shows their literacy and to explain in a page—that's 250-300 words, I say—who they are as literate people. They should think metaphorically, I say: literacy could mean reading and writing; it might take an adjective, as in scientific literacy; it might not involve reading and writing at all. (*What will it involve for this group, I wonder.*)

The second day: they comply, all of them. Each entry is the specified length, though one of the students, a commuter from a small town southeast of Charlotte, barely makes it to the bottom of the wide-ruled page. All but two of them have specified items, from a class ring to a Winnie-the-Pooh to a car and a candle. (*In 1996, only one has mentioned a computer.*) Most of them talk about the objects in a context of use: the reading of a book, the writing of a letter, the function of a refrigerator to demonstrate skills and accomplishments. Over twenty-five percent mention the Bible and/or religious readings (*Allan Bloom would be pleased*). Several of them begin, school style, with a dictionary definition of literacy that—all too well—grounds their own definition.

This is one way of reading the entries: it tells me something about these students. *But I can read these entries in other ways:* I can read for various populations—according to traits that are given, such as gender; how do the young men in the class think of literacy? What are the patterns here? And likewise, for the young women: do they construct literacy uniformly? Or for in-state and out-of-state differences, or for commuters as compared to residential students. I could look up their grades, and see what readings are motivated by that categorization.

Or I could just read to see what they think literacy is: to try to *learn from them* what they have brought to this classroom with them, to think about how that may and/or may not intersect with what I have planned. To do this, I read:

first, entry by entry, looking for patterns;

second, connecting those patterns with theory about literacy and reading and writing and processes;

third, across the entries and seeing what, if any, generalizations I can make about this group. How do they define literacy? Do they understand it to have played any particular role in their lives? Do they see it ideologically? and

fourth, how can I use what I understand about them in a curricular way?

As it turns out, these students understand what it is that I think is most important about literacy: that literacy is connected to our meaning-making. You'll see.

***

I focus on eight selections, eight rationales for those selections and what they tell me about my students' understandings of literacy and of themselves as literate human beings. I begin to understand the multiple contexts they bring with them to the shiny computer classroom and to the curriculum that I've planned for them.

Ann's is the first I read, the first that I'll try to pattern in some way. Hers is a rationale to warrant all the claims we like to make about the value of English studies. She suggests that she reads often and for different purposes, that she has a passel of books (*not articles, not short stories, but books*) awaiting her, and that she likes to read.

> Speaking of religion, my latest book is about vampires and priests. I have about twelve more waiting for me to read. I love to try to figure out how people imagine or live through certain situations. It is one of my favorite pastimes.
>
> One of my other favorite pastimes is, of course, food. I have several allergies and have to read labels and check ingredients on lots of foods. So even the gum I am chewing is a good example. It needs to be sugar free and peppermint, my favorite flavor.

It's true, of course, that these books probably don't appear on any of E. D. Hirsch's lists. And it's true that having 12 left to read doesn't say as much as one hopes about how many may actually have been completed; it only suggests. Still, isn't this a sign of literacy, of understanding what the average English teacher wants to hear? Besides, there is another way to frame this: Like any good eighteenth century essayist's, Ann's literacy both delights and instructs. It brings her pleasure as well as knowledge, as she uses it for a pastime and to read labels. In other words, for Ann, *literacy is a multiple construct.*

Kathy's chosen object is her high school class ring, and she writes of completing high school in the way someone a century ago might have: of the effort involved, the hard work. To her, it's an accomplishment. I'm surprised: for a minute, I'm back in the factory selling trailers.

> My class ring is probably my most prized possession. It signifies many things to me, but most important it signifies how hard I worked to get to this point in my life, which is graduated and in college. . . .
>
> I'm sure that when I have a daughter of my own she'll wear my class ring like I wore my mothers and she'll do her best to have one of her own. Now I can't wait until I get my college ring because it will mean as much or more to me than my high school ring does now.

I'm both impressed and disconcerted by what I read here. On the one hand, Kathy chooses a symbol, and that move to abstraction seems promising. And Kathy has linked this school accomplishment with the personal and the continuous, with her wearing her mother's high school ring, with her earning her own high school ring and now college ring, and then with her daughter carrying on what Kathy seems to be formulating as a family tradition of literacy. But, on the other hand, where is literacy? I see the symbol that apparently represents literacy, but I don't see the signs of literacy itself—texts of any variety, for instance, or processes. What I do see, in Berlin's terms, is a kind of naive faith in individual effort as the sole causal agent of progress. Perhaps what I see, too, is a need to locate literacy more specifically—in terms of Kathy's practices—and more contextually—in terms of the relationship between the individual and the cultural.

Faith begins her rationale with a school literacy concept that contradicts the current constructivist notion of meaning-making: the idea that literacy is indeed the "the ability to extract underlying meanings." (*Alas, the dental model of literacy, I lament.*) But the object she chooses to embody her literacy is something we wouldn't extract. It's human.

> My parents are an exhibit that prove my literacy very well. Through their actions, moods and tones of voice, I am able to conclude how they feel and what they are thinking. . . . my parents' body language and overall manners allow me to read them like a book.

I don't know if the pun is intended or not, but I like the comparison between Faith's reading her parents and her reading a book; I like the suggested movement back and forth between media, and the fact that one of the media is absolutely human. I am interested in how Faith understands and then interprets the ways her parents behave, and how we might use this understanding to talk about how behavior is represented in other media, including written text. In sum, I like the leap here, I like the confidence with which she seems to express it, and I like the possibilities that this rationale presents to us.

Michelle talks about her literacy in terms of an object that, at first glance, doesn't seem to connect: a bicycle.

> My bicycle is an exhibit that shows me as a literate person. First of all, I know how to use it; I then know how to fix it if it were to break down, and finally, I feel that I am able to teach someone else how to adequately use and fix my bicycle.

As I read over the rationale and Michelle explains how she uses the bicycle, I begin to see it through the lens of literacy. It is, after all, something that she uses. She knows how to fix it when it breaks, so she has a kind of knowledge, and she can apply it. And since she can teach someone else, there is a way to share what she knows: it's social. Yes, I think, the bicycle seems like a surprisingly good choice.

As important, I think I see some larger patterns emerging, patterns based on what is absent as much as what is present, patterns I don't expect. So far no one is talking about literacy connected to school: interesting? So far no one is talking about literacy connected to a job: interesting? What the students are talking about is how literacy involves knowledge, processes, pleasure, people. When it comes to literacy, these students seem (surprisingly) literate.

The next two rationales I read together. The first, composed by Janice, compares herself to a television.

> Each channel represents a different side of me. [She indicates different sides by way of different channels: news, religious, cartoon, music video.] A television is the most appropriate exhibit to show me as a literate person. Just like me, a television shelters all kinds of information, whether it be useful or useless.

The second, written by Kelly, brings together reading and television in the form of *The Mystery Science Theatre 3000 Colossal Episode Guide.*

> I feel that I have clearly illustrated why I have chosen the MST3K book as my exhibit to show my apparent literacy. The book is a form of printed media which I use to enhance my perception of visual media. I read it and comprehend its contents. I make practical use of the book and its contents. I find that at times it enables me to carry on more intelligent conversations with other "Mysties". Perhaps the most important characteristic of this exhibit is that it makes being a literate individual enjoyable. In one sentence, It makes reading fun.

Several observations interest me here. These students don't see television and literacy as either/or options: they see them operating together. Janice sees herself in a fairly postmodern way—as a self with different sides to her—and she understands that not all information is valuable. She reads herself into the television the way students used to read themselves into books, and she does so in a way that, as she links channels and selves, seems insightful. Kelly calls into question the very notion of literacy as it is currently understood when she talks of her own literacy as "apparent," but at the same time she makes a cross-media argument: that one literacy can be used in support of another, which results in more intelligent conversations. Like Ann before her, she finds it leads to enjoyment. And again, literacy is a multiple construct, particularly as it acts here as the *interface and interaction among media*.

In the penultimate rationale, Diane packages old style literacy in a new package, one that picks up themes we have heard already.

> The thing that exhibits my status as a literate person is my pink pen with praying hands. This pen shows my reading skills in that I personally had to read the bible and other religious material in order to grasp the concept of the praying hands. And because my religious views are so strong, I do a lot of biblical reading. The complexity of religious text helps my ease and comfort with reading. I also write with the pen, and therefore I must read my own writing in order to revise and edit.
>
> I understand that my pen is a pen. I understand that it has colors, pink and gold. I understand that it is a tool used for writing, and drawing, and many other things. I also know that my pen can be used to show the world what I see in my mind. The fact that I understand this object concretely and abstractly plainly shows the extent of my literacy.

Like Kathy, Diane reminds me of literacy past, in this case because of her use of the Bible: its complexity, she says, helps her learn to read. But this literacy is written as well as read, and it's packaged in a pink pen with praying hands—the pen that symbolizes as does Kathy's ring, but that also is used—to revise and edit. As important, Diane contextualizes what this pen signifies: she tells us what she understands, in ever-increasing ways, from the concrete object to its functionality to its link between her and the world. Literacy, for Diane as for Faith, is social, and the pen provides her an intersection for both concrete and abstract.

Finally, Josey writes of her certification as an EMT. Like her father, Josey is a volunteer firefighter, and her commitment to this avocation is shown by her willingness to learn more than the job actually requires. She undertakes this learning for reasons that she has articulated very well for herself, reasons that are highly ideological.

> Literacy is more than just having some fancy piece of sheepskin. It is more than being able to read Shakespeare. Literate people should be able to use what they have learned to benefit others.

***

If reflection is about learning, then I should have learned something here. To do that, I've started by inviting my students to foreground what they know and by reading those excerpts *to see what I can learn from them*, a reading for inquiry. For purposes of this exercise, I've then 1) chosen the exhibits that I've excerpted here, 2) shared them in a particular sequence for particular purposes, and 3) interpreted them all along. This reflection, we should note, is mine; if we had asked the students to join this chapter, we might have read another version of their literacy altogether.

The literacy I observe through these processes is both old and new, and highly situated, and I suppose that's what interests me. Here in North Carolina, these students do read the Bible, and it may be that their reading practices are more fluent, more comprehensive, more sophisticated because of it. Simply, they may read better because they read the Bible. Historically, the desire to read the word of God has moved citizens in this country to learn to read, of course. I'm just surprised that this motivation still operates—but I suspect that this observation says as much about my religious practices as it does about the students' reading habits. (It also reminds me how much I have still to learn about the people with whom I live.) Such familiarity with the Bible might also suggest that these students understand something about registers, depending on which version of the Bible they've been reading. It may be that they understand something about parable and image and interpretation. These are possibilities I now know that I need to consider with them and that we might use in class, ideas I have gathered from this assignment and my reading of it. My understanding of the *lived curriculum*, in other words, can now influence the curriculum I hope to *deliver*.

At the same time, the literacy of these students is unlike my mother's literacy, a point most of us don't quite yet fully appreciate. Our students' experiences with literacy are quite different from ours. Our literacy tends to be print-based, by history or preference; theirs video-based, certainly by history, often by preference. Does it matter? I think so. It means, for one thing, that our students' literacy is, from the get-go, cross-media in nature, the media building on and overlapping each other in patterns students understand as cohesive. It's also holistic, entailing both process and product. Several of them see literacy as vehicle for concrete thinking as well as for abstractions. It's linked to enjoyment rather than to school success or a job. And for some, literacy has ideological implications.

Overall, I think we may be in the middle of a major change. If we include electronic communication within our definition of literacy, as surely we must, we are clearly in the middle of change, whether you read it positively, as Tapscott does in *Growing Up Digital*—who says, "*These kids are going to have a much more open, interactive, collaborative, verbal, thoughtful environment, and that will change the way they will be as adults*" (qtd in Malinowski 45)—or read it negatively, as does Sven Birkerts in *The Gutenberg Elegies*, and, more recently, in the pages of *Teaching English in the Two-Year College*—who counters, "*These media—print and electronic—are different at the core. They derive from opposing premises. And one cannot, except by performing the most exhausting internal oscilliations, serve both*" (238).

Is this change paradigmatic? I'm not sure, and I don't think this one chapter will make that case. What I do know: the students who have shared with me their understandings of literacy are much more sophisticated about literacy than I'd expected, open to thinking about themselves as literate human beings in interesting ways. They don't seem to need to be persuaded of literacy's value, as I had expected. They need to do all the things that will enhance the literacy they bring with them to the classroom, including problematizing it.

There's a mixing of media involved here that explodes Selfe's "layered literacy" into multi-layered literacies; my students seem almost naturally to navigate among various kinds. *These students are redefining literacy, even as we don't watch them.*

And finally, if this assignment "worked," it's interesting to note what happened here. We can start with what I did *not* do: I did not say, please write a piece of reflective writing. What I did do: *I assumed that these students were literate, that they knew about their own literacies in ways I couldn't possibly, and I asked them to speak to that experience.* I asked them to conceive of that experience capaciously. I asked them, implicitly, to trust that I would respect their sharing. For their part, to accomplish the task I set, they had to *exercise reflection*: to think about what literacy means to them; to consider this in light of their own experiences; if possible, to consider literacy in multiple frames and theorize about it; to problematize it and perhaps call it into question; to make a judgment: to articulate all this for an other; to tell that other what literacy means to them.

What I also learned is that many of these students are already reflective; we have much to build on.

***

I'm using reflection here as a means of understanding how we might operate without replicating ourselves, and that is by 1) learning about and 2) incorporating the insights of those in our classrooms. What I like about this set of student reflections, among other things, is that it illustrates what I'm calling the *experienced curriculum*—which of course we see in various ways in reflection-in-action, in constructive reflection, and in reflection-in-presentation. (In fact, the exercise in literacy that I read is a good example of constructive reflection.) Who the students are is important for yet another reason: to show how this relates to pedagogy. As chapter one defines student-centered learning, a pedagogy meets that definition only to the extent that the real students in our real classes find a real place there. This chapter is one means of showing how to begin to do that: to learn about who our students are and how they do or do not see themselves as literate. Given the current velocity of technological change—which is transforming not only the delivery but also the nature of our courses and our literacies—this seems like a necessary starting place.

***

In theory, I know more about literacy than I did when I sold boxcars. I understand that literacy is contextual, that even as an English teacher (or perhaps *especially* as an English teacher), I cannot and do not "own" literacy, that we have many varieties of literacy, some of which I will never be expert in. In theory, however, I can both teach others about literacy—at least about some versions of literacy—and help them to become more literate in those practices and in their understandings of them. But it's important to take the *theory to practice and back*: to learn from other literate human beings about their literacies—in this case, about what literacy is to my students, about how they define it, about what it represents to them. To the extent that I do this, that I read my students reflectively and build in and on their lived curricula, I avoid what Bizzell calls the "'foundationalism' of humanist literacy work and of cultural literacy work such as Hirsch's" (525).

But I'm not sure that I've answered the question that selling boxcars raised for me: what is the role of literacy in the lives of people?

Of course, to the extent that literacy is pluralistic—and it is always pluralistic, I think—I could not have answered this question by myself. I could only have asked and learned, incorporating it into my own answer, using it to advance teaching and learning.

To understand that there is a lived curriculum, to learn what it is for a specific learner or group of learners, to have it articulated, to build upon it: we have to ask those whose literate practices are informed by it.

Reflection is one means to achieve that end.

Notes

1. This student's perception was presented anonymously in personal communication with Laura Julier and Paula Gillespie: October 10, 1996.
2. For an example of this work, see my "Teacher Portfolios: Lessons in Resistance, Readiness, and Reflection" in *Situating Portfolios*, and chapter six here.

CHAPTER NINE

Reflective Texts, Reflective Writers

Only connect.

E. M. Forster

What coherent whole can I make of snow on a beach?

Richard Rosenblatt

MY FRIEND CHARLES SCHUSTER ASKED ME ONCE, WHEN I BEGAN TO talk about reflection, "Are we looking for the reflection in the writing," he asked, "or reflection apart from the writing?"

"*Bothand*," I replied.

Bothand is the correct answer, I still think, but here I'll take the opportunity to elaborate more fully. Such elaboration teaches something else we need to know about reflection. After that, I'll over/view the larger argument about reflection, issue some cautions, and articulate some questions.

The conclusion of this text, of course, provides its own points of departure.

***

What does a reflective text look like? What about it makes it reflective? Tough questions, these are, and I'm not sure that I have the answers to them. I certainly don't have a definitive reply. But during the last several years as I've pursued reflection into every nook and cranny, I've found myself *noticing* reflective texts. My students', of course, but as we do with anything we become newly aware of and captivated by, I've also been seeing reflective texts in all kinds of reading materials, from Sherwin Nuland's *How We Die: Reflections on Life's Final Chapter*, to John Krakauer's *Into the Wild* and *Into Thin Air*, to shorter texts, also in the mainstream media, in magazines like

TIME and *Harper's*, and even sometimes in my local paper, *The Charlotte Observer*.

I first became aware of reflective texts in the mainstream media as a function of looking for them but failing: finding texts that, in spite of their good writing, didn't suffice as reflective texts. Thus, early on, I *located reflection by its absence*: in a text in the July 1995 issue of *Harper's* written by G. J. Meyer, "Dancing with Headhunters: Scenes from the Downsized Life." Meyer has lost his job (in this case as a public relations/communications executive), he has a year's severance pay to find another job, and the pickings, he finds, are thin indeed. He is unemployed for over a year. The experience prompts a vivid and smart narrative of the experience as well as a good deal of reflection: about how he grew up, went to school, and found himself earning annually a tidy six-figure sum. The problem with the text is that this reflection wasn't very reflective at all: though Meyer writes well, what he doesn't do is every bit as remarkable. He doesn't position himself except within the rather small community of executives. He doesn't see that perhaps getting paid a six-figure sum for hawking seed corn or farm implements is unreasonable, and *that's* why his former employer doesn't need him anymore. He doesn't make the connection between his situation and that of an unskilled laborer who has also lost his job permanently—in spite of his having been very good at it. He doesn't "get" the larger economic picture: the capitalistic system that rewards and punishes arbitrarily. Ultimately and most personally, he doesn't see how to rewrite this story—*his own story*—that has gone so awry.

The problem, then, is that Meyer cannot invent a new story. All he's able to do is cling to the old story, to his narrative of progress rudely derailed. He cannot get outside himself to see the contradictions, the associations, the incongruities that inhabit the new story he is living but that he still doesn't quite grasp. Indeed, as well-written as they may be, these *reflections* are little more than the reverberations of victimhood. It would be interesting, informative, and instructive to know, for example, what Meyer would make of his story for other readers–say, those of *Mother Jones* or the *Village Voice*. But neither story-making nor reflection is in evidence. In sum, Meyer's writing may be "good" in the conventional sense of the word: it is clear, its images are evocative, it's got a point of view that is consistently developed. On the other hand, that's part of its problem, for me: *it's got a single point of view, it's got a single story, and it's got a single voice.* The author seems unable to generate multiple versions of his own (life) text. So: multiplicity and community as keys to reflection, to whatever it is that I value in reflection, in reflective texts. I had made a start.

As I said in chapter four, however, it's only minimally instructive to locate what you value by its absence. Better to locate it by means of presence. I also thought that identifying reflective texts would prove useful in multiple ways: to make reflection *visible* and valuable—ie, *something to be valued*; to illustrate what I meant by reflection–by pointing to a wide range of texts, and I thought I would learn more about reflection in the process myself. I found the first in the spring of 1996, a short text authored for *TIME* by David Gelertner, one of the Unabomber's victims, on the occasion of Theodore Kaczynsky's arrest: "A Victim Reflects on the Evil Coward." In this text, a prelude to a book on the subject that Gelertner has just published, the computer scientist talks about how he makes sense of the experience of being the Unabomber's victim. As a computer wizard with symbolic import as victim, Gelertner says he is "unworthy . . . [in part] because I had written pieces that many colleagues regarded as traitorous" (44). His victimhood doesn't make sense. Still, *he can make his own sense of the event*, which he does by reference to E. B. White's essay "What Do Our Hearts Treasure?"

> The bright side, so to speak, of grave injury, discomfort, and nearness to death is that you emerge with a clear fix on what the heart treasures. Mostly I didn't learn anything new but had the satisfaction of having my hunches confirmed. I emerged knowing that, as I had always suspected, the time I spend with my wife and boys is all that matters in the end. I emerged as a practicing Jew. (Admittedly, I had always been one.) (45)

His response to the arrest?

> My response to this week's arrest is to congratulate the FBI on its fine work, thank once again the many people who helped us generously when we needed it, remember and honor the men who were bestially murdered and drink *l'chaim*—to the life of mind, to the human enterprise that no bomb can touch. (45)

Ultimately, if reflection is valuable, it's because—as reflection-in-action, as constructive reflection, as reflection-in-presentation, as reflective text—it enables us to *make sense*.

***

I want to look in some detail at two reflective texts: first, a text on breast cancer and healing written by a pathologist and published in a recent *Harper's*; and second, a student text, the narrative on her grandfather's death that Lara, the student we met in chapter three, wrote. In both of these texts, the authors *enact reflection*: conjoin our inside and outside lives, move to synthesize, reveal gaps, make some sense of the world, show us how it means. If we think reflection is important, we need, I think, to be able to point to texts that work *both* inside and outside of the academy, that suggest and echo and resonate in multiple worlds, that point us in directions we think are worthy.

These texts do all that.

***

In "A Woman with Breast Cancer: The Will to Live, as Seen Under a Microscope," Spencer Nadler, a surgical pathologist, tells the story of meeting a thirty-five-year-old woman who confronts breast cancer. Into this story, he weaves multiple narratives.

The first and in some ways the least important narrative is the story of the author himself, as pathologist: what a pathologist is, the attitude, the work, the demeanor belonging to pathology. (*We are indeed defined by our work.*) Another way to think about the opening of the text is through the idea of context. Like the reflective writers we've seen before, Nadler opens by providing context:

> Preoccupied with cancer cells, I have no social or psychological sense of a cancer patient. I retrieve this woman's biopsy slides from the file and review them in my office. I fix on elements of function, not form: milk-producing lobules, milk-transporting ducts, nipples, fat, connective tissue. I fix on cancer. After her surgery, my responsibility will be to classify the cancer, grade its aggressiveness, and determine the extent of its local spread. I will cull the facts that are pertinent to any use of radiation or chemotherapy, will help the physicians mount their therapeutic blows. (71)

It's a clean business, pathology, much cleaner than I'd imagined, and neater, too, orderly, focused on *biopsy slides*, on *elements of function, not form*. I can sense Nadler's satisfaction in making objective the *elements* of breast cancer—what my mother-in-law calls "the dread disease," the one that killed my maternal aunt, the one that has marked my mother, the one I don't particularly want to know myself.

And Nadler understands this, in an appropriately complex way: the value of being *detached*, the role he plays as Everyman, the price that this exacts:

> By confining myself to cells, I stay clear of the fiery trials of illness. I remain detached; I render my diagnosis with a cool eye. My fascination with the microscopic form, color, and disposition of cells drives me like a critic to interpret, to applaud or decry for the rest of us. Paradoxically, observing so much of life through a microscope has left me feeling that I've sampled too little, that I've missed the very warp and woof of it. (71)

Observing life through the microscope, Nadler tells us, with an almost Jamesian sensibility, is a life-excluding enterprise.

***

A second narrative Nadler weaves is that of the patient he calls Hanna, the woman he comes to know at first only routinely: by means of the slides; but then, very conventionally, in person. They meet three times: first, when she wants to see the slides of the cancer; second, when she has other tumors she wants to see; third, when she wants her son, an aspiring doctor, to meet the pathologist.

But as is characteristic in Nadler's world, he first meets the patient Hanna before these personal encounters: he first meets her *by means of the slides*. Hanna's not simply represented by the tumor, though: *she is the tumor*. As tumor, she is mundane, unremarkable, drawing enough attention to be *classified*, then to be put away.

> I classify this tumor as an infiltrating, modestly differentiated carcinoma arising from breast ducts.
>
> I have completed my evaluation of Hanna Baylan. I await two more breast biopsies, a lung biopsy, and three skin biopsies. All are suspected of being malignant. Hanna Baylan will fast become a memory, a name of yesterday's surgery schedule with a tumor attached. (71)

Typically, this classification and storage would have *been* the encounter. But Hanna is unusual: she becomes more and other than the tumor when she, suddenly, *appears* at Nadler's door. She wants to take up Nadler's vision: she too wants to see herself as tumor. She requests to see herself as biopsied slide. Surprised, Nadler complies, approaching the task methodically, first showing her healthy tissue:

> She listens quietly as I move the pointer across the microscopic land-scape. "These clustered islands of glands are lobules," I tell her. "Milk is produced here in the lactating breast."
>
> "They look like pink hydrangeas to me," she says, "a sprawling garden of them." She talks excitedly, asserting interpretive authority over her own cells. I can only imagine the variety of forms a cellular array such as this might suggest to the uninitiated eye. (71)

From the outset, Hanna understands that she may exert *interpretive authority*, that the cancer has made moot distinctions born of (mere) expertise. Nadler see things a little differently: Hanna's description of the healthy cells as *sprawling* life, he sees as merely *uninitiated*. Hanna is there, he seems to think, to be *initiated*. Which she is, soon enough:

> She stares into the microscope, transfixed by the disarray of her own malignant growth, a raw view of her life spread out before her. "It looks like distorted Hula Hoops twirling frantically," she says. "It's all damaged, isn't it? Just like my real world."
>
> "This is your real world, too," I say.
>
> She looks at me over the top of the microscope. "People don't shun me because my tumor ducts look like reckless Hula Hoops." (72)

Here, metaphor translates: the *damaged* cells aren't flowers, but *frantic Hula Hoops*. Here, real worlds both intersect and collide—the real world of the pathologist, the real world of the person. At the same time, they tell the same story, but it is plural and *differentiated*: a story of *damage* that plays out in the same life-altering yet divergent ways. Multiple real worlds coming together in Hanna, the one explaining and making sense of the other in some incomplete, not altogether coherent way.

Hanna returns later, six years later, numerous protocols of chemotherapy later, four more tumors later, "to see my cancer cells again," to "confront them one at a time, get a handle on their persistence." She is, Nadler says, "tired of all the pretty pictures, the metaphors. She's ready to deal with her cancer in a more direct way. I tell her that our dysfunctional and superfluous cells normally self-destruct in a programmed cellular suicide" (73). But he also has been *initiated*. He begins to use the metaphors that she is moving to give up: "I project one of her biopsy slides onto the screen, magnifying her cancer cells to the size of golf balls. They glare at us like cyclopean monsters—granular, pink bodies clinging to one another, each nuclear blue eye reflecting its own confusion" (73). Without intending to, Hanna has instructed the pathologist, just as he has instructed her. Multiple worlds, multiple ways of seeing.

Hanna returns for a third, quick visit, her last. She has brought her adolescent son, an aspiring doctor, the "flesh of Hanna's successful life" (75), to meet the pathologist who has helped her understand the Hanna on the slide. And, we sense, she has come to say goodbye.

She is leaving for Maine, to see the "leaves," "the fall."

***

A third narrative concerns what Hanna teaches Nadler about disease and healing. He knows much about the technical dimensions of disease, needs to learn much about the relationship between and among disease and healing and the human, about the relationship between the person and the disease. He learns not through any course of study, but from Hanna.

One of first things the pathologist learns is the need to personalize one's disease, to make it one's own, to give that disease *its own identity*. And Hanna does: through metaphor.

> She touches the screen, runs her fingers over the cancer cells as though she were gathering their random spread into some kind of order. The loveliness of cells on slides, all of the different shapes and colors, allows Hanna to give her breast cancer its own identity.
>
> "They're like moons," she says, "each with a different face, a different complement of light and dark."
>
> I turn off the auditorium lights. Her hands spread a silhouette that shadows her moons like eclipses.
>
> "I'd like to spend time here," she says. "Touch them, get to know them."
>
> "No rush." (74)

Another way to understand Nadler's narrative is to frame it in terms of knowledge and understanding. Knowledge and understanding, we know, aren't the same, and we see that here quite clearly: the knowledge that Nadler brought to this story; the understanding that he is acquiring, born of relationships and a human being and synthesis and even *disarray*. In fact, I think that's what Nadler wants us to see: *the knowledge that drew Hanna to him; the understanding that draws him to her.*

And not least important, he begins to understand the power of imagination: "She studies the micrographs, keeps an inquisitive silence. I await the new metaphors she'll conceive to keep her cancer at bay. Our imagination is what saves us" (74).

As Scott Momaday says, *we are what we imagine.*

***

A fourth narrative Nadler weaves tells quite specifically about how Hanna transforms him. Hanna initiates a process of intimacy that alters the way the pathologist sees disease and death: their relationship frames both. He starts his reflection on this change by invoking yet another context, that provided by Greek mythology:

> Like Charon ferrying between the living and the dead, she glides back and forth between her threatened life and her dead, stained biopsy cells. She quickly grasps the cause and effect—critical cell changes have twisted her life. For years I have processed thousands of such cases, determined the manifold forms of disease. But I've never been an intimate part of anyone's illness, never felt the connection between cells and a larger self. (72)

The *cells* have been isolated, as has Nadler. Hanna as patient and person contextualizes the *cells*, calling the doctor to a new, human interpretation of disease, calling him finally to disengage from disengagement, calling him instead to engage, to become: an intimate part of her illness. Context, it turns out, entails connection, connectedness.

In working with and watching Hanna, Nadler also learns from her about how we learn, more particularly about how we learn through and with language, about how language itself has instructive value, how it can teach us: "There is little need for pedagogy; she is finding her own truths with metaphor" (72). Together, both metaphor and intimacy come together in Nadler's embrace: "Although I've never done this before, I put my arms around her and give her a long, firm hug. Her bones seem as ungraspable as hope" (74).

***

The fifth and final narrative that Nadler weaves into his story of Hanna responds to the question so characteristic of classroom reflection-in-presentation: more generally, now, *what have you learned?*

Spencer Nadler, pathologist, has learned many and various lessons; his writing suggests that he has learned them well, or perhaps better than well. He has learned them profoundly.

He has learned about Hanna, of course; he thinks of her quite differently now. He can "no longer think of her in terms of the dead, stained cells I see on her slides" (75). Using Hanna as exemplar, Nadler has begun to think about how we represent death, which he talks about through invoking the contexts of print, genre, and obituary:

> I have never understood the purpose of a newspaper obituary. As a published notice of death, it certainly works well enough. As a biography filled with concrete facts—achievements, mostly—it gives the life in question a one-sided loftiness devoid of the flaws and failures that make it whole. And where is the mention of the individual's spirit, effectiveness as a human being, courage in adversity? What about people who successfully battle illness for many years before succumbing? What are their achievements in this regard, or do they simply "die after a long illness"? (74)

The life devoid is not the life, Nadler suggests. In metaphorical terms, pathology is the *obit*, providing the demographic or medical profile, the *concrete facts*, but deleting the stuff of life, *the flaws, the failures, the courage, the spirit*. This deletion is a dear purchase: in representing the one so well, it excludes, almost erases the other: the stuff of life.

Nadler learns also about the role of diagnosis in the healing process; like a teacher learning from a student, the doctor learns about healing from the patient.

> I begin to see that the diagnosis of a disease plays little part in the healing process; nor, for that matter, does the treatment strategy. Help attuned to individual needs is what heals. Disease seems to be more than a set of facts, and illness more than a diminished way of life. They are a strange tandem that plays out differently in every host—despair, terror, agony, a call to arms, newfound clarity, transcendence, metamorphosis. Those afflicted must have their needs satisfied on *their* terms. *They* must control, as much as possible, the progress of their own adversity. I can feel Hanna yearn for answers. I must give them to her, show her the pictures that help her. (74-75)

The *progress of adversity*: the paradoxical nature of illness: a moving forward of backwardness. The *control* of these processes, Nadler says, should not lie in *diagnosis* and *treatment* managed by dispassionate doctors, but rather in help provided by compassionate doctors who work with and learn from.

That Nadler has learned—and what he has learned—is also suggested by his final line. He ends as he began, looking through a microscope, but what he sees now is filled with image, with metaphor, with Hanna. "I return to my microscope. In the spread of a squamous skin cancer, I strain to see the deciduous leaves of Maine, so fiery when fallen, then turning slowly to compost, to nurture blanketed seeds" (75).

***

When we write text, more particularly when we read text, and certainly when we teach text (even in a postmodern age), we search for unity, for themes that resonate throughout, for the structures that bring order and pattern to such themes, for the (appropriate) voices to speak to us. Asking for such order in our students' texts resonates itself with echoes of middle class values that we inscribe, with our need to tidy up within our students' texts, to assure that they stay within the boundaries we have demarcated, to make sure that they take care, that they not go too far. It may be that we are only replicating the construct of writing that was inscribed in us—that is, writing as act with intellectual, ideological, and, indeed, moral consequences linked to a unified construct—as Richard Rosenblatt observes:

> Students of my generation were taught that E. M. Forster's *Howard's End* is an important novel because its central dictum, "Only connect," is a prescription for moral life. It was assumed that making connections was a sign for the mind's worth and purpose. Only connect; things fall apart; these fragments I have shored against my ruins. Perhaps this effort to bridge and yoke was a consequence of the big bad Bomb, and of a world growing up under the persistent threat of disintegration. Perhaps it was simply an invention of the academy in which exam questions insisted on one's making sense of this as related to that. (80)

Fragments and disconnects inhabit our daily lives every bit as much as the connects. Sometimes we can reconnect the disconnects, thread the fragments. Sometimes we can't. But identifying them is every bit as important as forging connections, sometimes more valuable because unless and until they are acknowledged, we rely on a detached and clean though ultimately false and much less human sense of: *what is.*

Reflection attempts to describe what is. Textually, it includes within its weavings the threads of disconnects as well as of connects, the threads composing what Louise Phelps calls the tapestry of reflection.

***

The first assignment in my section of English 1101 is a narrative: I ask that students create and develop a rhetorical situation, complete with purpose, audience, and scenes they will focus on, as a way of helping them frame the task at hand, a way of asking them to do what Polyani says we must, articulate and outline our own good problems. Lara, the commuting 18-year-old student we've met before, decides to write about the death of her grandfather. A Southern church-going non-smoker, he has lung cancer, and he will die before his time.

Although Lara is a fine student (and an interesting young woman), I don't want to make her a different kind of inverted exemplary narrative: I don't want to claim that she is extraordinary. What I do want to claim is that what she made of her experience is quite extraordinary. It is commonplace to ask students to write narratives. It is (all too) commonplace for people we love to die of cancer. What Lara does with the one in the framework of the other is to weave a tapestry of several stories that go by the title "Grandfather's Last Days."

***

Story One is the portrait of the grandfather as he spends his last days, as seen through Lara's eyes.

> Grandfather's once 300 pound frame, miniaturized now to less than 200 pounds. His throat and esophagus, like pieces of raw meat, causes him intense pain when he eats and drinks. He depends wholly on the I.V. to give his body substance to prolong living. Working its way speedily up Grandfather's weakened legs is another complication, gangrene, a painful disease that comes about when the body does not receive enough circulation. I look at his hands, knowing I will not see the soft, strong hands that held my own as a child. Almost the same color of the hospital sheets, they look like a mass of useless bones lying limp at his sides. The only time he moves them is when he grips the sheets as the pain overwhelms his body.

In this portrait, Lara doesn't blink, and she doesn't want us to blink, either. When the body isn't hosting *gangrene*, it looks like a *mass of useless bones lying limp at his sides*. The *IV* is keeping her grandfather alive, but implied here is the question as to why—or as to what we mean when we say the word alive.

The life described here, embodied in Lara's grandfather, is a painful means of death.

∗∗∗

Story Two is the story of medicine's limits, of what it cannot do, plotted against what we expect of it, a story of critical disconnects, of bitter ironies. One scene that tells this tale is within the hospital where Lara's grandfather will die.

> I will never grow accustomed to the smell of hospitals. The stench of sickness and death is everywhere—slipping stealthily through the black and white tiled corridors, falling heavily from the fluorescent lights and cutting swiftly through the white cinder block walls. The smell makes me nauseous. I fight the urge to turn and run back to my car. At least there I would be safe from the oppressing sight, smell and feeling of death that cling to my thoughts as I walk toward his room. I reach his room, plaster a smile on my face and enter. I catch my breath as I glimpse Grandfather for the first time in two days. My smile falters, and I recover quickly. I gaze unbelieving at the transformation that has occurred. A man, once full of life, lies motionless on the stark, white sheets of the hospital bed, suffocated in the blankets because he is always cold. The shiny steel bars on the side of the hospital bed usually constricting his movements are down "to allow maximum comfort," as the nurse says. Maximum comfort? Even minimum comfort seems unlikely in this hellish place.

The *hospital* that was to provide a healing place, at least a caring place, is, Lara says, a *hellish place*, a place where *comfort* is an oxymoron, where the *stench of death* is so powerful that is *cuts through cinder block walls.* And as bad, the treatment intended to save, at least to alleviate, becomes the problem: "And if he opened his eyes, their brilliant blue would be dulled with suffering, and their gaze would be vacant. All this is a result of the chemotherapy that Grandfather had hoped would ease the effects of cancer. My God, how can modern science do this to a body?" *Modern science,* and more particularly modern medicine, does not live up to its promise. Quite the reverse: it has become a monster rivaling the cancerous monster that first drew the grandfather's attention.

The limits of medicine silently mock its assumed purpose.

∗∗∗

In the third story, Lara, like Spencer Nadler, and like the writers of classroom reflection-in-presentation, takes up the question, what have I learned? And like these other writers, Lara has learned about what Laura Kaplan calls the outer life and about the inner life, about knowledges and about understandings.

Lara has learned about the disease of cancer, about one form of treatment that does not treat, about what the word "complication" means in this context, about how to explain it in a personal context:

> Three months ago my family clung to the hope that chemotherapy would cure the monster growing in Grandfather's lungs. We knew there were side effects to the treatment, but we were not prepared for the sickness that tore at his body. And now, three months later, I still visit him in the same hospital bed. Now, the cancer is gone, the complication is pneumonia. He has had it twice already, and the doctors say they can do nothing for him.

Lara has also learned about herself, and like Hanna, she has learned about *finding her own truths with metaphor.*

> I look around the room, realizing guiltily that I am trying to find something that will take my mind off Grandfather. The bright flowers, the encouraging cards and the sunlight streaming in through the windows do the opposite of their intent—to raise our spirits. My wandering eyes rest on one lone plant. Among all of the other flowers and plants in the room, this plant is dying. Suddenly, I feel an almost insane compassion for this single plant. I feel like bursting into tears, but I know how ridiculous that is. It's only a plant. I realize I reminds me of Grandfather. They are both losing the battle for life. It seems so unfair that this once beautiful plant should now wilt and die while so many around it burst with life.

The *single plant,* the single grandfather, the single writer: all deserving *compassion* that makes Lara feel *insane.* Lara brings together the outer life—the progress of cancer—to her inner life—her reaction to her grandfather's loss, to her loss, using image and metaphor to understand it, to re-contextualize it, to control it.

Lara learns about funerals, about death, about how it distorts the lives, feelings, faces of those we love; about how we shrink from witnessing such grief:

> I sit in the third pew of the church between my mother and my father, trying to hold in the sobs that so desperately want to escape. It has been two days since my mother received the call that her father, my grandfather, was

dead. I have yet to let the tears flow freely. I don't want to cry; I don't want people to know I'm weak. I look at the casket with the American flag draped across it. Is he really in there? I don't like looking at the casket, so I look around at the people. They fill every pew in the church, and some are standing. Expressions of pain and sorrow distort so many familiar faces. I don't like looking at them either. The only safe place to look is at my feet, so I stare at them intently.

And finally, Lara has learned how to make a tentative connection, a tenuous resolution: "I am no longer angry at myself, the doctors or God."

***

Chris Anson, in summarizing the qualities of reflective writers, says:

> In contrast to relativists, then, reflective writers eventually find stability and resolution in the chaos of diversity, by analyzing alternatives in the content and structure of their writing. These conclusions must remain to some degree tentative, since the acknowledged relativism of the world allows for modification. But even in grappling with the most difficult moral and intellectual questions, reflective writers assume that some perspectives are more logical, sensible, and well-supported than others. This is writing we are familiar with as professionals—balanced, informed, reasoned. (338)

Lara is such a reflective writer. As we saw earlier (chapter three), she writes reflection: what I've called reflection-in-action, constructive reflection, reflection-in- presentation. In those processes, she has learned not only how to talk about writing in a reflective way, but also how to write reflective texts. Reflection in the writing; reflection apart from the writing.
Bothand.

***

As I've presented it here, reflection seems devoid of action, and I want to correct that impression. In the summer of 1994, Nancy DeJoy first suggested to me that she saw a real linkage between reflection and action, an idea echoed by one of the reviewers of a draft of this text:

> I wanted the author to acknowledge the ways in which other texts might be obviously "reflective." I was thinking, for instance, of Jim Berlin's posthumously published book, *Rhetorics, Poetics, and Cultures,* in which Berlin

shares some of his career-long reflections on his field and his own teaching. Such a book isn't reflective perhaps in the way the two texts in the chapter are, but isn't Berlin's text the result of similar kinds of reflection?

Of course. (And: *thank you.*) In the conclusion to that text, Berlin reflects upon a critique of his own work offered by a listener: "My error, he explained, was that I grossly overestimated the influence of the English department in the lives of our students and the workings of our society. English teachers, he insisted, are in the larger scheme of things just not all that important" (177). Berlin then goes on to explain that while we English teachers may be less important than he believed when he was younger, we still contribute mightily—and not always well—to the identity formation of students. Because we do, he says, we must "take seriously our duty as public intellectuals inside and outside the classroom" (180). Clearly, that work included this book as well as Berlin's others, the pedagogical work that accompanied them, and the activism that marked his life.

And, I think, if we look around at the work conducted by *many* of our colleagues, we will find likewise. I think here of Wendy Bishop's *Teaching Lives* and her reflection on her own pedagogical practices and poetics of knowing; of Victor Villanueva's reflections on language and identity and schooling and the peronal in *Bootstraps;* of Jonathan Kozol's many volumes where his voice infuses the object of critique; of bell hooks's work on what it means to be black and female in America. Although differently, all of these projects, like Berlin's, are reflectively activist. Reflection does not always produce activism—unless (and this, in my view, is unless writ large) we see understanding itself as a form of activism. But reflection is not at odds with a conventional view of activism: often it motivates such engagement.

Reflection connects to many kinds of work.

***

In this text, I've tried to do the same thing: talk about reflection, be reflective, be aware of how such reflection can change classroom practice—by bringing identity formation into the center of class, by assuming agency on the part of students, by seeing learning and texts as negotiated. I've focused on reflection that takes place on multiple occasions for multiple purposes in multiple forms: a reflection that occurs during writing and after, between and among drafts; that occurs cumulatively over time; that we shape for presentational purposes. Although this reflection assists in the writing (process) of a particular text, it also makes possible a more general, generative understanding of writing. Put differently, working within a single rhetorical situation provides the stuff that writers talk about, and *through that talk we become.* Over time, then, reflection provides the ground where the writer invents, repeatedly and recursively, a composing self. Concurrently, reflection contributes to the writing of texts that themselves are marked by a reflective tenor—multicontextual, thoughtful, holistic.

My interest in reflection did not spring from an interest in theory. It developed in the ground of practice: as I watched students work, as I began to appreciate how little I knew without asking, to learn from my students when I did ask, to understand ever-so-gradually that the teaching of writing, like the writing of text, is a social process, an interaction, an exchange, and finally, that to learn from these experiences what they had to teach, I needed to structure them, to find several means of framing and ways of aligning them.

To provide the primary frame, I've taken the concepts of reflection-in-action and reflective transfer—the basic premises of Donald Schon's "reflective practice"—and re-theorized them specifically for work in the writing classroom, although they apply, I think, in any space where literacy and text and curriculum are topics of inquiry. At the heart of this practice-based theory are three concepts:

reflection-in-action, the process of reviewing and projecting and revising, which takes place within a composing event;

constructive reflection, the process of developing a cumulative, multi-selved, multi-voiced identity, which takes place between and among composing events; and

reflection-in-presentation, the process of articulating the relationships between and among the multiple variables of writing and the writer in a specific context for a specific audience.

I've talked here about those concepts in a progressive and yet recursive way—about the reflection-in-action that addresses a single text; about the constructive reflection that works cumulatively toward identity formation; about reflection-in-presentation, with its inward-outwardness; about reflective reading and responding, and how to learn to do both; about writing, identity, and reflection, and about learning, overlearning, and couterlearning, and about curriculum-for-students; about reflection and its complexities in assessment situations; about using reflection to understand literacy; about reflective texts and reflective human beings and making sense. Though I'm not quite out of breath, *it's a lot*, I know—a new way of seeing the classroom and the students in it, a new way of working with them, a new way of understanding our work. But *it offers a lot*. More than I think we—or I—understand. Coming in part from portfolios, reflection is not unlike portfolios in its potential: it too has the power to change the face of American education.

***

In developing this theory, I've made certain arguments. Like reflection itself, they are threads weaving whole cloth. I've argued

that reflection is a discipline, a habit of mind/spirit/feeling that informs what we do, always tacitly, sometimes explicitly, and that making such understanding explicit is a good

that regardless of how much our context shapes us, we have agency, and it is in the doubling of that agency, in what Patricia Carini calls "agency and the witnessing of agency," that we learn

that for reflection to be generative and constructive in a school setting, it must be practiced, must itself be woven not so much throughout the curricula as *into* it

that reflection is both individual and social; as such, reflection is always rhetorical

that through reflection, students learn to know their work, to like it, to critique it, to revise it, to start anew

that through reflection, students reveal a "native language" which we are only now beginning to study, a language that can tell us much about how they and we learn, about the multiple contexts through which and in which we learn

that through reflection we teach ourselves through metaphor, and that metaphor is the primary mode of students' native languages

that students should reflect on writings they care about, that they must be allowed to exercise some authority over their material (which is, after all, the product of their minds), that they have something to share with us, and not just in marginalized or unofficial places but in the assignments that "count," both in our terms and theirs

that through reflection, students invent identities, and that in general that identity-formation is the always unfolding purpose of the writing classroom and of the classroom where our prospective colleagues learn to teach and to tutor

that classroom reflection-in-presentation is characterized by certain features that we also find in reflective discourse: invocation of multiple contexts, for instance, and synthesis and use of metaphor

that through reflection, we understand curriculum pluralized: as lived, as delivered, as experienced: it is in the intersection of these curricula that identities are formed; students exert the most authority in that intersection since they are the ones who inhabit that place; learning more about that place is a prime goal of reflection used for educational purposes

that through our own reflections, we make knowledge and compose understandings: students about their work, teachers about theirs

that through the concepts of counter-learner and over-learner— separately *and* together—we can begin to explore in yet another way how and why it is that students resist learning to write

that reflection balances a tension between the impulse for coherence and a sense of discontinuity; it brings together the inner life and the outer life; it provides a place where such coherence and fragments and fissures can co-exist
that like rhetoric itself, *reflection is both practice and art*

***

This is not to say that we shouldn't mark possible dangers that reflection brings with it. Some will find the term reflection too slippery. Some will claim that reflection turns students inward at the expense of the social and at the neglect of the ideological. Some will claim that it inappropriately awards authority to the student. Some will argue that the only value of having students undertake reflection is to produce "better" primary texts. Some will assert that all we really need is the reflection-in-presentation, that there isn't time to cover to all the material that has to be covered and do all this as well. Or: that in order to do what is illustrated and theorized here, school will change. *Yes.*

I want to say that all of these concerns are valid. But even taken together, they do not refute what students and teachers have been doing now—reflectively—for some time. All I've tried to do is to organize and illustrate and theorize what we've been doing so as to offer a coherent, voiced, imaginable world, one where the *de facto* curricula come into contact with the school curricula: where students are the agents of their own learning, where they know and describe and like and critique and revise their own writing, their own learning, where we learn from and with them.

If it's imaginable, it's doable.

***

A second set of cautions obtains for those who do practice reflection and who use it in their practice. Robert Brookfield summarizes those cogently: "Working solely within the reflective practice tradition can cause us to lose a certain critical 'edge.' If we're not careful, our enthusiasm for reflection can be converted exclusively into a concern for technique. The temptation will then be to measure how much reflection we have performed on any given day or how we score on a scale of reflective competence"(216). And "Although it's important to know what reflection looks like, we must be wary of specifying universally applicable criteria that can be converted into standardized competencies" (216). And finally, "Reflection in and of itself is not enough; it must always be linked to how the world can be changed. We reflect on our teaching so that we can create the conditions under which both teachers and students become aware of their own power of agency" (217).

***

There are also many complex questions about reflection that we need to ask, to reflect upon. Some of them include:

is reflection a universal? does it vary along class lines, in different cultures, according to gender?

what kinds of questions should we be asking? when? should they always be sequenced? what sequences will work in which contexts? what response should we provide to those sequences?

how hospitable a medium is a computer network for reflection? are there certain conventions that will foster reflection? what is the effect of a public audience on reflection?

what would students tell us about reflection within disciplinary contexts? are the operations similar? different? how can they theorize about this? how can teachers theorize about the teaching in these contexts?

what would students tell us after the fact—2 months, 2 years, 20 years—about their reflective habits? what proved to be most useful and why? how are we defining useful? which habits of mind could they transfer into the world?

what other characteristics might we ascribe to reflective texts and to classroom reflection-in-presentation?

could we develop a corpus of reflective texts? how useful might they be in the classroom?

what would teachers tell us about how their teaching changes once they use reflection? or: does it change?

***

In many ways, this is my story, of course, or my stories. Like all the reflective writers we've seen, I am telling you (in the long version, I guess) what I've learned. Like Lara, I have named one topic only to show you much more about many others. One of them concerns the impact of this learning on me: it's not only what I learned, but as Brookfield implies, what the impact of the learning is. I think the evidence of that impact is woven throughout this text. My students have changed me at least as much as I have changed them, sometimes with some resistance on both sides, I acknowledge. Resistance and reflection are symbiotic (but that's a text for another day).

Teaching is a living thing: it changes.

In this text, I've also tried to model reflection both in process and in product. I've understood myself primarily in three roles here: first, always as teacher; later, more tentatively as researcher, studying my students not empirically, but observationally, descriptively, reflectively; later still, as writer. *Writing is so public*, as text, my story becomes in content and manner in ways I don't always apprehend, don't inevitably control, can't reliably predict. *Teaching is often still private*; I touch more lives directly, but I can keep those stories out of your line of vision. *Research carries more weight*, makes it more official, takes me back to the public sphere. Here, I've made the choice to bring the teacher, the researcher, and the writer into dialogue within the public view, to animate one inside of the others, each in terms of the others. In sum, I've tried to read my students, my classes, my teaching—and our texts—individually, collectively, together, in multiple contexts, so as to learn, to articulate, for both you and me: reflectively.

∗∗∗

Through such reflecting, within the multiplicity of these contexts, I create my truths, for today.

WORKS CITED

Allen, Michael. 1995. Valuing Differences: Portnet's First Year. *Assessing Writing* 2.1: 67-91.

————, William Condon, Marcia Dickson, Cheryl Forbes, George Meese, and Kathleen Yancey. 1997. Portfolios, WAC, Email and Assessment: An Inquiry on Portnet. Yancey and Weiser, *Situating Portfolios*: 370-384.

————, Jane Frick, Jeff Sommers, and Kathleen Yancey. 1997. Outside Review of Writing Portfolios: An On-Line Evaluation." *WPA: Writing Program Administration* 20.3: 64-88.

Anson, Chris, ed. 1989. *Writing and Response: Theory, Practice, Research.* Urbana, IL: NCTE.

————, 1994. Portfolios for Teachers: Writing our Way to Reflective Practice. Black et al., *New Directions*: 185-201.

————. 1989. Response Styles and Ways of Knowing. Anson *Writing and Response*: 332-367.

Applebee, Arthur. 1996. *Curriculum as Conversation: Transforming Traditions of Teaching and Learning.* Chicago: U of Chicago.

Bartholomae, David. 1995. Writing with Teachers: A Conversation with Peter Elbow. *College Composition and Communication* 46: 62-71.

Berlin, James. 1996. *Rhetorics, Poetics, and Culture.* Urbana, IL: NCTE.

————. 1984. *Writing Instruction in Nineteenth-Century American Colleges.* Carbondale: Southern Illinois U.

————. 1994 *The Subversions of the Portfolio.* Black et at., *New Directions:* 56–69

Birkerts, Sven. Reading against the Current. *Teaching English in the Two-Year College* 24: 235- 243.

Bitzer, Lloyd. The Rhetorical Situation. *Philosophy and Rhetoric* 1: 1–14.

Bizzell, Patricia. 1988. Arguing about Literacy. *College English* 50: 141–53.

Black, Laurel, Donald Daiker, Jeffrey Sommers, and Gail Stygall, eds. 1994. *New Directions in Portfolio Assessment: Reflective Practice, Critical Theory, and Large-Scale Scoring.* Portsmouth, NH: Boynton/Cook Heinemann.

————.1994. Writing Like a Woman and Being Rewarded for It: Gender, Assessment, and Reflective Letters from Miami University's Student Portfolios. Black et al., *New Directions*: 235-248.

Bridwell-Bowles, Lillian. 1992. Discourse and Diversity: Experimental Writing within the Academy. *College Composition and Communication* 43: 349-368.

Broad, Robert. 1997. Reciprocal Authority in Communal Writing Assessment: Constructing Textual Value in a New Politics of Inquiry. *Assessing Writing* 4.2.

Brookfield, Stephen D. 1995. *Becoming a Critically Reflective Teacher.* San Francisco: Josey Bass.

Brookhart, Susan. 1997. Looking under the Hood. *National Forum* 77.2: 3-5.

Camp, Roberta. 1993. Changing the Model for Direct Assessment of Writing. *Holistic Scoring: Theoretical foundations and validation research,* ed. Michael Williamson and Brian Huot. Cresskill, NJ: Hampton: 56-69.

———. 1992. Portfolio Reflections in Middle and Secondary School Classrooms. Yancey, *Portfolios:* 61-79.

Carini, Patricia. 1997. Refracting Reflection. Keynote address delivered at "Expanding the Conversation on Reflection: Innovative Practices, New Understandings, Current Challenges," Montreal.

———. 1994. Dear Sister Bess: An Essay on Standards, Judgment, and Writing. *Assessing Writing* 1.1: 29-67.

Connors, Robert J. and Andrea Lunsford. 1993. Teachers' Rhetorical Comments on Student Papers. *College Composition and Communication* 44: 200-223.

Conway, Glenda. 1994. Portfolio Cover Letters, Students' Self-presentation, and Teachers' Ethics. Black et al., *New Directions:* 83-93.

Delpit, Lisa. 1995. *Other People's Children: Cultural Conflict in the Classroom.* New York: Free Press.

Dewey, J. 1993. *How We Think* (2nd ed). Boston: D. C. Heath.

Edgerton, Russell, Pat Hutchings, and Kathleen Quinlan. 1991. *The Teaching Portfolio: Capturing the Scholarship in Teaching.* Washington, DC: American Association of Higher Education.

Elbow, Peter. 1986. *Embracing Contraries: Explorations in Teaching and Learning.* New York: Oxford U.

———. 1993. Ranking, Evaluating, Liking: Sorting Out Three Forms of Judgment. *College English* 55: 187-206.

———. 1995. Being a Writer vs. Being an Academic. *College Composition and Communication* 46: 72-83.

———. 1997. Time Out from Grading and Evaluating. *Assessing Writing* 4.1: 1-19.

——— and Kathleen Blake Yancey. 1994. On the Nature of Holistic Scoring and Reading: An Inquiry Composed on Email. *Assessing Writing* 1.1: 91-109.

Faigley, Lester. 1989. Judging Writing, Judging Selves. *College Composition and Communication* 40: 395-412.

———, Roger Cherry, David Jolliffe, and Anna Skinner. 1985. *Assessing Writers' Knowledge and Processes of Composing.* Norwood, NJ: Ablex.

Fisher, Walter R. 1995. Narration, Knowledge and the Possibility of Wisdom. *Rethinking Knowledge: Reflections across the Disciplines,* ed. Robert F. Goodman and Walter R. Fisher. Albany: SUNY Press: 169-195.

Flower, Linda and John Hayes. 1981. A Cognitive Process Theory of Writing. *College Composition and Communication* 32: 365-387.

Folkenfilk, Robert. 1993. The Self as Other. *The Culture of Autobiography,* ed. Robert Folkenfilk. Stanford: Stanford UP: 215-237.

Freedman, Sarah. 1984. The Registers of Student and Professional Expository Writing: Influences on Teachers' Responses. [rpt.] *Composition in Four Keys: Inquiring into the Field,* ed. Mark Wiley, Barbara Gleason, and Louise Phelps. Mountain View, CA: Mayfield. 302-310.

Gass, William. 1994. The Art of Self: Autobiography in an Age of Narcissim. *Harpers* (May): 43-52.

Geisler, Cheryl. 1994. *Academic Literacy and the Nature of Expertise.* Hillsdale, NJ: Erlbaum.

Gelertner, David. 1996. A Victim Reflects on the "Evil Coward." *TIME* (Apr. 15): 44-45.

Gere, Anne Ruggles. 1994. Kitchen Tables and Rented Rooms: The Extracurriculum of Composition. *College Composition and Communication* 45: 75-93.

Gergen, Kenneth. 1991. *The Saturated Self: Dilemmas of Identity in Comtemporary Life.* New York: Harper Collins.

Goffman, Erving. 1959. *The Presentation of Self in Everyday Life.* New York: Anchor Doubleday.

Hamp-Lyons, Liz and William Condon. 1993. Questioning Assumptions about Portfolio-Based Assessment. *College Composition and Communication* 44: 176-190.

Harrington, Susan Marie. 1997. Placing Reflection/Reflecting Placement. "Expanding the Conversation on Reflection: Innovative Practices, New Understandings, Current Challenges," Montreal.

Harris, Joseph. 1997. *A Teaching Subject: Composition Since 1966.* Upper Saddle River, NJ: Prentice Hall.

Harris, Muriel. 1989. Composing behaviors of one and multi-draft writers. *College English* 51: 174-191.

Hashimoto, Irvin. 1985. Structured Heuristic Procedures: Their Limitations. *College Composition and Communication* 36: 73-81.

Hilgers, Thomas. 1986. How Children Change as Critical Evaluators of Writing: Four Three-Year Case Studies. *Research in the Teaching of English* 20: 36-55.

Hillocks, George. 1995. *Teaching Writing as Reflective Practice.* New York: Teachers College Press.

Hull, Glynda and Mike Rose. 1990. This Wooden Shack Place: The Logic of an Unconventional Reading. *College Composition and Communication* 41: 287-298.

Hult, Christine. 1996. The Scholarship of Administration. *Resituating Writing: Constructing and Administering Writing Programs,* ed. Joseph Janangelo and Kristine Hanson. Portsmouth, NH: Boyton/Cook, Heinemann: 119-127.

Ingberg, Affhild. 1997. Personal Email.

Jamar, Steve. 11 June 1997. Posting to electronic listserv, *Writing Program Administration List (WPA-L).* Available fen00kby@unccvm.uncc.edu.

Janangelo, Joseph. 1996. Intricate Inscriptions: Negotiating Conflict between CollaborativeWriters. *Journal of Teaching Writing* 15.1: 91-105.

Jean Chandler. 1997. Positive Control. *College Composition and Communication* 48: 273-274.

Jolliffe. David. 1996. *Twelve Readers Reading:* Exemplary Responses, Thorny Problems. *Assessing Writing* 3.2: 221-233.

Kaplan, Laura. 1994. Speaking for Myself in Philosophy. *Philsophy in the Contemporary World.* 1.4: 20-24.

Light, Richard. 1991. *The Harvard Assessment Seminars: Second Report.* Cambridge: Harvard University Graduate School of Education and Kennedy School of Government.

Lucas, Catharine. 1992. Introduction: Writing Portfolios—Changes and Challenges. Yancey, *Portfolios:* 1-12.

Marrs, Robert. 14 Jan 1997. Posting to electronic listserv *Portnet-L.* Available **fen00kby@unccvm.uncc.edu.**

Marshall, Margaret. 1997. Marking the Unmarked: Reading Student Diversity and Preparing Teachers. *College Composition and Communication* 48: 231-249.

Meese, George. 10 Jan 1997. Posting to electronic listserv *Portnet-L.* Available **fen00kby@unccvm.uncc.edu**.

Metzger, Elizabeth and Lizbeth Bryant. 1993. Portfolio Assessment: Pedagogy, Power, and the Student. *Teaching English in the Two-year College* 20: 279-288.

Meyer, G. J. 1995. Dancing with Headhunters: Living the Downsized Life. *Harper's* (July): 37-56.

Miller, Susan. 1989. *Rescuing the Subject: A Critical Introduction to Rhetoric and the Writer.* Carbondale: Southern Illinois U P.

———. 1982. "How Writers Evaluate Their Own Writing." *College Composition and Communication* 44: 176-183.

Morrow, Nancy. 1997. The Role of Reading in the Composition Classroom. *Journal of Advanced Composition* 17: 453-473.

Moss, Pamela. 1994. Can There Be Validity without Reliability? *Educational Researcher* 23: 5- 12.

Murphy, Sandra. 1994. Reflection: New Standards Examples. Western Pennsylvania Teachers of English Conference on Writing, Pittsburgh.

———, and Mary Ann Smith. 1992. Looking into Portfolios. Yancey, *Portfolios:* 49-61.

Myers, Miles and David Pearson. 1996. Performance Assessment and the Literacy Unit of the New Standards Project. *Assessing Writing* 3.1: 5-31.

Nadler, Spencer. 1997. A Woman with Breast Cancer. *Harper's* (June): 70-76.

Nelson, Jennie. 1995. Reading Classrooms as Texts. *College Composition and Communication* 46: 411-30.

Owens, Derek. 1994. *Resisting Writings (and the Boundaries of Composition).* Dallas: Southern Methodist U P.

Paulson, L., P. Paulson, and Carol Meyer. 1991. What Makes a Portfolio a Portfolio? *Educational Leadership* 48: 60-63.

Perl, Sondra. 1997. Personal Email. Available **fen00kby@unccvm.uncc.edu**.

———. 1994. Introduction. *Landmark Essays on Writing Process,* ed. Sondra Perl. Davis, CA: Hermagoras Press: xi-xx.

———. 1980. Understanding Composing. *College Composition and Communication* 31: 363-370.

————, and Arthur Egendorf. 1979. The Process of Creative Discovery: Theory, Research, and Implications for Teaching. *Linguistics, Stylistics, and the Teaching of Composition*, ed. Donald McQuade. L&S Books.

Phelps, Louise Wetherbee. 1997. (Re)Weaving the Tapestry of Reflection: The Artistry of a Teaching Community. Keynote delivered at "Expanding the Conversation on Reflection: Innovative Practices, New Understandings, Current Challenges," Montreal.

————. 1989. Images of Student Writing: The Deep Structure of Teacher Response. Anson, *Writing and Response*. 37-68.

Pianko, Sharon. 1979. Reflection: A Critical Component of the Composing Process. *College Composition and Communication* 30: 275-278.

Polanyi, M. 1969. *Knowing and Being*. Chicago: U of Chicago P.

Purves, Alan. 1984. The Teacher as Reader: An Anatomy. *College English* 46: 259-265.

Rosenblatt, Roger. 1997. Only Disconnect. *Time* (Feb 24): 80.

Sadker, Myra and David Sadker. 1994. *Failing at Fairness: How Our Schools Cheat Girls*. New York: Simon and Schuster.

Salvatori, Mariolina. 1996. Conversations with Texts: Reading in the Teaching of Composition. *College English* 58: 440-454.

Schon, Donald. 1987. *Educating the Reflective Practitioner*. San Francisco: Josey-Bass.

————. 1995. Causality and Causal Inference in the Study of Organizations. *Rethinking Knowledge: Reflections across the Disciplines*, ed. Robert F. Goodman and Walter R. Fisher. Albany: SUNY Press: 69-103.

Schultz, Lucille, Russel Durst and Marjorie Roemer. 1997. Stories of Reading: Inside and Outside the Texts of Portfolios. *Assessing Writing* 4.2: forthcoming.

Schuster, Charles. 1994. Climbing the Slippery Slope of Writing Assessment: The Programmatic Use of Writing Portfolios. Black et al., *New Directions*: 314-325.

Schwalm, David. 9 Nov 1997. Posting to electronic listserv *Writing Program Administration List (WPA-L)*. Available **fen00kby@unccvm.uncc.edu**.

Selfe, Cynthia. 1989. Redefining Literacy: The Multilayered Grammars of Composition. *Critical Perspectives on Computers and Composition Instruction*, ed. Gail Hawisher and Cindy Selfe. New York: Teachers College Press: 3-15.

Shulman, Lee. 1996. "Course Anatomy: The Dissection and Transformation of Knowledge." American Association of Higher Education Conference on Faculty Roles and Rewards, Atlanta.

Sirc, Geoffrey. 1989. Response in the Electronic Medium. Anson, *Writing and Response*: 187-209.

Smagorinsky, Peter. 1996. Response to Writers, not Writing: A Review of *Twelve Readers Reading* by Richard Straub and Ronald Lunsford. *Assessing Writing* 3.2: 211-221.

Smith, Summer. 1997. The Genre of the End Comment. *College Composition and Communication* 48: 249-269

Sommers, Jeffrey. 1997. Portfolios in Literature Courses: A Case Study. *Teaching English in the Two-Year College* 24: 220-235.

————. 1989. The Writer's Memo: Collaboration, Response, and Development. Anson, *Writing and Response:* 174-86.

————, Laurel Black, Donald Daiker, and Gail Stygall. 1993. The Challenges of Reading Portfolios. *WPA: Writing Program Administration* 17: 7-31.

Sommers, Nancy. 1992. Between the Drafts. *College Composition and Communication* 43: 23- 31.

————. 1980. Revision Strategies of Student Writers and Adult Experienced Writers. *College Composition and Communication* 31: 378-388.

Straub, Richard and Ronald Lunsford. 1995. *Twelve Readers Reading.* Creskill, NJ: Hampton Press.

Sullivan, Francis. 1997. Calling Writers' Bluffs: The Social Production of Writing Ability in University Placement Testing. *Assessing Writing* 4.1: 53-81.

Sunstein, Bonnie. 1994. Handout from the New Standards Project, Palm Springs, CA.

Tapscott, Don. 1997. Interview, quoted in Jamie Malanowski. Generation WWW. *Time Digital* (Nov. 3): 43.

Thaiss, Chris and Terry Zawicki. 1997. How Portfolios for Proficiency Help Shape a WAC Program. *Assessing Writing across the Curriculum: Diverse Approaches and Practices,* ed. Kathleen Blake Yancey and Brian Huot. Greenwich, CT: Ablex: 79-97.

Vygotsky, L. 1978. *Mind in Society.* Cambridge, MA: Harvard University Press.

————. 1962. *Thought and Language.* Cambridge, MA: MIT Press.

Watson, Sam. 1991. Letters on Writing—A Medium of Exchange with Students of Writing. *Teaching Advanced Composition: Why and How,* ed. K. Adams and J. Adams. Portsmouth, NH: Boynton/Cook: 133-151.

Weiser, Irwin. 1997. Revising our Practices: How Portfolios Help Teachers Learn. Yancey and Weiser, *Situating Portfolios:* 293-305.

Wiggins, Grant. 1993. *Assessing Student Performance: Exploring the Purpose and Limits of Testing.* San Francisco: Josey-Bass.

Yancey, Kathleen Blake, ed. 1992. *Porfolios in the Writing Classroom: An Introduction.* Urbana, IL: NCTE.

————, and Irwin Weiser, eds. 1997. *Situating Portfolios: Four Perspectives.* Logan, UT: Utah State U P.

————. 1997. Teacher Portfolios: Lessons on Resistance, Readiness, and Reflection. Yancey and Weiser, *Situating Portfolios:* 244-263

————. 1996. Dialogue, Interplay, and Discovery: Mapping the Rhetoric of Reflection in Portfolio Assessment. *Portfolios in the Writing Classroom: Policy and Practice, Promise and Peril,* ed. Robert Calfee and P. Perfumo. Hillsdale, NJ: Lawrence Erlbaum Associates: 83-103.

————. 1996. Portfolio as Genre, Rhetoric as Reflection: Situating Selves, Literacies, and Knowledge. *WPA: Writing Program Administration:* 55-70.

————. 1992. Portfolios in the Writing Classroom: A Final Reflection. Yancey *Portfolios:* 102-117.

INDEX

ABOUT THE AUTHOR

KATHLEEN BLAKE YANCEY, AN ASSOCIATE PROFESSOR OF ENGLISH AT the University of North Carolina-Charlotte, teaches courses in writing, reading, rhetoric, and teaching. Her work has appeared in various journals (e.g., *College Composition and Communication; Writing Program Administration*), and she has edited or co-edited four collections of essays: two of them focused on portfolios, one on voice in writing, and one on program assessment for writing-across-the-curriculum programs. She also co-founded and co-edits the journal *Assessing Writing*. She consults frequently with faculty across the country. Her current projects include work in reflective reading across the curriculum, in the electronic environment as reflective practicum, and in the poetics and rhetorics of discourse.